Operating OpenShift
An SRE Approach to Managing Infrastructure

Rick Rackow and Manuel Dewald

Beijing · Boston · Farnham · Sebastopol · Tokyo

Operating OpenShift

by Rick Rackow and Manuel Dewald

Published by O'Reilly Media, Inc., 1005 Gravenstein Highway North, Sebastopol, CA 95472.

O'Reilly books may be purchased for educational, business, or sales promotional use. Online editions are also available for most titles (*http://oreilly.com*). For more information, contact our corporate/institutional sales department: 800-998-9938 or corporate@oreilly.com.

Acquisitions Editor: John Devins	**Indexer:** Amnet Systems LLC
Development Editor: Corbin Collins	**Interior Designer:** David Futato
Production Editor: Ashley Stussy	**Cover Designer:** Karen Montgomery
Copyeditor: Piper Editorial Consulting, LLC	**Illustrator:** Kate Dullea
Proofreader: Judith McConville	

November 2022:   First Edition

Revision History for the First Edition

2022-11-07:   First Release

See *http://oreilly.com/catalog/errata.csp?isbn=9781098106393* for release details.

978-1-098-10639-3

[LSI]

To Linus

— R.R.

To Marie

— M.D.

Table of Contents

Preface. ix

1. Introduction. 1
    Traditional Operations Teams   2
    How Site Reliability Engineering Helps   3
    OpenShift as a Tool for Site Reliability Engineers   4
    Individual Challenges for SRE Teams   5

2. Installing OpenShift. 7
    OKD, OCP, and Other Considerations   7
        OKD   7
        OCP   8
        OSD, ROSA, and ARO   8
    Local Clusters with OpenShift Local   8
    Planning Cluster Size   12
        Instance Sizing Recommendations   12
        Node Sizing Recommendations   12
        Master Sizing Recommendations   13
        Infra Nodes   15
    Basic OpenShift Installations   17
        Installer-Provisioned Infrastructure   17
        Self-Provisioned Infrastructure   24
    Summary   24

3. Running Workloads on OpenShift. 25
    Deploying Code   26
        Deploying Existing Container Images   27
        Deploying Applications from Git Repositories   29

Accessing Deployed Services   31
   Accessing Services from Other Pods   31
   Distribution of Requests   32
Exposing Services   33
   Route by Auto-generated DNS Names   34
   Route by Path   35
   External Load Balancers   37
Securing Services with TLS   40
   Specifying TLS Certificates   40
   Redirecting Traffic to TLS Route   42
   Let's Encrypt Trusted Certificates   44
   Encrypted Communication to the Service   51
Summary   57

4. Security. 59
Cluster Access   59
Role-Based Access Control   61
   Roles and ClusterRoles   62
   RoleBindings and ClusterRoleBindings   63
   CLI   65
ServiceAccounts   66
Threat Modelling   67
Workloads   68
Summary   72

5. Automating Builds. 73
OpenShift Image Builds   73
   Docker Build   74
   Source to Image (S2I) Build   81
   Custom S2I Images   84
Red Hat OpenShift Pipelines   87
   Overview   88
   Install Red Hat OpenShift Pipelines   90
   Setting Up the Pipeline   92
   Turning the Pipeline into Continuous Integration   104
Summary   110

6. In-Cluster Monitoring Stack. 111
Cluster Monitoring Operator   111
   Prometheus Operator   114
   User Workload Monitoring   130
Visualizing Metrics   136

	Console Dashboards	136
	Using Grafana	137
	Summary	141

7. Advanced Monitoring and Observability Strategies. **143**

Service Oriented Monitoring	143
Service Level Indicators	144
Service Level Objectives	145
Tools	150
Logging	154
ClusterLogging	154
Log Forwarding	158
Loki	158
Visualization	159
Installation	159
Creating a Grafana Instance	161
Data Source	161
Dashboards	164
Summary	166

8. Automating OpenShift Cluster Operations. **167**

Recurring Operations Tasks	168
Application Updates	169
Certificate Renewals	169
OpenShift Updates	169
Backups	170
Automating Recurring Operations Tasks	170
Persistence	170
Creating Snapshots	173
Using CronJobs for Task Automation	176
Cluster Configuration	182
Manage Cluster Configuration with OpenShift GitOps	184
Installing OpenShift GitOps	185
Managing Configuration with OpenShift GitOps	189
Managing Configuration of Multiple Clusters with OpenShift GitOps	193
Summary	197

9. Developing Custom Operators to Automate Cluster Operations. **199**

Operator SDK	201
Operator Design	202
Bootstrapping the Operator	203
Setting Up a CA Directory for Development	207

Designing the Custom Resource Definition   209
Installing the CustomResourceDefinition   212
Local Operator Development   213
The Reconcile Function   216
Deploying the Operator   217
Creating and Updating OpenShift Resources   220
Specifying RBAC Permissions   223
Routing Traffic to the Operator   225
Adding Additional Controllers   227
Updating Resource Status   229
Summary   231

10. **Practical Patterns for Operating OpenShift Clusters at Scale**. **233**
Cluster Lifecycle   233
Cluster Configuration   235
Logging   235
Monitoring   236
Alerting   237
Automation   238
On Call   238
Primary On Call   239
Backup On Call   239
Shift Rotation   239
Ticket Queue   239
Incident Management   240
When to Declare an Incident   241
Inform the Customer   241
Define Roles   241
Incident Timeline   242
Document the Process   242
Postmortem   243
Accessing OpenShift Clusters   243
The Stage Is Yours   243

Index. **245**

Preface

In late December 2020, a Slack notification from Rick popped up on Manuel's laptop.

"You know what?" it said, "You and I, we're going to write a book!"

"What are we going to write about?"

"Operating OpenShift!"

Fast-forward almost two years, and that very book is now before your eyes.

The backstory is that over the past several years, more and more people reached out to us to ask if we would be able to share some of our OpenShift insights with them—to help them operate their OpenShift clusters more efficiently.

At that time the two of us worked as site reliability engineers for OpenShift clusters at Red Hat. Efficiently operating OpenShift clusters was indeed our day-to-day challenge, and we had accumulated a lot of knowledge and expertise. We used that experience to create this book.

We divided the 10 chapters of this book according to our personal interests and depth of experience. Chapters 1, 3, 5, 8, 9, and 10 are written by Manuel. Chapters 2, 4, 6, and 7 are by Rick.

We learned a lot more about OpenShift in the past two years working on the book. Even with our experience operating OpenShift at Red Hat, many of the tools for operating and automating operations still required further research and experimentation. We've done our best to compile the results of our experiments into simple steps that you can follow to get started. Of course, you'll need to adjust the examples to apply them to your specific needs as soon as you start using the tools.

All the examples use the simplified scenario of an arcade gaming platform that you'll deploy to your cluster as you follow the book. You'll find the resources of this example workload in the corresponding GitHub repository (*https://github.com/Opera tingOpenShift/s3e*).

Conventions Used in This Book

The following typographical conventions are used in this book:

Italic
> Indicates new terms, URLs, email addresses, filenames, and file extensions.

`Constant width`
> Used for program listings, as well as within paragraphs to refer to program elements such as variable or function names, databases, data types, environment variables, statements, and keywords.

`Constant width bold`
> Shows commands or other text that should be typed literally by the user.

`Constant width italic`
> Shows text that should be replaced with user-supplied values or by values determined by context.

> This element signifies a tip or suggestion.

> This element signifies a general note.

> This element indicates a warning or caution.

Using Code Examples

Supplemental material (code examples, exercises, etc.) is available for download at *https://github.com/OperatingOpenshift*.

If you have a technical question or a problem using the code examples, please send emails to *bookquestions@oreilly.com*.

This book is here to help you get your job done. In general, if example code is offered with this book, you may use it in your programs and documentation. You do not need to contact us for permission unless you're reproducing a significant portion of the code. For example, writing a program that uses several chunks of code from this book does not require permission. Selling or distributing examples from O'Reilly books does require permission. Answering a question by citing this book and quoting example code does not require permission. Incorporating a significant amount of example code from this book into your product's documentation does require permission.

We appreciate, but generally do not require, attribution. An attribution usually includes the title, author, publisher, and ISBN. For example: "*Book Title* by Some Author (O'Reilly). Copyright 2012 Some Copyright Holder, 978-0-596-xxxx-x."

If you feel your use of code examples falls outside fair use or the permission given above, feel free to contact us at *permissions@oreilly.com*.

O'Reilly Online Learning

 For more than 40 years, *O'Reilly Media* has provided technology and business training, knowledge, and insight to help companies succeed.

Our unique network of experts and innovators share their knowledge and expertise through books, articles, and our online learning platform. O'Reilly's online learning platform gives you on-demand access to live training courses, in-depth learning paths, interactive coding environments, and a vast collection of text and video from O'Reilly and 200+ other publishers. For more information, visit *http://oreilly.com*.

How to Contact Us

Please address comments and questions concerning this book to the publisher:

O'Reilly Media, Inc.
1005 Gravenstein Highway North
Sebastopol, CA 95472
800-998-9938 (in the United States or Canada)
707-829-0515 (international or local)
707-829-0104 (fax)

We have a web page for this book, where we list errata, examples, and any additional information. You can access this page at *https://oreil.ly/operating-openshift-1e*.

Email *bookquestions@oreilly.com* to comment or ask technical questions about this book.

For news and information about our books and courses, visit *https://oreilly.com*.

Find us on LinkedIn: *https://linkedin.com/company/oreilly-media*

Follow us on Twitter: *https://twitter.com/oreillymedia*

Watch us on YouTube: *https://www.youtube.com/oreillymedia*

Acknowledgments

Over the past two years, a lot of people have been supportive of our idea for this book, and we would like to thank everyone who helped us stay motivated and finish this work.

We'd like to thank the following people who worked with us from the O'Reilly team:

John Devins helped us finalize the book proposal and convinced the right people that it's worth to invest in the topic. Corbin Collins, our development editor, was always the first to review our raw material and patiently corrected our formatting and grammar mistakes. He also always had an eye on our roadmap and reached out in time if adjustments needed to be made. Along with him, we also want to thank Sara Hunter and Ashley Stussy for their thorough reviews and incredibly helpful feedback.

Our technical editors Andrew Block and Bilgin Ibrayam were incredibly helpful and contributed lots of good ideas to improve the content. They even mentioned alternatives that we'd overlooked in our research.

A lot of the research done for this book involved chatting with the right people, both inside Red Hat and in the open source communities, who have been hard at work on the respective components covered in this book. We'd like to thank everyone who helped us get things up and running.

Finally, we want to thank our families, Stephanie, Linus, Julia, and Marie, who have been supportive of the idea from the beginning and helped us free up time to focus on writing this book and put up with our moods when things didn't go too well.

This book would not exist without you.

## CHAPTER 1

Introduction

Manuel Dewald

Operating distributed software is a difficult task. It requires humans with a deep understanding of the system they maintain. No matter how much automation you create, it will never replace highly skilled operations personnel.

OpenShift is a platform, built to help software teams develop and deploy their distributed software. It comes with a large set of tools that are built in or can be deployed easily. While it can be of great help to its users and can eliminate a lot of traditionally manual operations burdens, OpenShift itself is a distributed system that needs to be deployed, operated, and maintained.

Many companies have platform teams that provide development platforms based on OpenShift to software teams so the maintenance effort is centralized and the deployment patterns are standardized across the organization. These platform teams are shifting more and more into the direction of Site Reliability Engineering (SRE) teams, where software development practices are applied to operations tasks. Scripts are replaced by proper software solutions that can be tested more easily and deployed automatically using continuous integration/continuous delivery (CI/CD) systems. Alerts are transformed from simple cause-based alerts like "a high amount of memory is used on Virtual Machine 23" into symptom-based alerts based on Service Level Objectives (SLO) that reflect customer experience, like "processing of requests takes longer than we expect it to."

OpenShift provides all the tools you need to run software on top of it with SRE paradigms, from a monitoring platform to an integrated CI/CD system that you can use to observe and run both the software deployed to the OpenShift cluster, as well as the cluster itself. But building the automation, implementing a good alerting strategy, and finally, debugging issues that occur when operating an OpenShift cluster, are still difficult tasks that require skilled operations or SRE staffing.

Even in SRE teams, traditionally a good portion of the engineers' time is dedicated to manual operations tasks, often called *toil*. The operations time should be capped, though, as the main goal of SRE is to tackle the toil with software engineering.

O'Reilly published a series of books (*https://sre.google/books*) written by site reliability engineers (SREs) at Google, related to the core SRE concepts. We encourage you to take a look at these books if you're interested in details about these principles. In the first book, *Site Reliability Engineering* (*https://sre.google/sre-book/table-of-contents*), the authors mostly speak from their experience as SREs at Google, suggesting to limit the time working on toil to 50% of an engineering team's time.

Traditional Operations Teams

The goal of having an upper limit for toil is to avoid shifting back into an operations team where people spend most of the time working down toil that accumulates with both the scale of service adoption and software advancement.

Part of the accumulating toil while the service adoption grows is the number of alerts an operations team gets if the alerting strategy isn't ready for scaling. If you're maintaining software that creates one alert per day per tenant, keeping one engineer busy running 10 tenants, you will need to scale the number of on-call engineers linearly with the number of tenants the team operates. That means in order to double the number of tenants, you need to double the number of engineers dedicated to reacting to alerts. These engineers will effectively not be able to work on reducing the toil created by the alerts while working down the toil and investigating the issues.

In a traditional operations team that runs OpenShift as a development platform for other departments of the company, onboarding new tenants is often a manual task. It may be initiated by the requesting team to open a ticket that asks for a new OpenShift cluster. Someone from the operations team will pick up the ticket and start creating the required resources, kick off the installer, configure the cluster so the requesting team gets access, and so forth. A similar process may be set up for turning down clusters when they are not needed anymore. Managing the lifecycle of OpenShift clusters can be a huge source of toil, and as long as the process is mainly manual, the amount of toil will scale with the adoption of the service.

In addition to being toil-packed processes, manual lifecycle and configuration management are error prone. When an engineer runs the same procedure several times during a week, as documented in a team-managed Wiki, chances are they will miss an important step or pass a wrong parameter to any of the scripts, resulting in a broken state that may not be discovered immediately.

When managing multiple OpenShift clusters, having one that is slightly different from the others due to a mistake in the provisioning or configuration process, or even due to a customer request, is dangerous and usually generates more toil.

Automation that the team generated over time may not be tailored to the specifics of a single snowflake cluster. Running that automation may just not be possible, causing more toil for the operations team. In the worst case, it may even render the cluster unusable.

Automation in a traditional ops team can often be found in a central repository that can be checked out on engineer devices so they can run the scripts they need as part of working on a documented process. This is problematic not only because it still needs manual interaction and hence doesn't scale well but also engineer's devices are often configured differently. They can differ in the OS they use, adding the need to support different vendors in the tooling, for example by providing a standardized environment like a container environment to run the automation.

But even then, the version of the scripts to run may differ from engineer to engineer, or the script to run hasn't been updated when it should've been as a new version of OpenShift has been released. Automated testing is something that is seldomly implemented for operations scripts made to quickly get rid of a piece of toil. All this makes automation in scripts that are running on developer machines brittle.

How Site Reliability Engineering Helps

In an SRE team, the goal is to replace such scripts with actual software that is versioned properly, has a mature release strategy, has a continuous integration and delivery process, and runs from the latest released version on dedicated machines, for example, an OpenShift cluster.

OpenShift SRE teams treat the operations of OpenShift clusters, from setting them up to tearing them down, as a software problem. By applying evolved best practices from the software engineering world to cluster operations, many of the problems mentioned earlier can be solved. The software can be unit-tested to ensure that new changes won't break existing behavior. Additionally, a set of integration tests can ensure it works as expected even when the environment changes, such as when a new version of OpenShift is released.

Instead of proactively reacting to more and more requests from customers as the service adoption grows, the SRE team can provide a self-service process that can be used by their customers to provision and configure their clusters. This also reduces the risk of snowflakes, as less manual interaction is needed by the SRE team. What can and cannot be configured should be part of the UI provided to the customer, so requests to treat a single cluster differently from all the others should turn into a feature request for the automation or UI. That way, it will end up as a supported state rather than a manual configuration update.

To ensure that the alerting strategy can scale, SRE teams usually move from a cause-based alerting strategy to a symptom-based alerting strategy, ensuring that only problems that risk impacting the user experience reach their pager. Smaller problems that do not need to be resolved immediately can move to a ticket queue to work on as time allows.

Shifting to an SRE culture means allowing people to watch their own software, taking away the operations burden from the team one step at a time. It's a shift that will take time, but it's a rewarding process. It will turn a team that runs software someone else wrote into a team that writes and runs software they're writing themselves, with the goal of automating the lifecycle and operations of the software under their control. An SRE culture enables service growth by true automation and observation of customer experience rather than the internal state.

OpenShift as a Tool for Site Reliability Engineers

This book will help you to utilize the tools that are already included with OpenShift or that can be installed with minimal effort to operate software and OpenShift itself the SRE way.

We expect you to have a basic understanding of how containers, Kubernetes, and OpenShift work to be able to understand and follow all the examples. Fundamental concepts like pods will not be explained in full detail, but you may find a quick refresher where we found it helpful to understand a specific aspect of OpenShift.

We show you the different options for installing OpenShift, helping you to automate the lifecycle of OpenShift clusters as needed. Lifecycle management includes not only installing and tearing down clusters but also managing the configuration of your OpenShift cluster in a GitOps fashion. Even if you need to manage the configuration of multiple clusters, you can use Argo CD on OpenShift to manage the configuration of a multitude of OpenShift clusters.

This book shows you how to run workloads on OpenShift using a simple example application. You can use this example to walk through the chapters and try out the code samples. However, you should be able to use the same patterns to deploy more serious software, like automation that you built to manage OpenShift resources—for example, an OpenShift operator.

OpenShift also provides the tools you need to automate the building and deployment of your software, from simple automated container builds, whenever you check in a new change, to version control, to full-fledged custom pipelines using OpenShift Pipelines.

In addition to automation, the SRE way of managing OpenShift clusters includes proper alerting that allows you to scale. OpenShift comes with a lot of built-in alerts that you can use to get informed when something goes wrong with a cluster. This book will help you understand the severity levels of those alerts and show you how to build your own alerts, based on metrics that are available in the OpenShift built-in monitoring system.

Working as OpenShift SREs at Red Hat together for more than two years, we both learned a lot about all the different kinds of alerts that OpenShift emits and how to investigate and solve problems. The benefit of working close to OpenShift Engineering is that we can even contribute to alerts in OpenShift if we find problems with them during our work.

Over time, a number of people have reached out, being interested in how we work as a team of SREs. We realize there is a growing interest in all different topics related to our work: From how we operate OpenShift to building custom operators, people show interest in the topic at conferences or reach out to us directly.

This book aims to help you take some of our learnings and use them to run OpenShift in your specific environment. We believe that OpenShift is a great distribution of Kubernetes that brings a lot of additional comfort with it, comfort that will allow you to get started quickly and thrive at operating OpenShift.

Individual Challenges for SRE Teams

OpenShift comes with a lot of tools that can help you in many situations as a developer or operator. This book can cover only a few of those tools and does not aim to provide a full overview of all OpenShift features. Instead of trying to replicate the OpenShift documentation, this book focuses on highlighting the things we think will help you get started operating OpenShift. With more features being developed and added to OpenShift over time, it is a good idea to follow the OpenShift blog (*https://blog.openshift.com*) and the OpenShift documentation (*https://docs.openshift.com*) for a more holistic view of what's included in a given release.

Many of the tools this book covers are under active development, so you may find them behaving slightly differently from how they worked when this book was published. Each section references the documentation for a more detailed explanation of how to use a specific component. This documentation is usually updated frequently, so you can find up-to-date information there.

When you use Kubernetes as a platform, you probably know that many things are automated for you already: you only need to tell the control plane how many resources you need in your deployment, and Kubernetes will find a node to place it. You don't need to do a rolling upgrade of a new version of your software manually, because Kubernetes can handle that for you. All you need to do is configure the Kubernetes resources according to your needs.

OpenShift, being based on Kubernetes, adds more convenience, like routing traffic to your web service from the outside world: exposing your service at a specific DNS name and routing traffic to the right place is done via the OpenShift router.

These are only a few of the tasks that used to be done by operations personnel but can be automated in OpenShift by default.

However, depending on your specific needs and the environment you're running OpenShift in, there are probably some very specific tasks that you need to solve on your own. This book cannot tell you step-by-step what you need to do in order to fully automate operations. If it were that easy to fit every environment, it would most probably be part of OpenShift already. So, please treat this book as an informing set of guidelines, but know that you will still need to solve some of the problems to make OpenShift fit your operations strategy.

Part of your strategy will be to decide how and where you want to install OpenShift. Do you want to use one of the public cloud providers? That may be the easiest to achieve, but you may also be required to run OpenShift in your own data center for some workloads.

The first step for operating OpenShift is setting it up, and when you find yourself in a place where you'll need to run multiple OpenShift clusters, you probably want to automate this part of the cluster lifecycle. Chapter 2 discusses different ways to install an OpenShift cluster, from running it on a developer machine, which can be helpful to develop software that needs a running OpenShift cluster during development, to a public reachable OpenShift deployment using a public cloud provider.

Installing OpenShift

Rick Rackow

As with any piece of software, the story of OpenShift starts by installing it. This chapter walks you through some scenarios that reach from small to scale. This chapter focuses on a single cluster installation and explores the limits of different sizes of clusters. However, at some point, scaling a cluster may either not be enough or may not serve the use case very well. In those cases you will want to look into multicluster deployments. Those are covered as part of Chapter 10.

OKD, OCP, and Other Considerations

OpenShift can be considered as a distribution of Kubernetes, and it is available in different ways. We will go over each of them in this section, draw a small comparison, and point out how they relate to one another.

OKD

OKD is not an acronym. Before its rebranding, OKD used to be called OpenShift Origin. Now it's OKD, and that is how it should be referred to, for trademark reasons. Namely, the Linux Foundation does not allow Red Hat to use "Kubernetes" in products or projects further than referencing it.

> OKD is a distribution of Kubernetes optimized for continuous application development and multi-tenant deployment. OKD also serves as the upstream code base upon which Red Hat OpenShift Online and Red Hat OpenShift Container Platform are built.
>
> —docs.okd.io

In other words, OKD is where upstream Kubernetes is vendored and the core of OpenShift starts to exist. It serves as the base for everything else that is OpenShift.

OCP

OCP stands for OpenShift Container Platform. This is what people (especially inside Red Hat) most commonly mean when they mention OpenShift. OCP is positioned downstream of OKD. Different support levels are available. You can try it out for free during an evaluation period. All you need is a Red Hat account. It is not required for you to make any purchase of a Red Hat product or support to follow this book.

OCP is what is covered in this book. If there is a difference between how OCP and OKD work, we default to OCP.

OSD, ROSA, and ARO

In addition to a self-hosted and self-installed OpenShift, Red Hat also offers OpenShift-as-a-Service as a fully managed offering on Amazon Web Services, Microsoft Azure, and Google Cloud Platform. We don't go into much detail with those, as you wouldn't really need to read this book if you were to buy a subscription for any of those, but for future reference, the terminology is:

Acronym	Name	Available On
OSD	OpenShift Dedicated	AWS, GCP
ROSA	Red Hat OpenShift Service on AWS	AWS
ARO	Azure Red Hat OpenShift	Azure

All of those are viable options for anyone who wants to run production workloads on OpenShift as they are all very closely connected to one another with direct dependencies. The dependency tree is OKD $\Rightarrow$ OCP $\Rightarrow$ OSD, ROSA, ARO.

Which one you decide on depends on your needs in terms of support, environment, ease of use, ease of operation, and cost per cluster. We decided to default to OCP for this book because it strikes a balance between upstream and downstream position. It is more feature complete than OKD and offers support but not to a level of a fully managed solution like OSD or the other managed solutions.

Local Clusters with OpenShift Local

OpenShift Local is the easiest way to launch a full OpenShift cluster locally. If you have touched Kubernetes before, you have probably heard of Minikube (*https://mini kube.sigs.k8s.io/docs*) and OpenShift Local, the OpenShift equivalent.

Its developers describe it as "OpenShift 4 on your laptop" (*https://oreil.ly/lGsnm*). In fact, you can install it not just on laptops but almost everywhere: workstations, Cloud VMs, or laptops. At its core, OpenShift Local is a virtual machine that serves as both OpenShift Worker and Master.

OpenShift Local is ephemeral by nature and should not be used for production use cases.

The documentation (*https://code-ready.github.io/crc*) is your best friend. Make sure to consult it whenever you get stuck. It is the condensed start-to-finish guide for OpenShift Local, and it's open source. That means it's frequently updated, and you can contribute to it, in case you find something along the way that you think isn't covered enough yet.

Head on over to OpenShift Cluster Manager (OCM) (*https://cloud.redhat.com/open shift*). We reference this page frequently throughout this chapter, specifically when we talk about the installers. It serves as your overview and starting point for all clusters that you registered, regardless if they are OpenShift Local, OCP, or managed clusters.

Sign in with your Red Hat account. If you don't have one, create one. You should be presented with a view similar to the one in Figure 2-1.

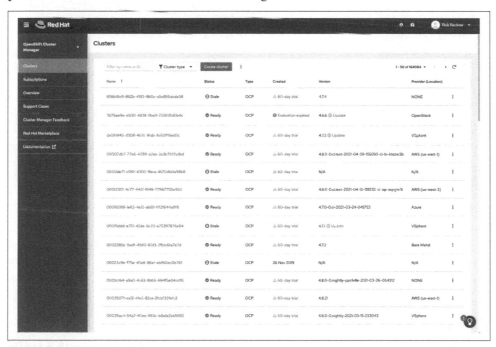

Figure 2-1. OCM start view

Click the Create cluster button and then choose "Local" in the next view.

Choose the platform that you want to install OpenShift Local on. Note that it has your current platform auto-selected, based on your browser's user agent. The example shown in Figure 2-2 was created on macOS, and it is auto-selected.

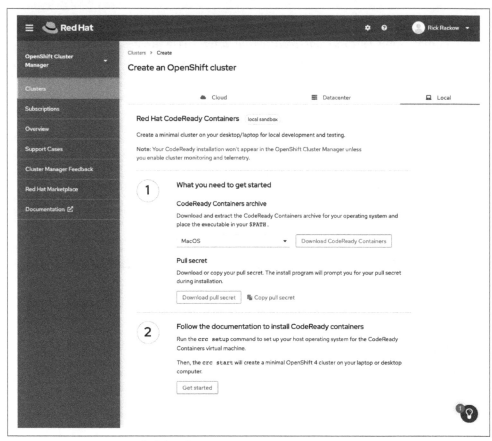

Figure 2-2. OCM OpenShift local view

Next, download the archive. Also download and save your "Pull secret" by clicking the Download Pull Secret button, shown in Figure 2-2. After the download has finished, extract the archive into any location that is in your $PATH.

```
$ tar -xJvf crc-macos-amd64.tar.xz
```

Since you have extracted into your $PATH, you will now be able to use the included binaries right away. Two important files are packaged in the archive. The first is *crc*, which is the binary to interact with your OpenShift Local cluster, and its name is an acronym for CodeReady Containers, the former name of OpenShift local. The second is *oc*, which is the OpenShift command line utility to interact with generally all OpenShift clusters. It is the equivalent of *kubectl* for Kubernetes. Those two files together allow you to effectively set up and manage your OpenShift Local cluster, as well as interact with it afterward as you would with any other OpenShift cluster.

The basic interaction with your cluster will be to set it up. This can be done as follows:

```
$ crc setup
INFO Checking if podman remote executable is cached
INFO Checking if admin-helper executable is cached
INFO Caching admin-helper executable
INFO Uncompressing crc_hyperkit_4.7.5.crcbundle
crc.qcow2: 10.13 GiB / 10.13 GiB [------------------] 100.00%
Your system is correctly setup for using CodeReady Containers.
You can now run 'crc start' to start the OpenShift cluster
```

During your first setup, you will be prompted to opt into sending telemetry data. This is a very limited set of on-cluster data that gets forwarded to Red Hat. You can see the full list of what gets sent online (*https://oreil.ly/hvTF6*).

> Opting out of sending telemetry data can impact certain features in OpenShift Cluster Manager that rely on telemetry data.

Now that the setup is done, go ahead and launch the cluster with the following command:

```
$ crc start
INFO Checking if running as non-root
INFO Checking if podman remote executable is cached
INFO Checking if admin-helper executable is cached
INFO Checking minimum RAM requirements
INFO Checking if HyperKit is installed
INFO Checking if crc-driver-hyperkit is installed
INFO Checking file permissions for /etc/hosts
INFO Checking file permissions for /etc/resolver/testing
CodeReady Containers requires a pull secret to download content from Red Hat.
? Please enter the pull secret
```

At this point, paste the content of the pull secret you downloaded earlier. The pull secret will allow you to pull the required images from Red Hat's container registry as well as associate the cluster to your Red Hat user, which ultimately also will make it show up in OpenShift Cluster Manager. Your OpenShift Local installation is completed after this step. You can use this cluster to familiarize yourself with the oc command line tool as well as the web console. Remember that this cluster is ephemeral. In case you need to restore the state of installation, you can start over with the following command:

```
$ crc delete && crc start
```

Planning Cluster Size

In this section you will deploy a multinode OpenShift Cluster. There are some considerations to go over, and one of the most important is planning the cluster's size and capacity.

Instance Sizing Recommendations

OpenShift documentation has some pointers for how to scale your clusters' instances. Let's examine what potential issues you can run into if you scale too small. You can safely assume that scaling too big is not an issue, other than cost. You will also find remarks about that throughout the following sections.

The instance size is directly related to your workloads, and master and nodes behave similarly to some extent. The more workloads you plan to run, the bigger your instances have to become. However, the way they scale is fundamentally different. Whereas nodes directly relate to workload almost linearly, masters don't. That means that a cluster's capacity can be scaled out to a certain extent without any adjustments to the control plane.

Node Sizing Recommendations

To better illustrate the scaling behavior of nodes, let's look at an example.

Think of a cluster of three nodes; ignore the masters for now. Each of them is an AWS m5.xlarge, so 4 vCPU and 8 GB of ram. That gives you a total cluster capacity of 12 vCPU and 24 GB ram. In this virtual scenario you can try to run workloads in perfect distribution and use up all the resources, and then you will either need to scale nodes to bigger instances (horizontally) or more of them (vertically). Add another instance and the cluster capacity grows linearly. Now you have 16 vCPU and 32 GB for our workloads.

The above scenario disregards a small but important detail: system reserved and kube reserved capacity. Since OpenShift release 4.8, OpenShift can take care of that automatically. To enable this functionality, add the following to the KubeletConfig:

```
apiVersion: machineconfiguration.openshift.io/v1
kind: KubeletConfig
metadata:
  name: dynamic-node
spec:
  autoSizingReserved: true
```

It is possible to adjust the KubeletConfig post-install as well as before creating a cluster. Forcing OpenShift to take on the system-relevant resources is a recommended setting to ensure the cluster's functionality and should not be omitted unless explicit reasons exist.

Think of it like this: 10 pods that run an m5.xlarge node and each of those pods has a requested set of resources of 0.4 CPU, and they actually use that. Naturally, your system process gets into trouble and that node becomes unstable. In the worst case, the node becomes unresponsive and crashes, the workloads on it get reallocated to other nodes, overloading those, and you end up with a chain reaction: your whole cluster becomes unresponsive. From that perspective it's a small price to pay to sacrifice some of that precious capacity to ensure cluster stability.

So we know that nodes scale linearly with their workloads and that we need to add a bit of reserved capacity on top of that. So how big should your node be? We have to consider three questions:

- How big is your single biggest workload?
- How much can you utilize a big node?
- How fast can you deploy more nodes?

The single biggest workload determines the minimum size of a node. The explanation is that if you can't fit the workload on a node, you have a problem, because you want to be able to deploy all your workloads to the cluster.

The flip side of that is the efficiency you want to achieve. Having a node idle at only 50% usage all the time is really just burning money. You want to find the sweet spot between being able to fit all your workloads, while at the same time making the most of your nodes. Those two points together lead to the point that we want to be using nodes that are as small as possible and if you need more, deploy another one, so the utilization per node is still high even with an extra node added to the cluster.

The factor that can make you go down a different path is time: the time it takes to deploy another node, in case you hit capacity. Certain ways to deploy are faster than others. For example, having set up automation that allows you to deploy another node to the cluster within 5 minutes makes a great difference from having to manually provision a new blade in a datacenter and waiting for it for a day until the datacenter team has mounted and connected it.

The rule here is the slower you can provision new nodes, the bigger a single node needs to be, and the earlier you have to provision new nodes. The time to new node directly works against the max utilization you want to aim for per node.

Master Sizing Recommendations

Nodes are important for giving a home to your workloads, but masters are the heart of OpenShift.

The masters, or control plane nodes, are what keep the cluster running since they are hosting:

- etcd
- API server (kube and OpenShift)
- Controller manager (kube and OpenShift)
- OpenShift Oauth API server
- OpenShift Oauth Server
- HA proxy

The masters don't directly run workloads; therefore, they behave differently when it comes to scalability. As opposed to the linear scalability needs of nodes, which depend on the workloads, the master capacity has to be scaled alongside the number of nodes.

Another difference compared to the node scalability is that you need to look at vertical scaling over horizontal scaling. You cannot simply scale out master nodes horizontally because some components that run on masters require a quorum as well as replication. The most prominent case is etcd. The central store for state, secrets, and so on is just one of the components to name. Theoretically, almost any arbitrary number of masters is possible in an OpenShift cluster as long they can form a quorum. This means that a leader election needs to happen, with a majority of votes. This can become rather tricky, for example with an even number of nodes like "4" or "2." In those cases, there is no guarantee that any given node will have a majority, and leader election can get stuck or, worse, multiple leaders can be elected, which might break the cluster. The question is, "Why not just 1?" and the answer to that is the cluster's resilience. You cannot risk your whole cluster, which is basically unusable without masters, by having only a single point of failure. Imagine a scenario where you have one master instance, and it crashes because of a failure in the underlying infrastructure. The whole cluster is completely useless at this point, and recovery from that kind of failure is hard. The next smallest option is 3, and that is also our recommendation. In fact, the official documentation states that exactly three master nodes must be used for all production deployments (*https://oreil.ly/Izxdc*).

With the count set, we have the option left of vertical scaling. However, with masters being the heart of the cluster, you have to account for the fragile state you take a cluster into when you resize an already running master node, since it will need to be shut down to be resized.

Make sure to plan for growth. If you plan to have 20 nodes at the very beginning in order to have room for your workloads, choose the next bigger size master instances. This comes at a small price point but will save you massive amounts of work and risk by avoiding a master scaling operation.

Infra Nodes

Infra nodes are worker nodes with an extra label. Other than that, they are just regular OpenShift nodes. So if they're "just" nodes, why do they get the extra label? Two reasons: cost and cluster resilience.

The easy one is cost: certain infrastructure workloads don't trigger subscription costs with Red Hat. What that means is if you have a node that exclusively runs infrastructure workloads, you don't have to pay your subscription fee for that node. Seems like an easy way to save money. For the sake of completeness, the full list of components that don't require node subscriptions can be found in the latest documentation (*https://oreil.ly/ef1Ea*). Some components run on masters and also need to be there, like the OCP control plane. Others can be moved around. So you create a new set of nodes, with the `infra` label.

Reason number two: the cluster's resiliency. Regular workloads as well as infra workloads don't make a difference to OpenShift when they're on the same node. Imagine a regular cluster with just masters and nodes. You deploy all your applications as well as the infra workloads that come out of the box to nodes. Now when the unfortunate situation happens that you run out of resources, it may just as well be that an "infra" workload gets killed as a "regular" application workload. This is, of course, not the best situation. On the other hand, when all infrastructure-related workloads are safely placed on their own set of nodes, the "regular" applications don't impact them at all, creating better resilience and better performance. Good candidates to be moved around are:

- In-cluster monitoring (configmap)
- Routers (IngressController)
- Default registry (Config)

Moving them by adding a label to the corresponding elements that are noted inside the parenthesis. The following example shows how it is done for the in-cluster monitoring solution.

```
apiVersion: v1
kind: ConfigMap
metadata:
  name: cluster-monitoring-config
  namespace: openshift-monitoring
data:
  config.yaml: |+
    alertmanagerMain:
      nodeSelector:
        node-role.kubernetes.io/infra: ""
    prometheusK8s:
      nodeSelector:
        node-role.kubernetes.io/infra: ""
    prometheusOperator:
      nodeSelector:
        node-role.kubernetes.io/infra: ""
    grafana:
      nodeSelector:
        node-role.kubernetes.io/infra: ""
    k8sPrometheusAdapter:
      nodeSelector:
        node-role.kubernetes.io/infra: ""
    kubeStateMetrics:
      nodeSelector:
        node-role.kubernetes.io/infra: ""
    telemeterClient:
      nodeSelector:
        node-role.kubernetes.io/infra: ""
    openshiftStateMetrics:
      nodeSelector:
        node-role.kubernetes.io/infra: ""
    thanosQuerier:
      nodeSelector:
        node-role.kubernetes.io/infra: ""
```

Add that to your already existing configmap or create a new one with just this. For the latter option, we would create the preceding file and apply it as follows:

```
$ oc create -f cluster-monitoring-configmap.yaml
```

Follow it with the following command:

```
$ watch 'oc get pod -n openshift-monitoring -o wide'
```

A last note on the scaling of infra nodes: They scale almost the same way as master nodes. The reason they need to be scaled vertically in the first place is that Prometheus as part of the in-cluster monitoring solution requires more memory with more metrics it is storing.

Basic OpenShift Installations

This section discusses the first way to install an actual production OpenShift cluster. There are two different ways that come in different shapes but do the same thing, just for your respective infrastructure.

Installer-Provisioned Infrastructure

Think of this as an all-in-one solution. The installer creates the underlying infrastructure, networking infrastructure, and OpenShift cluster on the cloud provider of your choice (or compatible bare metal options). Run a single command, pass in your credentials, and what you get back is an up-and-running OpenShift cluster.

The starting point is again the OpenShift Cluster Manager landing page, which you can see in Figure 2-3.

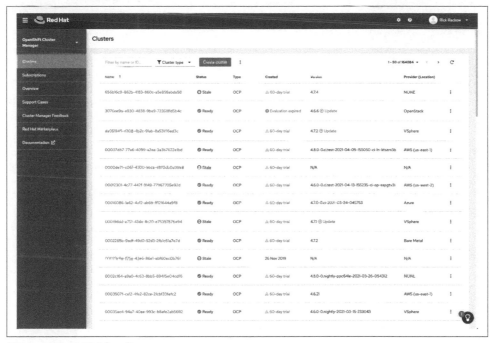

Figure 2-3. OCM landing page

Click the Create cluster button again, but this time choose your cloud provider, in our case Google Cloud Platform (GCP). This takes you to the next page, shown in Figure 2-4, where we choose "Installer-provisioned infrastructure."

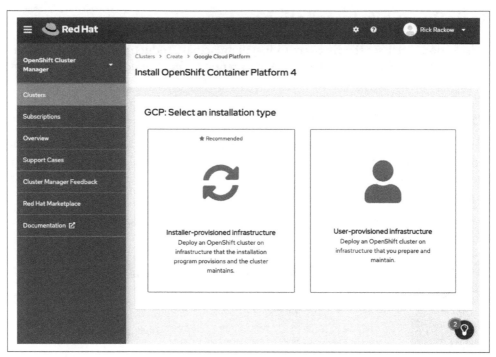

Figure 2-4. OCM installer choice

Figure 2-5 shows the main installer page. In the first part, you can see all required artifacts. Part two gives you the absolute basic installation command, and part three contains some minor information about subscriptions.

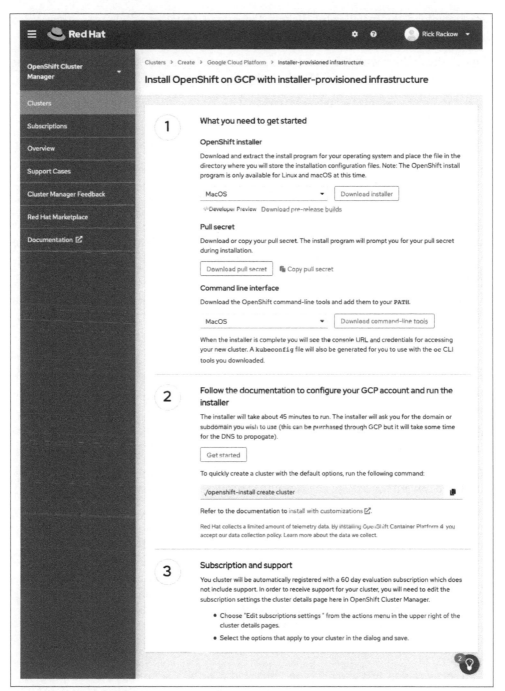

Figure 2-5. OCM installer-provisioned infrastructure landing page

Let's download the installer by clicking Download Installer. While we're there, also download the pull secret and `oc` binary.

Unpack the archive with the binaries to somewhere in your $PATH to have easy access to them on the command line. Use the following command:

```
$ tar -xzvf openshift-client-mac.tar.gz
x README.md
x oc
x kubectl
```

Now unpack the installer in the same way:

```
$ tar -xzvf openshift-install-mac.tar.gz
x README.md
x openshift-install
```

You can move *openshift-install* into a directory in your $PATH too, in case you plan to access it rather frequently, for example. Otherwise, just keep it in a location that suits you and reference it by absolute or relative path.

In our example, we unpacked in the *~/Downloads* directory, so we would access the installer as follows:

```
$ ./Downloads/openshift-install
```

Prerequisites

Make sure that your cloud provider is set up and ready. The installer will also let you know if any configuration is missing. A whole section in the documentation (*https://oreil.ly/XIJrM*) discusses just the setup of the prerequisites, but we want to go over it anyway, just to be sure you have a good overview of what you need.

To begin, we need a project. You can create that from the console or from the command line interface (CLI) by running the following command:

```
gcloud projects create openshift-guinea-pig
```

Your GCP project must use the Premium Network Service Tier if you are using installer-provisioned infrastructure. The Standard Network Service Tier is not supported for clusters installed using the installation program. The installation program configures internal load balancing for the api-int.<cluster_name>.<base_domain> URL; the Premium Tier is required for internal load balancing.

In the project you just created, you also need a certain set of application programming interfaces (APIs) to be enabled. Table 2-1 shows you which ones are needed.

Table 2-1. GCP required API overview

API service	Console service name
Compute Engine API	compute.googleapis.com
Google Cloud APIs	cloudapis.googleapis.com
Cloud Resource Manager API	cloudresourcemanager.googleapis.com
Google DNS API	dns.googleapis.com
IAM Service Account Credentials API	iamcredentials.googleapis.com
Identity and Access Management (IAM) API	iam.googleapis.com
Service Management API	servicemanagement.googleapis.com
Service Usage API	serviceusage.googleapis.com
Google Cloud Storage JSON API	storage api.googleapis.com
Cloud Storage	storage-component.googleapis.com

You can leverage the `gcloud` CLI tool again to enable all of those or any other method that you prefer.

```
$ gcloud services enable compute.googleapis.com cloudapis.googleapis.com \
  cloudresourcemanager.googleapis.com \
  dns.googleapis.com \
  iamcredentials.googleapis.com \
  iam.googleapis.com \
  servicemanagement.googleapis.com \
  serviceusage.googleapis.com \
  storage-api.googleapis.com \
  storage-component.googleapis.com
Operation "operations/acf.p2-10448422-91a9fd12a64b" finished successfully.
```

Make sure that you have enough quota in your project. Please see the OpenShift documentation (*https://oreil.ly/uTABD*) for the latest requirements.

You also need a dedicated public domain name system (DNS) zone in the project, and it needs to be authoritative for the domain. If you don't have a domain, you can purchase one from your preferred registrar.

Now create the managed zone like this but with your domain:

```
$ gcloud dns managed-zones create ocp-cluster \
  --description=openshift-cluster \
  --dns-name=operatingopenshift.com \
  --visibility=public
```

Get the authoritative name servers from the hosted zone records:

```
$ gcloud dns managed-zones describe ocp-cluster
creationTime: '2021-04-22T11:13:17.236Z'
description: openshift-cluster
dnsName: operatingopenshift.com.
id: '9171610950957705760'
kind: dns#managedZone
name: ocp-cluster
nameServers:
- ns-cloud-d1.googledomains.com.
- ns-cloud-d2.googledomains.com.
- ns-cloud-d3.googledomains.com.
- ns-cloud-d4.googledomains.com.
visibility: public
```

The last step here is to point your registrar to the name servers that you just extracted as authoritative.

Now create the service account:

```
$ gcloud iam service-accounts create ocp-cluster \
    --description="Service account for OCP cluster creation" \
    --display-name="OCP_CREATOR"
Created service account [ocp-cluster].
```

Afterward assign it the required roles in order to get the needed permissions. The list of required permissions is in the documentation (*https://oreil.ly/hJzZ1*).

```
$ gcloud projects add-iam-policy-binding innate-attic-182119 \
    --member="serviceAccount:ocp-cluster\
             @innate-attic-182119.iam.gserviceaccount.com" \
    --role="roles/owner"
Updated IAM policy for project [innate-attic-182119].
bindings:
- members:
  - serviceAccount:ocp-cluster@innate-attic-182119.iam.gserviceaccount.com
  role: roles/owner
etag: BwXAjkFSyZw=
version: 1
```

The last step before you can actually install our cluster is to get your local environment ready.

Create a secure shell protocol (SSH) key-pair and add it to your ssh-agent (after you enabled the agent) with the following command:

```
$  ssh-keygen -t ed25519 -N ''
Generating public/private ed25519 key pair.
Enter file in which to save the key (/Users/rrackow/.ssh/id_ed25519):
Your identification has been saved in /Users/rrackow/.ssh/id_ed25519.
Your public key has been saved in /Users/rrackow/.ssh/id_ed25519.pub.
The key fingerprint is:
SHA256:c0y9aLQMnv6lBd51Hdrw4q4muNwAeExxdWvauvhwTtk rrackow@MacBook-Pro
```

```
The key's randomart image is:
+--[ED25519 256]--+
|    . ... .      |
|     o  ...      |
|    . . oo.. .   |
|    +  . B+o .= o|
|   . + S.0..o.oo|
|    . .. =+o....  |
|      oo=.E+.     |
|      ..Oo.=.     |
|      +o==...     |
+----[SHA256]-----+
$ eval "$(ssh-agent -s)"
Agent pid 49003
$ ssh-add /Users/rrackow/.ssh/id_ed25519
Identity added: /Users/rrackow/.ssh/id_ed25519 (rrackow@MacBook-Pro)
```

Now create a key-file and download it. Once that is done, export its path.

```
$ gcloud iam service-accounts keys create servicce-account-keys \
    --iam-account=ocp-cluster@innate-attic-182119.iam.gserviceaccount.com
created key [b8879741ba8850edcadd9840996e882adc05e228]
$ export GOOGLE_APPLICATION_CREDENTIALS='~/service-account-keys'
```

Installation

The installer, if you don't pass in any arguments, works in an interactive mode, which looks something like this: it will prompt you for choices, and you can move around with the arrow keys and make an appropriate selection with the return key.

```
$ ./Downloads/openshift-install create cluster --dir='ocp-cluster-install'
? SSH Public Key  [Use arrows to move, enter to select, type to filter]
> /Users/rrackow/.ssh/id_ed25519.pub
  /Users/rrackow/.ssh/libra.pub
  /Users/rrackow/.ssh/openshift-gcp.pub
  /Users/rrackow/.ssh/rpi-ocp-discovery.pub
  /Users/rrackow/.ssh/rrackow_private.pub
  /Users/rrackow/.ssh/rrackow_redhat_rsa.pub
  <none>
? Platform  [Use arrows to move, enter to select, type to filter]
  aws
  azure
> gcp
  openstack
  ovirt
  vsphere
INFO Credentials loaded from file "/Users/rrackow/.gcp/osServiceAccount.json"
? Project ID  [Use arrows to move, enter to select, type to filter]
> openshift-guinea-pig (innate-attic-182119)
? Region  [Use arrows to move, enter to select, type to filter]
  europe-west6 (Zürich, Switzerland)
  northamerica-northeast1 (Montréal, Québec, Canada)
  southamerica-east1 (São Paulo, Brazil)
```

```
 > us-central1 (Council Bluffs, Iowa, USA)
   us-east1 (Moncks Corner, South Carolina, USA)
   us-east4 (Ashburn, Northern Virginia, USA)
   us-west1 (The Dalles, Oregon, USA)
   ? Base Domain  [Use arrows to move, enter to select, type to filter]
 > operatingopenshift.com
   rackow.io
   ? Cluster Name ocp-cluster
   ? Pull Secret [? for help] *****************
INFO Creating infrastructure resources...
INFO Waiting up to 20m0s for the Kubernetes API
INFO Install complete!
INFO To access the cluster as the system:admin user when using 'oc': run
'export KUBECONFIG=/home/myuser/install_dir/auth/kubeconfig'
INFO Access the OpenShift web-console here:
https://console-openshift-console.apps.ocp-cluster.operatingopenshift.com
INFO Login to the console with user:
"kubeadmin", and password: "4vYBz-Ee6gm-ymBZj-Wt5AL"
INFO Time elapsed: 36m22s
```

 You don't have to write the credentials as you can find them in your
install dir, for example *ocp-cluster-install/.openshift_install.lo*.

Each option will collapse once you make a selection, so don't be confused if it looks
slightly different for you. The last two require a manual input.

After you make your last selection, the installer will work its magic. This commonly
takes around 45 minutes.

Self-Provisioned Infrastructure

You can also install OpenShift on preexisting infrastructure. That puts you in full
control of absolutely everything and also allows for a better incorporation in any sort
of pipeline. Imagine you ran a pipeline, with just a create cluster command, and
it fails at some point. Probably not very pretty to sort out what went wrong and even
worse to actually automate error handling.

Summary

In this chapter, we discussed how to install a local cluster all the way through with
considerations on how to plan your production cluster size. Each type of instance
was highlighted, and lastly, you learned how to install production clusters with the
OpenShift installer, using Installer Provisioned Infrastructure.

## CHAPTER 3

Running Workloads on OpenShift

Manuel Dewald

At this point you should already have an OpenShift cluster that you can use to deploy applications. It may be a cluster running on VMs provisioned by a cloud provider or even a small cluster on your notebook using OpenShift Local. You can access the console and log in to the cluster with the oc command-line utility. But how do you deploy an application that your team built to the cluster?

Most applications running on OpenShift clusters are web-based. Such applications are usually accessed by users via a web browser, or as backends by apps installed to user-owned devices. For the sake of this chapter you can use an arranged deployment consisting of three different services to practice deploying application code to your OpenShift cluster. A small OpenShift Local cluster should provide enough capacity to deploy this application. However, to follow some parts of the chapter you will need a cluster that is accessible externally.

The application used in this chapter is the arcade gaming platform of a fictitious game publisher. It consists of the following components:

- Games, each running in its own service (for now there is only one game).
- A highscore service where the scores of every game and player can be shown.
- The platform service, used as entry point where customers can browse, start, and purchase games.

Figure 3-1 gives you an overview of the involved components and how they interact.

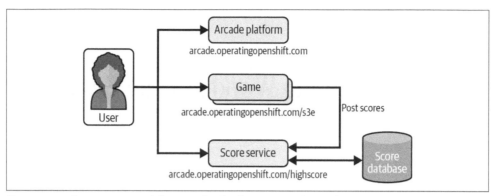

Figure 3-1. Components of the arcade platform example application

The code is organized in a Git repository on GitHub (*https://github.com/OperatingO penShift/s3e*), where each developer of the company can contribute to every service when necessary. All three services of this small sample application are located in the same Git repository. This is so you need to look at only one repository and do not need to clone several different ones. The code from this example is used in all of the following sections. If you want to follow along with this example code, use this command to check out the latest version:

```
$ git clone https://github.com/OperatingOpenShift/s3e
```

Deploying Code

To have all services you want to run on your OpenShift cluster contained in the same namespace, first create a new project:

```
$ oc new-project arcade
```

This command will automatically switch your context to the newly created `arcade` project. All further commands automatically target this project without the need to mention it in every command.

A *project* in OpenShift is a namespace with additional annotations. In most cases the differentiation between project and namespace is not relevant for the examples in this book, so the two terms are mostly interchangeable.

To switch to a different project, you can use the following command:

```
$ oc project default
```

To switch back to the `arcade` project, run the following command accordingly:

```
$ oc project arcade
```

Instead of running the `oc project` command before subsequent commands, you can also execute all the commands against a certain namespace by selecting the namespace in each command. All oc commands support the -n flag (shorthand for --namespace), which can be used to specify a namespace to run the command in.

In practice, when you know you'll execute a number of commands against the same namespace, switching to it using oc project saves some typing time and also saves you from executing commands against the "default" namespace and wondering where all your resources went.

Deploying Existing Container Images

The quickest way to start a container in the new project is using oc run. Since the game service of the application you want to deploy is already built into a container image, you can start it on the cluster using the following command:

```
$ oc run game --image=quay.io/mdewald/s3e
pod/game created
```

This will spin up a new pod on the cluster. Use the following command to observe it while it's starting up. As soon as it's ready, you should see the status "Running":

```
$ oc get pods
NAME   READY   STATUS    RESTARTS   AGE
game   1/1     Running   0          24s
```

At this point, you're probably curious to take a look at the game you just deployed. However, the oc run command just spins up a pod without an exposed endpoint, so you need to find a way to access the game UI (which is exposed at port 8080 in this container image). A quick and simple approach to confirm the UI is working is to forward the port from the container to your local machine. To do so, run the following command:

```
$ oc port-forward game 8080
Forwarding from 127.0.0.1:8080 -> 8080
```

While oc run is a quick and easy way to verify that the cluster can access your built container image and runs as expected, it is not the method of choice to continuously run an application on your cluster, as it doesn't provide advanced concepts that some of the abstractions around deploying pods provide. The standard way to deploy an application is a *deployment* resource. Deployments provide additional features to plain pods. For example, they can be used for rolling upgrades or to run multiple instances distributed across nodes. To create a deployment game with the same container image, run oc create deployment and oc get pods to observe the pod coming up:

```
$ oc create deployment game --image=quay.io/mdewald/s3e
deployment.apps/game created

$ oc get pods
NAME                     READY   STATUS    RESTARTS   AGE
game                     1/1     Running   0          13m
game-c6fb95cc6-bk6zp     1/1     Running   0          78s
```

Security context constraints

When you deploy a container using oc create deployment the pod will run with different parameters. One difference is the annotation openshift.io/scc. Compare the output of the following two commands, adjusted to the pod generated for your deployment:

```
$ oc get pod game \
-o "jsonpath={.metadata.annotations['openshift\.io/scc']}"
anyuid

$ oc get pod game-c6fb95cc6-bk6zp \
-o "jsonpath={.metadata.annotations['openshift\.io/scc']}"
restricted
```

The restricted security context constraint (SCC) means the pods of this deployment will not be able to run privileged containers or mount host directories, and containers must use a unique identifier (UID) from the allowed range. That means, for applications running a web server (in this example, NGINX), they need to be configured accordingly. They cannot run on port 80 or specify a UID that will be mapped automatically to a high UID within the range configured by the project.

See the NGINX documentation (*https://oreil.ly/Z1Wp8*) for an explanation on how to configure NGINX to serve on a specific port.

Scaling and exposing deployments

You can now scale the game Deployment using oc scale deployment. You will see additional pods coming up immediately.

```
$ oc scale deployment game --replicas=3
deployment.apps/game scaled

$ oc get pods
NAME                     READY   STATUS             RESTARTS   AGE
game                     1/1     Running            0          16m
game-c6fb95cc6-bk6zp     1/1     Running            0          3m24s
game-c6fb95cc6-bmxzd     0/1     ContainerCreating  0          3s
game-c6fb95cc6-q8bp8     0/1     ContainerCreating  0          3s
```

To access those different instances, you need to create a *service* resource and tell it to expose port 8080 from your pods. To create the service, run the following command:

```
$ oc expose deployment game --port=8080
service/game exposed

$ oc get service
NAME    TYPE        CLUSTER-IP       EXTERNAL-IP    PORT(S)     AGE
game    ClusterIP   172.25.113.82    <none>         8080/TCP    6s

$ oc get endpoints
NAME    ENDPOINTS                                              AGE
game    10.116.0.57:8080,10.116.0.59:8080,10.116.0.60:8080    22s
```

As you can see from the output of `oc get endpoints`, OpenShift has registered three different endpoints for the service, one for each instance running. To test the connection, you can again forward port 8080 to localhost, this time using the service instead of the pod:

```
$ oc port-forward service/game 8080
Forwarding from 127.0.0.1:8080 -> 8080
Forwarding from [::1]:8080 -> 8080
```

To get the second service of the arcade platform application deployed, repeat the preceding steps for the platform service:

```
$ oc create deployment platform --image=quay.io/mdewald/s3e-platform
```

```
$ oc expose deployment platform --port=8080
```

Use port-forwarding again to check if the service is accepting requests:

```
$ oc port-forward service/platform 8080
```

As you have probably already realized, port-forwarding is not how your users would want to access your service. Before we dive into exposing the services to the outside of the cluster in "Accessing Deployed Services" on page 31, the following section takes a look at a third way to deploy your application.

Deploying Applications from Git Repositories

The arcade platform contains a service that collects the scores per user of all games. The service is written in Go (*https://golang.org*) and can be found in the *highscore* subfolder of the Git repository. To deploy this service, this example does not use an already existing image from a container registry but instead uses OpenShift's built-in build infrastructure.

To deploy the application right from the Git repository, run the following command:

```
$ oc new-app https://github.com/OperatingOpenShift/s3e \ ❶
--context-dir=highscore ❷
--name=highscore ❸
--> Found container image 28f6e27 (13 days old) from Docker Hub for
    "alpine:latest"
```

```
      * An image stream tag will be created as "alpine:latest" that will track
        the source image
      * A Docker build using source code from
        https://github.com/OperatingOpenShift/s3e will be created
        * The resulting image will be pushed to image stream tag
          "highscore:latest"
        * Every time "alpine:latest" changes a new build will be triggered

  --> Creating resources ... ❹
      imagestream.image.openshift.io "alpine" created
      imagestream.image.openshift.io "highscore" created
      buildconfig.build.openshift.io "highscore" created
      deployment.apps "highscore" created
      service "highscore" created
  [...]
```

❶ Git repository containing the application

❷ Subfolder in the repository to deploy

❸ Name of the application used in resources

❹ Resources created for the application

When reading the output of this command, you can see OpenShift does a lot of work for you in maintaining this application. Chapter 5 takes a closer look at OpenShift's built-in build system.

What's important for now is that OpenShift created a build pod that checked out the Git repository and built a container image using the Dockerfile in the *highscore* subfolder. It automatically created a service for the application in the same step.

It will take some time to finish the build. When running `oc get pods` you will see a build pod running, and after the state of this pod turns to "Completed" the application pod will come up:

```
$ oc get pods
NAME                          READY   STATUS      RESTARTS   AGE
game                          1/1     Running     0          33h
game-c6fb95cc6-vj2qh          1/1     Running     0          20h
highscore-1-build             0/1     Completed   0          4m12s
highscore-56656f848c-k542p    1/1     Running     0          2m57s
```

There is no owning resource for all the resources created by `oc new-app`. You can follow the logs to get an understanding of which resources the command created for you on the OpenShift cluster.

Cleaning up an application

The following sections still use the resources created by the oc
new-app command to expose them to the outside of the cluster.
However, you may wonder how to uninstall an application, since
there is no resource owning everything that OpenShift created
automatically. You can run the following command to clean up
everything that relates to the highscore application, as OpenShift
adds the app=highscore label to everything it creates:

```
$ oc delete all --selector app=highscore
service "highscore" deleted
deployment.apps "highscore" deleted
buildconfig.build.openshift.io "highscore" deleted
build.build.openshift.io "highscore-1" deleted
imagestream.image.openshift.io "alpine" deleted
imagestream.image.openshift.io "highscore" deleted
```

Alternatively, if you want to get rid of the whole platform, you can
also delete the project:

```
$ oc delete project arcade
project "arcade" deleted
```

Accessing Deployed Services

After deploying all three services of the arcade platform application as described
in the previous section, you should now have three services running in the arcade
namespace:

```
$ oc get services
NAME         TYPE        CLUSTER-IP       EXTERNAL-IP   PORT(S)    AGE
game         ClusterIP   172.25.113.82    <none>        8080/TCP   35h
highscore    ClusterIP   172.25.32.245    <none>        8080/TCP   45s
platform     ClusterIP   172.25.170.245   <none>        8080/TCP   6s
```

All three services expose port 8080 of the pods. For game and platform you used your
knowledge of the services to expose the right port. In case of the highscore service,
OpenShift detected the exposed port from the container it built.

Accessing Services from Other Pods

All three services are of type *ClusterIP*, which allows other components of the cluster
to access it. This is helpful for services that are used only by components communicating to each other within the cluster. To test this, you can deploy a pod to interact
with the services:

```
$ oc run curl --image=curlimages/curl --command sleep 30h
```

This command will create a pod in the cluster that you can use to query one of the
services using the curl command. The hostname of the service is the name you gave

the service, so in this case you can query *http://platform:8080* to reach the platform web service:

```
$ oc exec curl -- curl -s http://platform:8080
<html>
  <head>
[...]
```

The preceding `oc run` command created a pod in the namespace `arcade`, where all the services of the arcade platform are deployed as well. That's why you can access the service just by specifying the service name as hostname. If you create the curl pod in another namespace, for example the `default` namespace, this would not be possible, as the following snippet shows:

```
$ oc -n default run curl --image=curlimages/curl --command sleep 30h
$ oc -n default exec curl -- curl -s platform:8080
command terminated with exit code 6
```

As you can see, the curl pod in the `default` namespace cannot resolve the hostname `platform`. However, we still can query a service in a different namespace by specifying the full internal domain name of the service:

```
$ oc -n default exec curl -- curl -s platform.arcade.svc.cluster.local:8080
<html>
  <head>
[...]
```

The internal DNS name of OpenShift services is set to *<service-name>.<namespace>.svc.cluster.local*.

> Depending on the network configuration of the cluster you're using, communication across specific namespaces may be blocked. NetworkPolicies can be used to allow or to block communication between services of specific namespaces.

Distribution of Requests

In the previous section, you scaled the `game` deployment up to three running pods. If you have not done this until now or scaled it back down, use the following command to scale it up:

```
$ oc scale deployment game --replicas=3
deployment.apps/game scaled
```

OpenShift will distribute the requests across all the endpoints of the service. To make this visible, the `game` deployment writes a header `instance-ip` to responses, which you can query from your curl pod. Use the following command to list all endpoints of the `game` service:

```
$ oc get endpoints game
NAME    ENDPOINTS                                              AGE
game    10.116.0.62:8080,10.116.0.63:8080,10.116.0.64:8080    35h
```

The following command runs an endless loop with curl commands to send HTTP requests to the game service:

```
$ oc exec curl -- sh -c \
'while true; do curl -si game:8080 | grep instance-ip; sleep 1s; done'
instance-ip: 10.116.0.62
instance-ip: 10.116.0.63
instance-ip: 10.116.0.62
instance-ip: 10.116.0.64
instance-ip: 10.116.0.63
instance-ip: 10.116.0.64
instance-ip: 10.116.0.63
[...]
```

The -i flag tells curl to print response headers. Each output of the curl command is filtered with grep to only print the response header instance-ip. This results in a list, showing the distribution of requests.

As you can see in the output of the command, the requests are distributed randomly to all three deployed pods.

To exit from the endless loop, press Ctrl+C.

 The "instance-ip" header is a custom header added for the purpose of this chapter. If you want to replicate this with your own application you can add the following line to your NGINX configuration:

```
add_header instance-ip $server_addr always;
```

However, this is not something we recommend for production deployments but just to visualize which endpoint receives the request.

Exposing Services

So far, you've seen how to access services from within the cluster using the hostname or the cluster-internal DNS name of a given service. To access a service from your local machine for debugging you can use port-forwarding. In most cases, however, you want your users to reach the web services, or at least parts of them, via the network, for example using their web browser. For that, you need to expose your services. OpenShift provides easy-to-use tooling to create a public DNS name as subdomain of the cluster domain that can be reached from outside of the cluster. To use it, you can create *route* resources for the services you want to expose to the network or internet.

Route by Auto-generated DNS Names

The first service to expose is the main entrance point of the arcade gaming platform, the `platform` service. To do so, just run `oc expose` again, this time specifying the *service* you want to expose to the outside world:

```
$ oc expose service platform
route.route.openshift.io/platform exposed
```

After running this command, a route resource has been created in the "arcade" namespace. Use the following command to see the route that has been generated:

```
$ oc get routes
NAME        HOST/PORT                           PATH    SERVICES    PORT
platform    platform-arcade.apps-crc.testing            platform    8080
```

Next, expose the `game` service. Run `oc expose` again and inspect the routes that OpenShift created in the namespace:

```
$ oc expose service game
route.route.openshift.io/game exposed

$ oc get routes
NAME        HOST/PORT                           PATH    SERVICES    PORT
game        game-arcade.apps-crc.testing                game        8080
platform    platform-arcade.apps-crc.testing            platform    8080
```

You can now see that for the different routes for the services, each was assigned a unique DNS name. Open a browser to verify the two web pages can be reached.

Figure 3-2 shows how the arcade gaming platform page should look. If you're running OpenShift Local, those will be *http://platform-arcade.apps-crc.testing* and *http://game-arcade.apps-crc.testing/s3e*. Remember the game service only serves the */s3e* path.

Figure 3-2. Example application: Arcade gaming platform front-end

Route by Path

From the platform page, you will notice that neither the link to the highscore page nor the button to the game is currently working. This is because the highscore service is not yet exposed, and because the game service is currently exposed with a different domain name. By default, OpenShift creates unique subdomains for each exposed service, composed from namespace and service name. You can see them in the output of the preceding oc get routes command. However, you can tell Open-Shift to route the requests based on the path in a URL instead of generating unique names per service. If you look back at the architecture of the example application in Figure 3-1, routing by path using the same domain name is what you need to get the application running.

You can reuse the domain name generated for the platform service, platform-arcade.apps-crc.testing for the complete application, specifying paths that should be routed to the different services. Since the platform service is meant as the main entrypoint to the application and expects requests at /, you don't need to alter this route. Expose the highscore service at */highscore* with the following command:

```
$ oc expose service highscore \
   --hostname=platform-arcade.apps-crc.testing --path=/highscore
route.route.openshift.io/highscore exposed
```

To change the hostname of the game service, you can edit the generated route with the following command. It opens an editor where you can adjust the generated hostname to platform-arcade.apps-crc.testing and set the path to /s3e:

```
$ oc edit route game
apiVersion: route.openshift.io/v1
kind: Route
metadata:
  [...]
  name: game
  namespace: arcade
spec:
  host: platform-arcade.apps-crc.testing
  path: /s3e ❶
  port:
    targetPort: 8080
  to:
    kind: Service
    name: game
    weight: 100
  wildcardPolicy: None
status:
  [...]
```

❶ Sets the path of this route to /s3e so all requests to this path will be forwarded to the game service.

After saving your changes and exiting the editor, you can get a list of the routes again. All three routes should now be assigned to the same hostname:

```
$ oc get routes
NAME        HOST/PORT                           PATH         SERVICES    PORT
game        platform-arcade.apps-crc.testing    /s3e         game        8080
highscore   platform-arcade.apps-crc.testing    /highscore   highscore   8080-tcp
platform    platform-arcade.apps-crc.testing                 platform    8080
```

When you revisit the main page *http://platform-arcade.apps-crc.testing* in your browser, the game button should work. The link to the highscore page should work as well, which will look similar to Figure 3-3 after finishing some games.

Figure 3-3. Example application: Arcade gaming platform highscore

External Load Balancers

Instead of using the OpenShift router to expose and access your services, you can use infrastructure-provided load balancers. For example, if you have deployed your OpenShift cluster to Google Cloud Platform (GCP), you can create GCP load balancers that will distribute the requests to your service across the OpenShift nodes.

On all nodes of the cluster a port will be open that listens for traffic directed to a specific service. The load balancer will distribute the requests to the nodes at this specific port. Requests to the load balancer IP will be forwarded to the right pod. This concept is called *NodePort* in OpenShift.

OpenShift will take care of configuring the load balancer in the infrastructure. All you need to do is specify the type LoadBalancer when exposing the deployment.

 To follow the examples of this section, you will need an OpenShift cluster that is deployed on infrastructure that provides load balancers, like GCP or Amazon Web Services (AWS). Although you can execute all the commands and create services of type LoadBalancer on OpenShift Local, it won't be different from a service of type NodePort.

Use the following command to create a new service with name game-lb to expose the game deployment with a service of type LoadBalancer. Afterward, inspect the created service with oc describe:

```
$ oc expose deployment game --type=LoadBalancer --port=8080 --name=game-lb
service/game-lb exposed

$ oc describe service game-lb
Name:                     game-lb
Namespace:                arcade
Labels:                   app=game
Annotations:              <none>
Selector:                 app=game
Type:                     LoadBalancer
IP:                       172.30.248.198
LoadBalancer Ingress:     34.71.94.126
Port:                     <unset>  8080/TCP
TargetPort:               8080/TCP
NodePort:                 <unset>  30547/TCP
Endpoints:                0.116.0.62:8080,10.116.0.63:8080,10.116.0.64:8080
Session Affinity:         None
External Traffic Policy:  Cluster
Events:
  Type    Reason         Age    From          Message
  ----    ------         ----   ----          -------
```

```
Normal   EnsuringLoadBalancer   46s   service-controller   Ensuring load balancer
Normal   EnsuredLoadBalancer    8s    service-controller   Ensured load balancer
```

You can compare this service to the original game service.

```
$ oc describe service game
Name:              game
Namespace:         arcade
Labels:            app=game
Annotations:       <none>
Selector:          app=game
Type:              ClusterIP
IP:                172.25.113.82
Port:              <unset>  8080/TCP
TargetPort:        8080/TCP
Endpoints:         10.116.0.62:8080,10.116.0.63:8080,10.116.0.64:8080
Session Affinity:  None
Events:            <none>
```

You can see that OpenShift has created a service of LoadBalancer as opposed to ClusterIP. Additionally, a NodePort has been allocated for this service that can now be used to access the service. You should be able to query any node at this port and reach the game-lb service, which will distribute the requests across the same endpoints as the game service.

Get an IP address of any of your nodes from oc get nodes -o wide or oc describe nodes. If your nodes are reachable externally and the ports are exposed, you can use the external IP to query the service right from your computer. In most cases, the nodes are not exposed to the internet directly or the ports are behind a firewall, so they cannot be reached from the internet. However, you can still deploy a pod inside the cluster and query the internal IP to observe the service behavior.

```
$ oc describe node | grep InternalIP
  InternalIP:  192.168.126.11
[...]

$ oc run curl --image=curlimages/curl --command sleep 30h ❶

$ oc exec curl -- sh -c \
  'while true; do curl -si 192.168.126.11:32167 | \
  grep instance-ip; sleep 1s; done' ❷
instance-ip: 10.116.0.63
instance-ip: 10.116.0.62
instance-ip: 10.116.0.62
instance-ip: 10.116.0.63
instance-ip: 10.116.0.62
instance-ip: 10.116.0.64
[...]
```

❶ If the curl pod is already running from a previous example, this command might return an error. You can either delete the pod or reuse the existing one.

❷ The same command as above, which will run forever. To exit from it, press Ctrl+C.

In the preceding command, one node is queried using the allocated port of the service. From the headers you can see that the requests are distributed to the same endpoints as the requests you directed to the game service before.

In addition to the NodePort, OpenShift exposed the service using a load balancer in the infrastructure you deployed your cluster on.

For this example, an OpenShift cluster on GCP has been created. In the GCP console, you can find the load balancer that is associated with this service by comparing the public IP associated with the load balancer. Figure 3-4 shows an example configuration of a load balancer, created by OpenShift.

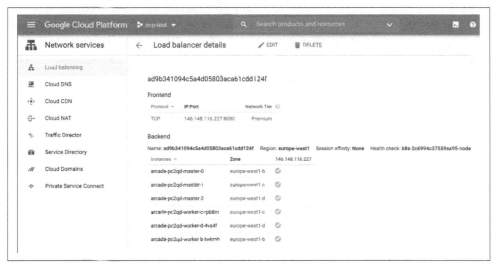

Figure 3-4. Load balancer details in the GCP console

Just as you queried the NodePort before, you can use curl from your local machine to access the service behind the load balancer using the external IP:

```
$ while true; do curl -si 34.71.94.126:8080/s3e/ | \
  grep instance-ip; sleep 1s; done
instance-ip: 10.116.0.63
instance-ip: 10.116.0.62
instance-ip: 10.116.0.63
instance-ip: 10.116.0.62
instance-ip: 10.116.0.62
instance-ip: 10.116.0.64
```

Press Ctrl+C again to stop the Curl loop.

Be aware that using infrastructure-provided load balancers for your services comes with additional costs for your project. We recommend using the OpenShift router as a default (also for its ease of use). Only if it doesn't provide the performance you need, or you need an external load balancer for a different reason, should you consider creating one for your service.

Securing Services with TLS

When following the examples in this chapter so far, you probably have realized or have even been warned by your web browser that the web services you've been accessing were insecure. Most browsers indicate that you're looking at a website that uses HTTP over HTTPS in some way, be it a small icon or a full-screen warning that you need to click your way through before you're able to visit the web page. This is a good reminder for everyone that all web pages should use secure connections. It may not be important when deploying a web service that you access only from your local device, but in most cases, you will have real users on another device, accessing your web service via the internet. In those cases, you should provide an HTTPS connection to your users so the data they enter is secured on its way to your web server. The warnings that web browsers show also tell the user in one glance whether or not you care for their privacy.

Luckily, providing officially signed certificates is very easy using Let's Encrypt (*https://letsencrypt.org*). Let's Encrypt is a service run by the Internet Security Research Group (ISRG). It aims to provide trusted, free transport layer security (TLS) certificates to anyone who runs a website on any public domain. Let's Encrypt certificates are valid for three months, which is much shorter than certificates provided by many paid providers, so the renewal process needs to be automated or you'll find yourself renewing certificates every three months. Luckily, Let's Encrypt itself provides good options to automate the certificate renewal, and there are even web servers like Caddy (*https://caddyserver.com*) hiding the certificate renewal process from administrators (or SREs).

For services deployed using the OpenShift router, you can provide TLS certificates in the route configuration. In the following examples, you will first deploy fake certificates and later request trusted certificates with Let's Encrypt. You can use a very similar procedure to provide custom certificates from trusted issuers with your route.

Specifying TLS Certificates

Before looking into automating the renewal of certificates issued by Let's Encrypt, take a look at how TLS routes are configured in OpenShift: For that, first create a self-signed certificate for the DNS name you use. This example is created on a OpenShift Local cluster using the base domain name *apps-crc.testing*, so for domain names of routes in this cluster, it is not possible to generate a publicly trusted certificate. You can run this example with any domain name, but please be advised that self-signed certificates should only be used to help you understand the process and must not replace trusted certificates for your web services.

All the routes you deployed in this chapter use the same domain name *platform-arcade.apps-crc.testing*, so you need to create and provide only a single certificate:

```
$ oc get routes
NAME        HOST/PORT                             PATH        SERVICES    PORT
game        platform-arcade.apps-crc.testing      /s3e        game        8080
highscore   platform-arcade.apps-crc.testing      /highscore  highscore   8080-tcp
platform    platform-arcade.apps-crc.testing                  platform    8080
```

To create a self-signed certificate, you can use the `openssl` command-line tool. Run the following command to generate a certificate:

```
$ openssl req -x509 -newkey rsa:4096 -nodes \
  -keyout tls.key -out tls.crt -days 90
```

This will create a certificate and a key file that you can use to encrypt the traffic to your services. For this purpose, recreate the `game` route with the following two commands:

```
$ oc delete route game
route.route.openshift.io `game` deleted

$ oc create route edge \ ❶
--cert=tls.crt --key=tls.key \ ❷
--hostname=platform-arcade.apps-crc.testing \
--port=8080 --path=/s3e --service=game
route.route.openshift.io/game created
```

❶ Specify the route type `edge`, which means the router will handle the TLS handshake.

❷ Enter the two files you generated above.

You just specified the certificate and key to use for HTTPS traffic to the game service. You can see them now in the route specification:

```
$ oc get route game -o yaml
apiVersion: route.openshift.io/v1
kind: Route
metadata:
  labels:
    app: game
  name: game
  namespace: arcade
spec:
  host: platform-arcade.apps-crc.testing
  path: /s3e
  tls:
```

```
    certificate: |
      -----BEGIN CERTIFICATE-----
      [...]
      -----END CERTIFICATE-----
    key: |
      -----BEGIN PRIVATE KEY-----
      [...]
      -----END PRIVATE KEY-----
    termination: edge
  to:
    kind: Service
    name: game
    weight: 100
  wildcardPolicy: None
status:
  [...]
```

Accessing the service should now be possible using the HTTPS scheme. Open a web browser to check if you can access your service. In the preceding example, it is accessible at *https://platform-arcade.apps-crc.testing/s3e*. Though it now uses HTTPS, the web browser still warns you that the web page is using a self-signed certificate.

Redirecting Traffic to TLS Route

Accessing the service with HTTP instead of the HTTPS scheme will no longer be possible in the current configuration. This allows you to deploy a second route using HTTP instead of HTTPS. You can also redirect the user automatically to the secure route, which should be the preferred option for most cases. To do so, set the `insecureEdgeTerminationPolicy` to `Redirect`. This setting has three different options:

- `None`: The default configuration. Only connection to HTTPS service is possible for this route.

- `Allow`: Allow traffic to both HTTP and HTTPS.

- `Redirect`: When accessing the HTTP scheme, the web server redirects the client to HTTPS.

To update this setting, edit the route as shown:

```
$ oc edit route game
apiVersion: route.openshift.io/v1
kind: Route
metadata:
  [...]
  name: game
  namespace: arcade
spec:
  [...]
```

```
  tls:
    [...]
    termination: edge
    insecureEdgeTerminationPolicy: Redirect
  to:
    [...]
status:
  [...]
```

The new configuration will also show up in the TERMINATION column in oc get
route:

```
$ oc get route game
NAME   HOST/PORT                         [...] PORT   TERMINATION    WILDCARD
game   platform-arcade.apps-crc.testing [...] 8080   edge/Redirect  None
```

You now can test and observe the redirected workflow using either the network
section of the debug tools of your web browser, or using curl, as shown in the
following listing:

```
$ curl -ikl http://platform-arcade.apps-crc.testing/s3e/ ❶
HTTP/1.1 302 Found ❷
Cache-Control: no-cache
Content-length: 0
Location: https://platform-arcade.apps-crc.testing/s3e/ ❸

HTTP/1.1 200 OK ❹
Server: nginx/1.19.7
Date: Mon, 05 Apr 2021 09:49:28 GMT
Content-Type: text/html
Content-Length: 7085
[...]
Cache-control: private

<!DOCTYPE html> ❺
<html xmlns='http://www.w3.org/1999/xhtml' lang='' xml:lang=''>
<head>
[...]
```

❶ Use -k to tell curl to trust the self-signed certificate, -i to show headers, and -L to
follow redirects.

❷ The first response is a 302, asking the client to execute the same request with a
different URL.

❸ This URL, using the HTTPS scheme, is returned by the original server, which
used the HTTP scheme.

❹ The next request is sent to the URL returned by the server (3) and returns status
code 200 (OK).

❺ The web page containing the game is returned.

Redirecting your users to the secure HTTPS scheme is a good practice especially for services that are directly user facing as in the example of the gaming platform. With redirection, the scheme used by the web service is nothing the user needs to care or think about. For example, users don't need to worry about typing `http://` or `https://`.

Now that you have enabled TLS encryption for one of the routes, the other two routes still use unencrypted HTTP. Since they all share the same hostname, you can reuse the same certificate and do not need to create or request new ones.

Use the following commands to extract the TLS property from the game route and apply it to the platform and highscore route, or recreate the routes as you did before with the game route:

```
$ oc patch route platform \
  --patch="{\"spec\":{\"tls\":$(oc get route game -o jsonpath='{.spec.tls}')}}"
route.route.openshift.io/platform patched

$ oc patch route highscore \
  --patch="{\"spec\":{\"tls\":$(oc get route game -o jsonpath='{.spec.tls}')}}"
route.route.openshift.io/highscore patched
```

Now you should see all routes are showing "edge/redirect" in the `TERMINATION` column and a check with the browser should show you're redirected to the right scheme. Since you're still using the self-signed certificate, a warning will be present.

```
$ oc get routes
NAME       HOST/PORT                              [...] PORT     TERMINATION
game       platform-arcade.apps-crc.testing [...] 8080         edge/Redirect
highscore  platform-arcade.apps-crc.testing [...] 8080-tcp edge/Redirect
platform   platform-arcade.apps-crc.testing [...] 8080         edge/Redirect
```

Let's Encrypt Trusted Certificates

Now that you know how to configure a certificate for a given route with a self-signed certificate, you can use the same process to use an officially signed and trusted certificate in your routes. However, updating certificates by hand when they are getting close to expiry—or even worse, when somebody first notices they're expired—is a tedious process, even if the certificates are valid for more than 90 days, as are the self-signed certificates in the previous example. Imagine your cluster serves more than a couple of routes, or you maintain more than one cluster and need to care for all those certificates.

A typical SRE task would be to automate this process so you don't ever again have to renew the certificates manually. If you decide to use Let's Encrypt, a lot of the automation process is already provided either by the Let's Encrypt service itself (automatic requesting of certificates) or by the community, as this service is quite popular.

For OpenShift, you can use cert-manager (*https://cert-manager.io*) to automatically request certificates for all the exposed services that you want to configure for TLS encrypted traffic.

 Using Let's Encrypt with cert-manager requires a cluster with a public-accessible domain name to perform the certificate renewal. Using OpenShift Local for it may be possible but difficult, so to practice this part you should deploy a cluster that is publicly accessible using one of the methods described in Chapter 2.

To install cert-manager on your OpenShift cluster, you can use cert-manager Operator, which is available on OperatorHub.

Visit the OperatorHub page on the OpenShift Console and search for cert-manager Operator, select it, and click Install on the screen shown in Figure 3-5 to install it.

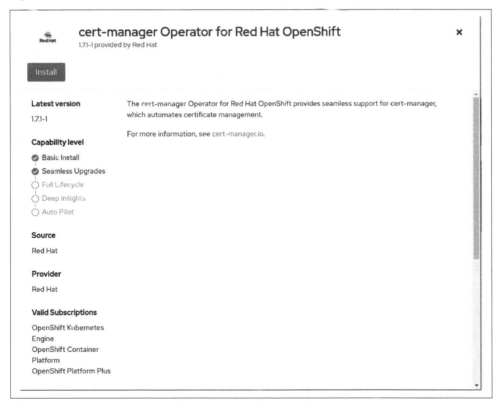

Figure 3-5. Installing cert-manager Operator from OperatorHub

The default options include observing all namespaces for resources to work on, which will be fine for this use-case.

 As of OpenShift 4.10, cert-manager Operator is in technology preview, so usage may be slightly different in upcoming versions of OpenShift.

One current limitation of cert-manager is that it works only with ingress resources, not directly with routes. This is because cert-manager is built to support all Kubernetes installations, where ingresses are default resources. Routes, as an OpenShift concept, are not yet supported.

Since OpenShift also supports ingress resources and can expose them via the router as well, this is not a big obstacle, but it does require you to replace your routes with an ingress.

First, remove the routes that you created to expose your services previously:

```
$ oc delete route game
route.route.openshift.io `game` deleted

$ oc delete route highscore
route.route.openshift.io `highscore` deleted

$ oc delete route platform
route.route.openshift.io `platform` deleted
```

Now, you need to tell cert-manager how you want to supply your ingresses with certificates. It supports many different configuration options that you can look up in the cert-manager documentation (*https://oreil.ly/kY3Sf*). As you now want to automate the renewal with Let's Encrypt, you need to configure it to use the Automatic Certificate Management Environment (ACME) protocol.

For that, create a ClusterIssuer resource and specify the ACME endpoint to use. For experimentation, you can use the staging endpoint provided by Let's Encrypt. As soon as you verify the workflow works, you can replace it by the production endpoint to get trusted certificates.

Create a file with the following content to configure a ClusterIssuer with the Let's Encrypt staging environment:

```
apiVersion: cert-manager.io/v1
kind: ClusterIssuer
metadata:
  name: le-staging ❶
spec:
  acme:
```

```
    preferredChain: ""
    privateKeySecretRef:
      name: le-staging-key
    server: https://acme-staging-v02.api.letsencrypt.org/directory ❷
    solvers:
    - http01:
        ingress: {} ❸
```

❶ The name of the ClusterIssuer will be referenced in the ingress to tell cert-manager to use this configuration to obtain certificates.

❷ The URL of the ACME directory to use. This is the staging endpoint provided by Let's Encrypt.

❸ Configure the operator to use the HTTP01 challenge to renew a certificate. This configuration is required so OpenShift can route challenge traffic to cert-manager via the router.

Apply the resource to the OpenShift cluster with oc apply:

```
$ oc apply -f le-staging.yaml
clusterissuer.cert-manager.io/le-staging created
```

You can also create it directly from the GitHub repository (*https://github.com/Opera tingOpenShift/s3e*) containing the example application using the following URL:

```
$ oc apply -f https://raw.githubusercontent.com/OperatingOpenShift/\
  s3e/main/cert-manager/le-staging.yaml

clusterissuer.cert-manager.io/le-staging created
```

Now create an ingress that instructs cert-manager to obtain new certificates using the ClusterIssuer you created. The following ingress configuration replaces the three routes of the example application:

```
apiVersion: networking.k8s.io/v1
kind: Ingress
metadata:
  annotations:
    cert-manager.io/cluster-issuer: le-staging ❶
    route.openshift.io/termination: edge
  name: platform
  namespace: arcade
spec:
  rules:
  - host: arcade.apps.<cluster-domain> ❷
    http:
      paths: ❸
      - backend:
          service:
            name: platform
```

```
            port:
              number: 8080
          path: /
          pathType: Prefix
        - backend:
            service:
              name: game
              port:
                number: 8080
          path: /s3e
          pathType: Prefix
        - backend:
            service:
              name: highscore
              port:
                number: 8080
          path: /highscore
          pathType: Prefix
  tls:
  - hosts:
    - arcade.apps.<cluster-domain> ❹
    secretName: platform-secret
```

❶ This annotation will instruct cert-manager to use the ClusterIssuer `le-staging` to get new certificates.

❷ The hostname where the application will be available.

❸ The paths referencing the different services the gaming platform is composed of. Each service you exposed using a route previously is replaced by a path in this ingress.

❹ The same hostname specified in (2). This will instruct cert-manager which hostnames the certificates are required to be valid for.

Create the ingress using `oc apply`:

```
$ oc apply -f ingress.yaml
ingress.networking.k8s.io/platform created
```

Once created, the OpenShift router will detect the ingress configuration and generate routes to expose the specified services. You need to select a hostname that is valid within the cluster, similar or equal to the hostname used earlier, so the router can generate valid routes.

When running `oc get ingress` during the renewal process, you should find an ingress created by cert-manager to execute the HTTP01 challenge. The OpenShift router will expose this ingress via a route. Use `oc get route` to follow this process:

```
$ oc get ingress
NAME                            HOSTS             PORTS      AGE
cm-acme-http-solver-4t6bb arcade.apps... 80         5s
platform                        arcade.apps... 80, 443    6s

$ oc get routes
NAME                                     HOST/PORT    PATH
cm-acme-http-solver-4t6bb-dmlq2 arcade...    /.well-known/acme-challenge/
```

You can follow the renewal process in the OpenShift Console by looking at the All Instances section of the cert-manager Operator page as shown in Figure 3-6. As soon as the status of all resources moves to Approved, Ready, and Valid, depending of the type of the resource, you can expect the certificate renewal to be completed.

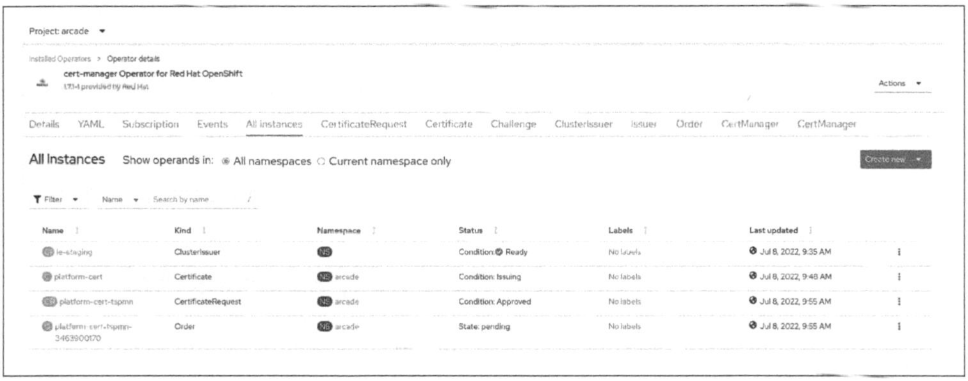

Figure 3-6. Listing all instances managed by cert-manager Operator

When the renewal process is done, cert-manager will store the certificate in the secret `platform-secret`, as specified in the ingress. This enables the router to generate route resources, finally exposing the services of the arcade gaming platform:

```
$ oc get routes
NAME             HOST/PORT    PATH         SERVICES    PORT       TERMINATION
platform-6trrx   arcade...    /s3e         game        <all>      edge/Redirect
platform-fbddd   arcade...    /            platform    <all>      edge/Redirect
platform-fdq4g   arcade...    /highscore   highscore   8080-tcp   edge/Redirect
```

The TLS configuration of the route will be filled with the contents of the secret that is referenced in the ingress. As you can see, the router is again configured to use edge termination and to redirect requests to the HTTPS endpoint.

Use Curl to verify a certificate is generated by Let's Encrypt staging endpoint, although it is still not a trusted certificate:

```
$ curl -kiv https://arcade.apps.arcade.ocp.operatingopenshift.com 2>&1 | grep issu
*  issuer: C=US; O=Let's Encrypt Staging Environment; CN=R3
```

After verifying the certificate renewal process works, you can replace the staging endpoint by the production one. To do that, apply the following ClusterIssuer, which differs only in the ACME directory URL:

```
$ oc apply -f https://raw.githubusercontent.com/OperatingOpenShift\
  /s3e/main/cert-manager/le-prod.yaml

clusterissuer.cert-manager.io/le-prod created
```

Now update the annotation in the ingress to tell cert-manager to use the new Cluster-Issuer:

```
$ oc annotate --overwrite ingress/platform \
    cert-manager.io/cluster-issuer=le-prod

ingress.networking.k8s.io/platform annotated
```

The renewal process will start again, updating the secret and finally the TLS configuration in the generated route resources. When the renewal is done, visiting the URL of the platform route in the browser will show you're now using a trusted certificate, which is indicated by the shield icon in the URL bar of the browser, as shown in Figure 3-7.

Figure 3-7. Using a trusted certificate for the example application

Using this setup allows you to switch between staging and production environments or even different TLS certificate providers just by changing an annotation on the ingress object.

To troubleshoot issues that occur in the renewal process, you can look up error messages in the resources created by cert-manager that are listed in the OpenShift Console. Cert-manager provides a guideline for troubleshooting this kind of issue in the documentation (*https://oreil.ly/4fBY8*). You can follow these steps to resolve the most common issues.

Encrypted Communication to the Service

The previous section talked about the encryption of the communication between a client outside a cluster and the cluster. TLS has been terminated on the router (edge termination), and the requests were forwarded to the web services in an unencrypted fashion.

In some cases this is fine, but in many cases you also want the communication between the router and the pods of the OpenShift cluster to be encrypted, that is, the router should use HTTPS to forward the requests. To achieve this, you have two different options. You can either not do the TLS termination on the router and instead forward the HTTPS requests to the target service (*passthrough*), or terminate the request and send a new HTTPS request to the target service (*reencrypt*). Compare the different termination modes in Figure 3-8.

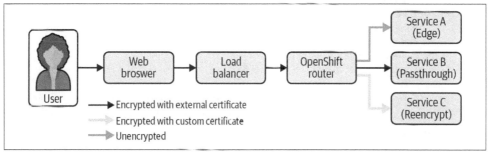

Figure 3-8. Comparison of TLS termination modes

Passthrough

A service that uses the passthrough TLS termination mode must handle the TLS termination on its own. The router does not decrypt the requests and passes them right to the receiving service. A web server of some sort that is part of the application needs to accept TLS-encrypted traffic and decrypt it accordingly. That means the web service you're using must support communicating via HTTPS, and you must provide the certificate to the service. If you're using Let's Encrypt with the cert-manager Operator, you can leave the requests and renewal of certificates to cert-manager and use the certificates it writes to the secret by mounting them into your web service's pods.

As an example for a passthrough route, you can use the platform deployment, which supports TLS communication when a certificate is mounted at a predefined path.

The secret `platform-secret` that is created by cert-manager is in the same namespace as the ingress. The operator takes care of updating the secret when a new certificate is requested.

Now you can mount that secret at the path */etc/nginx/certs/tls.crt* and */etc/nginx/certs/tls.key* in the platform pod, where the platform NGINX service expects the certificates to exist.

```
$ oc edit deployment platform
apiVersion: apps/v1
kind: Deployment
[...]
spec:
  template:
    spec:
      containers:
      - image: quay.io/mdewald/s3e-platform
        [...]
        volumeMounts: ❶
        - mountPath: /etc/nginx/certs
          name: tls-certs
          readOnly: true
      volumes:
      - name: tls-certs
        secret:
          defaultMode: 420
          secretName: platform-secret ❷
```

❶ The volumeMounts specify where the certificates should be mounted. Mount the certificates into the folder */etc/nginx/certs*, which is where the application container expects them.

❷ The secretName references the secret you specified in the ingress.

 How does the service know it should use those certificates? The platform service is based on NGINX and uses the following configuration to listen on HTTP (port 8080) and HTTPS (port 4443) at the same time. When no certificate is mounted, the service uses a self-signed default certificate that is included in the container image. Without those files, the service would not start:

```
[...]
ssl_certificate     certs/tls.crt;
ssl_certificate_key certs/tls.key;

server {
  listen 0.0.0.0:8080;
  listen 0.0.0.0:4443 ssl;
  [...]
}
```

The next step is to expose the port used for HTTPS communication in the platform pod instead of the HTTP port. Change port and target port in the `platform` service from 8080 to 4443:

```
$ oc edit service platform
apiVersion: v1
kind: Service
metadata:
  name: platform
  namespace: arcade
spec:
  ports:
  - port: 4443
    protocol: TCP
    targetPort: 4443
[...]
```

Finally, update the termination annotation and the rules in the ingress. Path-based routing is not possible using passthrough termination as the router doesn't decrypt requests, and hence can't know which path is requested. That means you need to remove all rules except the platform one from the ingress. The other services won't be reachable anymore.

```
$ oc edit ingress platform
apiVersion: v1
items:
- apiVersion: networking.k8s.io/v1
  kind: Ingress
  metadata:
    annotations:
      cert-manager.io/cluster-issuer: le-prod
      route.openshift.io/termination: passthrough ❶
    name: platform
    namespace: arcade
  spec:
    rules:
    - host: arcade.apps.<your-cluster-domain>
      http:
        paths:
        - backend:
            service:
              name: platform
              port:
                number: 4443 ❷
          pathType: ImplementationSpecific ❸
          path: '' ❹
    tls:
    - hosts:
      - arcade.apps.<your-cluster-domain>
      secretName: platform-secret
[...]
```

❶ Change the termination annotation to `passthrough` to advise OpenShift to create a passthrough route.

❷ Change the port number to the exposed TLS port.

❸ Change `pathType` to `ImplementationSpecific`.

❹ Change the path itself to an empty string.

 It's sufficient to change the "targetPort" setting on the service only so you don't have to update the port in the ingress as well to switch the port. However, consistency in port numbers helps understand and debug a system, so you should also update the port used for the communication between router and service.

You should now see the route being updated to use passthrough termination:

```
$ oc get route
NAME            HOST/PORT      PATH   SERVICES   PORT    TERMINATION
platform-4r77g  arcade.apps...        platform   <all>   passthrough/Redirect
```

To verify that the route now uses TLS to communicate with the pod, the platform service modifies the log output to print the protocol used. You can follow the logs of the service and send requests to the router from a browser or a second terminal and should see output similar to the following:

```
$ oc logs -lapp=platform -f
[...]
10.116.0.1 - [..] TLSv1.2 "GET / HTTP/1.1" 200 587 "-" "curl/7.68.0" "-"
```

The string `TLSv1.2` tells you that TLS has been terminated in the pod. Without the settings you changed in this section, the log line would look similar to the following:

```
10.116.0.1 - [...] - "GET / HTTP/1.1" 200 587 "-" "curl/7.68.0" "192.168.130.1"
```

 NGINX by default doesn't log if TLS is used or not. The variable `$ssl_protocol` is added to the default log line in the NGINX configuration specifically to visualize the differences between the termination settings.

If passthrough was a requirement for the application, you would need to change the architecture of the arcade platform to route based on DNS names rather than paths. A different option for the requirement to have encrypted communication between the services is to use the reencrypt termination mode.

Reencrypt

For the edge as well as passthrough termination modes, there is only one certificate in use for the encryption of the request from the client to the place where it's terminated. The termination happens either in the router, or the pod running the service itself. For the reencrypt termination mode, a second certificate comes into play: The certificate presented to external clients will remain the same, but now the router will communicate with the service's pod via HTTPS, using a different TLS certificate. This certificate is one that the router needs to trust and that is valid for the internal DNS name of the service. To generate one, add the following annotation to the platform service:

```
$ oc annotate service/platform \
  service.alpha.openshift.io/serving-cert-secret-name=platform-internal-cert
service/platform annotated
```

You should now see a new secret coming up. Update the platform deployment to use this secret to serve TLS encrypted traffic:

```
$ oc get secrets
NAME                       TYPE                    DATA
platform-secret            kubernetes.io/tls       2 ❶
platform-internal-cert     kubernetes.io/tls       2 ❷

$ oc edit deployment platform
apiVersion: apps/v1
kind: Deployment
[...]
spec:
  template:
    spec:
      containers:
      - image: quay.io/mdewald/s3e-platform
        [...]
        volumeMounts:
        - mountPath: /etc/nginx/certs
          name: tls-certs
          readOnly: true
      volumes:
      - name: platform-internal-cert ❸
        secret:
          defaultMode: 420
          secretName: self-signed
```

❶ The Let's Encrypt TLS secret used for external traffic from clients to the router.

❷ The generated TLS secret used for internal traffic from the router to the platform service.

❸ Reference the secret for internal communication as listed in (2).

Finally, update the termination annotation of the ingress to reencrypt traffic between the router and the platform pod:

```
$ oc edit ingress platform
apiVersion: networking.k8s.io/v1
kind: Ingress
metadata:
  annotations:
    cert-manager.io/cluster-issuer: le-prod
    route.openshift.io/termination: reencrypt ❶
  name: platform
  namespace: arcade
spec:
  rules:
  - host: arcade.apps.<cluster-domain>
    http:
      paths: ❷
      - backend:
          service:
            name: platform
            port:
              number: 4443
        path: /
        pathType: Prefix
      - backend:
          service:
            name: game
            port:
              number: 8080
        path: /s3e
        pathType: Prefix
      - backend:
          service:
            name: highscore
            port:
              number: 8080
        path: /highscore
        pathType: Prefix

  tls:
  [...]
```

❶ Instruct OpenShift to set up the route for reencrypt termination.

❷ Reencrypt allows you to use path-based routing again, so you can add back the additional paths.

You should now see the termination mode change to reencrypt at the generated route:

```
$ oc get route
NAME             HOST/PORT      PATH        SERVICES    TERMINATION
platform-kmppf   arcade.apps... /           platform    reencrypt/Redirect
platform-rhq66   arcade.apps... /highscore  highscore   reencrypt/Redirect
platform-srpqb   arcade.apps... /s3e        game        reencrypt/Redirect
```

Querying the service while observing the logs should again show the requests are using TLS:

```
$ oc logs -lapp=platform -f
[...]
10.116.0.1 - [...] TLSv1.2 "GET / HTTP/1.1" 200 587 "-" "curl/7.68.0" "-"
```

The reencrypt termination mode combined with the autogenerated certificates provides an easy way to have encrypted traffic from the client to the backend pod, while still allowing some insights into the request in the router. This allows you to use path-based routing and still encrypt the traffic from end to end.

 Only the platform service is enabled for TLS traffic, so only traffic to the platform service can be served. You could split out the highscore and game service into a separate ingress that uses edge termination.

Summary

In this chapter you successfully deployed different services onto an OpenShift cluster of your choice, using different deployment methods. You are now able to access any web service on a cluster whether it is exposed as a service, route, or not all. Even if you won't use port-forwarding very often to access your services, some services provide maintenance UI, logging, or monitoring interfaces that you can quickly access when debugging an issue.

You are now able to expose a web service using the built-in OpenShift router and encrypt traffic to your web services with TLS certificates that renew themselves automatically. You can even decide to implement different places where TLS is terminated: On the edge or in the destination service.

You tied different services together and figured out how to reach a service on the cluster using the internal domain name. To access services from outside of the cluster, you now know how to route requests based on an automatically generated hostname or a predefined path using the same domain name.

You probably used an admin used in this chapter to execute all the commands, so access control was probably not an issue for you. While this is good for experimenting, running proof of concepts or even in a development environment, in production you need to care about who has access to which parts of the cluster.

Developers may need access to the services deployed to a specific namespace. Other parts, which are only relevant for OpenShift, like the configuration of a ClusterIssuer, may be accessible only by the operations team.

Chapter 4 will explain how resources in a cluster can be protected using fine-grained Role-Based Access Control (RBAC).

Security

Rick Rackow

Security is an incredibly wide field and can definitely require multiple books on its own. In fact, there are a lot of great books on Kubernetes security already. However, operating OpenShift clusters cannot be done without security in mind. The cost of mistakes when it comes to security-related tasks is higher than in most other areas of operating a cluster. Recent data breaches and hacks have cost companies hundreds of millions of dollars, and that is even without potentially still uncovered issues.

This chapter covers the fundamental concepts of securing your cluster and your workloads, while staying more abstract than other chapters, focusing on concepts over implementation.

Cluster Access

When you have your cluster set up, you will have access to it using the kubeadmin account, but that is not very secure, and it also doesn't really scale, because you would need to hand out the password to everyone who wants to use the clusters and have them be admin. Instead, you will want to provision users, for which there are different methods, starting with the easiest: create a user by hand using the CLI. That doesn't scale very well either, so OpenShift comes with the ability to provision users automatically with the help of identity providers (IdP). Currently, the following identity providers can be used with OpenShift:

- HTPasswd
- Keystone

- LDAP
- Basic Authentication
- Request Header
- GitHub
- GitLab
- Google
- OpenID Connect

The implementation can vary a bit, but generally the steps are:

- Create Oauth app with Identity Provider
- Add Client secret to OpenShift
- Add Client ID to OpenShift
- Optionally add a Certificate Authority (CA) for your IdP instance to OpenShift

After you create the Oauth app with your identity provider of choice, you will be shown the Client ID and Client Secret. Usually, you will not be able to view the secret again, so you might want to save that in a password store; otherwise, you will have to regenerate it later.

You will now have to put the information you have into OpenShift objects. The Client Secret goes into a secret with the following command:

```
$ oc create secret generic github-client-secret \
--from-literal=clientSecret=superSecretClientSecret -n openshift-config
secret/github-client-secret created
```

Now that this is accessible for OpenShift, you can create the required Custom Resource, which will look something like Example 4-1. You have to fill in your Client ID and also the organization and teams. This is to ensure only users that are part of those organizations and teams will have access.

Example 4-1. Oauth Configuration

```
apiVersion: config.openshift.io/v1
kind: OAuth
metadata:
  name: cluster
spec:
  identityProviders:
  - name: githubidp
    mappingMethod: claim
    type: GitHub
    github:
```

```
ca:
  name: ca-config-map
clientID: 1234ClientID5678
clientSecret:
  name: github-client-secret
hostname: ...
organizations:
- myorganization
teams:
- myorganization1/team-a
```

One other interesting and important value is the `mappingMethod`. This determines how users are created on cluster. The options here are:

- claim
- lookup
- generate
- add

Not all of them are available for all identity providers, but in the case of GitHub as an identity provider, they are.

Logically they all do different things, and *claim* has become the most common for most users. When setting the mapping to *claim*, OpenShift will attempt to create a new user on the cluster, when someone logs in through the identity provider for the first time, and will fail if there is a user already on this cluster that authenticated through a different method.

The lookup method will check whether a given user for the identity they are trying to log in with exists. This requires an additional process, because users will not be provisioned on cluster automatically.

The slightly more generous alternative to *claim* is *generate*. It works similarly to *claim* but, if a given user exists on cluster already with a different identity, OpenShift will try to provision a new user. For example if *manuel* logged in via the also provisioned Google identity provider and now tries to log in via GitHub, the *generate* mapping-Methods will try to create a new user: *manuel2* or similar.

If you want to avoid that, you need to use the *add* method. Here OpenShift adds the new identity to the existing user.

Role-Based Access Control

Besides gaining access to your cluster, if you need to perform any actions on the cluster, you need a specific set of privileges to do so. Kubernetes has the concept of Role-Based Access Control (RBAC) that therefore is also used by OpenShift.

The following sections go over the nuances of RBAC in more detail.

Roles and ClusterRoles

A *role* is a specific set of permissions. The permissions start from nothing and then add up. There is no denying anything explicitly, mainly because a denial to certain privileges is only required if they have been granted before, which *should* not happen, since you start from zero privileges. It is thereby crucial to follow the principle of the least privilege: only assign any privileges that are absolutely required.

To assign a certain set of privileges, you need to understand how OpenShift resources work: every API has resources that you can execute certain actions against. Those actions are defined as verbs. The following example shows an interaction against the core API, using the *GET* verb for any resources of type pod:

```
$ oc get pods
```

All interactions with any OpenShift resource follow this concept, and while you can extend OpenShift with Custom Resource Definitions and thereby add new resources and APIs, the list of verbs is fixed to the following:

- GET
- CREATE
- APPLY
- UPDATE
- PATCH
- DELETE
- PROXY
- LIST
- WATCH
- DELETECOLLECTION

When you start to create a role, you have to ask yourself, "What do I want to do against which resource for which API?" From there you go ahead and build a role definition. The following example shows a role definition that would allow the example command oc get pods:

```
apiVersion: rbac.authorization.k8s.io/v1
kind: Role
metadata:
  namespace: default
  name: pod-reader
rules:
- apiGroups: [""] # "" indicates the core API group
```

```
  resources: ["pods"]
  verbs: ["get", "list"]
```

You might have noticed that in addition to the pure *GET* verb, there is also the *LIST* permission. If you were to leave that, you could get only one specific pod, which you already know about, whereas the `oc get pods` command has to list all pods to get them.

You can also see that there is a `namespace` parameter. This is the difference between a *Role* and a *ClusterRole*: Roles are namespaced, so the preceding definition only permits the actions in the `default` namespace. The following example for a *ClusterRole* will give the same permissions, but cluster wide:

```
apiVersion: rbac.authorization.k8s.io/v1
kind: ClusterRole
metadata:
  name: pod-reader-cluster
rules:
- apiGroups: [""] # "" indicates the core API group
  resources: ["pods"]
  verbs: ["get", "list"]
```

In addition to removing the namespace limitation, ClusterRoles are also the only means to give access to cluster-wide resources, such as *nodes*. That means you cannot use a Role to grant access to cluster-wide resources and *must* use a ClusterRole instead.

RoleBindings and ClusterRoleBindings

Now that you have defined a certain set of privileges that you want or need, you actually need a way to assign that to a user or a system account. That is the task of *RoleBindings*. A RoleBinding has a set of subjects, which are the users. Think of it as "They are subject to be assigned those permissions." The other part is the `roleRef`, which is the role you want to bind to the subjects. The following example assigns our `pod-reader` role to the user `Manuel`:

```
apiVersion: rbac.authorization.k8s.io/v1
kind: RoleBinding
metadata:
  name: read-pods
  namespace: default
subjects:
- kind: User
  name: Manuel
  apiGroup: rbac.authorization.k8s.io
roleRef:
  kind: Role
  name: pod-reader
  apiGroup: rbac.authorization.k8s.io
```

After the preceding is applied, Manuel would be granted the permissions to get and list pods in the default namespace.

You can assign the same role to multiple users in the same `RoleBinding`. In the next example, we assign the `pod-reader` role to `Manuel` and `Rick`:

```
apiVersion: rbac.authorization.k8s.io/v1
kind: RoleBinding
metadata:
  name: read-pods
  namespace: default
subjects:
- kind: User
  name: Manuel
  apiGroup: rbac.authorization.k8s.io
- kind: User
  name: Rick
  apiGroup: rbac.authorization.k8s.io
roleRef:
  kind: Role
  name: pod-reader
  apiGroup: rbac.authorization.k8s.io
```

Note that the name variable is case-sensitive. That means that `Manuel` is not the same user as `manuel`, and it is easy to trip over because an IDE will commonly not detect this as an issue.

The equivalent to a RoleBinding is the ClusterRoleBinding. It allows for granting cluster-wide accessing of resources. The following example will grant Rick and Manuel access to get and list all pods in all namespaces:

```
apiVersion: rbac.authorization.k8s.io/v1
kind: ClusterRoleBinding
metadata:
  name: read-pods-cluster
subjects:
- kind: User
  name: Manuel
  apiGroup: rbac.authorization.k8s.io
- kind: User
  name: Rick
  apiGroup: rbac.authorization.k8s.io
roleRef:
  kind: Role
  name: pod-reader-cluster
  apiGroup: rbac.authorization.k8s.io
```

Every permission in your OpenShift cluster is set up this way, and you should be wary about granting too many permissions even if it might become cumbersome at some point. This is especially true when you are starting to put workloads on your cluster and have to start to use ServiceAccounts.

CLI

The oc command line interface gives you the ability to perform some of the preceding actions ad hoc as well as get an overview of the roles and bindings that currently exist on your cluster.

To check which roles exist in your current namespace and what permissions they grant, execute the following command:

```
$ oc describe role.rbac
Name:         prometheus-k8s
Labels:       app.kubernetes.io/component=prometheus
              app.kubernetes.io/instance=k8s
              app.kubernetes.io/name=prometheus
              app.kubernetes.io/part-of=openshift-monitoring
              app.kubernetes.io/version=2.32.1
Annotations:  <none>
PolicyRule:
Resources                     Non-Resource URLs  Resource Names  Verbs
---------                     -----------------  --------------  -----
endpoints                     []                 []              [get list watch]
pods                          []                 []              [get list watch]
services                      []                 []              [get list watch]
ingresses.extensions          []                 []              [get list watch]
ingresses.networking.k8s.io   []                 []              [get list watch]
```

The same command works respectively for ClusterRoles; just be prepared for a lot more output, given the vast number of moving bits and pieces that are on an OpenShift cluster out of the box.

You can also find out which RoleBindings are in the current namespace using the following command:

```
$ oc describe rolebindings.rbac
Name:         prometheus-k8s
Labels:       app.kubernetes.io/component=prometheus
              app.kubernetes.io/instance=k8s
              app.kubernetes.io/name=prometheus
              app.kubernetes.io/part-of=openshift-monitoring
              app.kubernetes.io/version=2.32.1
Annotations:  <none>
Role:
  Kind:  Role
  Name:  prometheus-k8s
Subjects:
```

```
Kind              Name             Namespace
----              ----             ---------
ServiceAccount    prometheus-k8s   openshift-monitoring
```

Other than purely displaying existing state on a cluster, you can also use the CLI to apply changes. For example, you can add `Manuel` to the `pod-reader`:

```
$ oc adm policy add-role-to-user pod-reader Manuel -n default
clusterrole.rbac.authorization.k8s.io/pod-reader added: "Manuel"
```

ServiceAccounts

When you have certain tasks to automate, you might want to use a system account rather than an actual user and its token, respectively. ServiceAccounts obey the exact same rules for permissions as any other user on the cluster, so the important aspect here is to know how to create a ServiceAccount and then use it.

To create a service account, run the following command:

```
$ oc create sa my-bot
serviceaccount/my-bot created
```

You can also retrieve a ServiceAccount and its information:

```
$ oc get sa my-bot -o yaml
apiVersion: v1
imagePullSecrets:
- name: my-bot-dockercfg-bpf5n
kind: ServiceAccount
metadata:
  creationTimestamp: "2022-08-03T13:57:30Z"
  name: my-bot
  namespace: default
  resourceVersion: "25019623"
  uid: f718f7be-abce-47f0-a43b-0dc02b044bcf
secrets:
- name: my-bot-token-zwskx
- name: my-bot-dockercfg-bpf5n
```

You can now add any privileges to it. In the following example, we add the pod-reader role to the bot account:

```
$ oc policy add-role-to-user pod-reader system:serviceaccount:default:my-bot
ClusterRole.rbac.authorization.k8s.io/pod-reader added:
```

```
"system:serviceaccount:default:my-bot"
```

Now that the my-bot account can do something, you can go ahead and start to use it from outside the cluster. In this simple example we could use it in the following command to list all pods in the default namespace, without being authenticated ourselves:

```
$ export TOKEN=$(oc sa get-token my-bot)

$ oc get pods -n default --token $TOKEN
NAMESPACE NAME
grafana    grafana-deployment-787fd449f4-z5vkf
grafana    grafana-operator-controller-manager-5b5d45b9bd-wrnsv

$ oc whoami --token $TOKEN
system:serviceaccount:default:my-bot
```

The last command is not needed but makes it clear that the command was executed as the ServiceAccount.

The use cases for ServiceAccounts are wide, but generally if you need to perform any action from outside the cluster in an automated way, you probably should be using ServiceAccounts, and since there is no limit to the number of ServiceAccounts that can exist on a given cluster, it is a great way to follow the idea of the least privilege again.

For deployments, each app can have its own ServiceAccount with privileges scoped just to what is needed to deploy, so there is no scenario in which a single compromised token or account can interfere with all of your platform at once. This separation adds extra layers of rudimentary protection that you should have enabled in all of your infrastructure. You would not grant a user pseudoprivileges on a Linux host just to create a deployment, would you?

Now that you got access to a cluster and subsequently assigned some privileges, it is time to remove the default `kubeadmin` user. You should not log in as `kubeadmin` anymore, and while the password is fairly complex and therefore not easy to guess or brute force, an unused admin account is definitely not what you want. Before you do that, double check on the following:

- You have configured an Identity Provider
- You have assigned the *cluster-admin* role to a user

Both of these are crucial as you will otherwise lock yourself out of admin access.

If you have done both of these, you can now log in as a user with the cluster-admin role and execute the following command:

```
$ oc delete secrets kubeadmin -n kube-system
```

Threat Modelling

Threat modelling means that you look at potential threats to your system, mapping out their likeliness and impact. While your security team is busy doing that, it is good to think about and evaluate the risks to your platform and how to best protect against those risks.

To get started, think about the following scenario: someone writes all their passwords on a little notepad in their home. Is this good or bad?

You might be quick to say that they should be using a safe password store or something similar, but is it a realistic scenario that someone breaks into their home and steals the notepad to get their passwords? For the average citizen, no. It is not a real issue. Yes, there are better ways, but generally a notepad is OK and definitely better than using the same password everywhere.

But if the person using a notepad for all their passwords is the CEO of a Fortune 500 company, that's different, and there is, in fact, some chance that someone will try to steal their password notepad.

The same applies to your OpenShift cluster, and you should keep that in mind when you are hardening your cluster. If you are running CodeReadContainers on your laptop to learn and understand OpenShift, it is probably fine to just keep using the kubeadmin user. If you run a production cluster for your company that is exposed to the internet, you probably want to lock it down as described in the preceding sections with access control and RBAC rules.

Threat modelling a little in your head before you do things makes life easier for you and for your security team, as you will be able to explain what you did to protect your infrastructure and why you might not have done certain other actions.

Workloads

Locking down your cluster is one thing, but you want to use your cluster at some point, and that is when you start to deploy workloads, which need some security considerations as well. You want to be in a state where you make it as hard as possible to compromise a given workload and then even harder for a potential attacker to make lateral movements from there. This means even a single compromised workload should not lead to a compromise of your whole cluster.

One common type of workload to deploy is web services and anything else that is exposed via a route, and unless it is customer facing and open for the world, you most definitely should lock this down. The easiest way to do this out of the box is to use OpenShift's native capabilities. OpenShift allows you to deploy an Oauth-proxy in front of your application and thereby leverage the RBAC permission model you already have to define access rights for your exposed service.

In the following example, you will deploy a simple game, but since it's still a prototype, you only want the users who work on it to be able to access it.

First, you need a new namespace:

```
$ oc create namespace s3e
namespace/s3e created

$ oc project s3e
Now using project "s3e" on server "https://api.crc.testing:6443".
```

Now that you have a place for your game to live, it's time to get started with the proxy. You need a ServiceAccount for it to use:

```
apiVersion: v1
kind: ServiceAccount
metadata:
  name: proxy
  annotations:
    serviceaccounts.openshift.io/oauth-redirectreference.primary: >
      '{"kind":"OAuthRedirectReference",
      "apiVersion":"v1",
      "reference":{"kind":"Route","name":"proxy"}}'
```

Next, get your app deployment ready that includes the proxy:

```
apiVersion: apps/v1
kind: Deployment
metadata:
  name: proxy
spec:
  replicas: 1
  selector:
    matchLabels:
      app: proxy
  template:
    metadata:
      labels:
        app: proxy
    spec:
      serviceAccountName: proxy
      containers:
      - name: oauth-proxy
        image: openshift/oauth-proxy:latest
        imagePullPolicy: IfNotPresent
        ports:
        - containerPort: 8443
          name: public
        args:
        - --https-address=:8443
        - --provider=openshift
        - --openshift-service-account=proxy
        - --upstream=http://localhost:8080
        - --tls-cert=/etc/tls/private/tls.crt
        - --tls-key=/etc/tls/private/tls.key
        - --cookie-secret=SECRET
```

```
      volumeMounts:
      - mountPath: /etc/tls/private
        name: proxy-tls
    - name: app
      image: quay.io/operatingopenshift/s3e-game:latest
    volumes:
    - name: proxy-tls
      secret:
        secretName: proxy-tls
```

If you use a different image, make sure that the upstream variable still works correctly. In this case the game exposes itself on port 8080, so this is perfectly fine.

You can configure the proxy further using the --openshift-sar= argument to lock down specifically based on RBAC permissions. If you do not set this argument, as in this case, every user who can log in to OpenShift can also access whatever is behind the proxy, which seems sane for this scenario.

From here on you will also need a service and a route:

```
apiVersion: v1
kind: Route
metadata:
  name: proxy
spec:
  to:
    kind: Service
    name: proxy
  tls:
    termination: Reencrypt

apiVersion: v1
kind: Service
metadata:
  name: proxy
  annotations:
    service.alpha.openshift.io/serving-cert-secret-name: proxy-tls
spec:
  ports:
  - name: proxy
    port: 443
    targetPort: 8443
  selector:
    app: proxy
```

The selector here is specifying that the proxy is the backend to send traffic to.

You can put all of the above in a single YAML file and then deploy it to the cluster like so:

```
kind: List
apiVersion: v1
items:
```

```yaml
# Create a proxy service account and ensure it will use the route "proxy"
- apiVersion: v1
  kind: ServiceAccount
  metadata:
    name: proxy
    annotations:
      serviceaccounts.openshift.io/oauth-redirectreference.primary: >
        '{"kind":"OAuthRedirectReference",
        "apiVersion":"v1",
        "reference":{"kind":"Route","name":"proxy"}}'
# Create a secure connection to the proxy via a route
- apiVersion: v1
  kind: Route
  metadata:
    name: proxy
  spec:
    to:
      kind: Service
      name: proxy
    tls:
      termination: Reencrypt
- apiVersion: v1
  kind: Service
  metadata:
    name: proxy
    annotations:
      service.alpha.openshift.io/serving-cert-secret-name: proxy-tls
  spec:
    ports:
    - name: proxy
      port: 443
      targetPort: 8443
    selector:
      app: proxy
# Launch a proxy as a sidecar
- apiVersion: apps/v1
  kind: Deployment
  metadata:
    name: proxy
  spec:
    replicas: 1
    selector:
      matchLabels:
        app: proxy
    template:
      metadata:
        labels:
          app: proxy
      spec:
        serviceAccountName: proxy
        containers:
        - name: oauth-proxy
```

```
image: openshift/oauth-proxy:latest
imagePullPolicy: IfNotPresent
ports:
- containerPort: 8443
  name: public
args:
- --https-address=:8443
- --provider=openshift
- --openshift-service-account=proxy
- --upstream=http://localhost:8080
- --tls-cert=/etc/tls/private/tls.crt
- --tls-key=/etc/tls/private/tls.key
- --cookie-secret=SECRET
volumeMounts:
- mountPath: /etc/tls/private
  name: proxy-tls

- name: app
  image: quay.io/operatingopenshift/s3e-game:latest
volumes:
- name: proxy-tls
  secret:
    secretName: proxy-tls
```

To apply the configuration, execute the following command:

```
$ oc apply -f deploy-snake-proxy.yaml
serviceaccount/proxy created
route.route.openshift.io/proxy created
service/proxy created
deployment.apps/proxy created
```

You can now get the route URL via oc get route like so:

```
$ oc get route -o json | jq .items[].spec.host
"proxy-s3e.apps-crc.testing"
```

If you bring that up in your browser, you will now be presented with a login screen. This also lets you know that you secured your app via Oauth-proxy.

Summary

In this chapter, we discussed security best practices and considerations to make when planning and operating your OpenShift cluster. These will give you a starting point. However, as clusters as well as adversaries are ever evolving, it is of major importance to revise the steps you took.

## CHAPTER 5

Automating Builds

Manuel Dewald

Chapter 3 looked at how applications can be deployed to an OpenShift cluster by running commands to create Kubernetes objects and pulling container images from a central container registry. However, most applications are developed and updated over time after their first deployment.

This is especially true for software that is not running on a local device (such as a word processor) but on a cloud platform, like an OpenShift cluster. Shipping software to consumer devices is a much more involved process than updating cloud software, which is one reason many products move to produce cloud software.

Software that is running as a web service is usually accessed from a consumer device with a web browser or client. The software itself can be upgraded by the developing company at any time. Many companies even deploy updates multiple times a day.

For a company that is running all workloads in containers on OpenShift, such as the example game developer described in this book, the process of creating and updating container images needs to be automated and reproducible. Nobody wants to just sit there and create and deploy container images all day long.

This chapter is all about creating an automated procedure to bring code that developers wrote on their machines to the OpenShift cluster where it's meant to run.

Luckily, OpenShift already brings several tools to help with this process.

OpenShift Image Builds

The first of the tools this chapter looks at is the built-in build machinery that comes with every OpenShift installation. You already used this once to build a container image based on the code in a Git repository in Chapter 3, where you built and deployed the highscore service of the example application.

OpenShift supports three different build strategies:

- *Docker build:* Building a container image from a Dockerfile
- *Source to Image (S2I) build:* Building a container image from source code using a builder image
- *Custom build:* Run a custom container image to build the application image

The following sections describe those strategies in detail and help you to choose which strategy for your use case.

Docker Build

Try the docker build strategy first. It allows you to easily onboard the build of container images that already have a Dockerfile in place. The Dockerfile describes how the application container image should be built.

Often, an application is in development for some time before how it will be deployed is even decided. That it will run in a container eventually could already be clear at this point, so developers may start by building a container that runs the application.

To get started with a good development setup, developers create a Dockerfile that they can use to build and run the application locally. Using this Dockerfile for deployment as well is only natural: It already exists and is proven to be able to run the software. In addition, using this Dockerfile for the official build helps keep the development setup close to the production environment. This is useful later in the application life to prevent bugs that occur only in production and cannot be reproduced locally.

Developers of the highscore service build and run the container image based on the Dockerfile multiple times during their development workflow. However, for the production deployment, the team decides that they need to have a central build system that is based on what's currently checked into version control.

To build the application container, the team came up with a Dockerfile that packages all the dependencies of the application and can be used to build a container image that runs the highscore service.

It's a good practice to split Dockerfiles up into two separate stages, one for building the application and one for running, as the requirements can be quite different. In this example service, written in Go, the build image needs the Go compiler at compile time, but it is not needed at runtime. Here is what the Dockerfile of the highscore service looks like:

```
FROM golang:1.14 AS build ❶
COPY . /src
WORKDIR /src
RUN CGO_ENABLED=0 GOOS=linux go build ❷

FROM alpine:latest ❸
RUN apk --no-cache add ca-certificates
WORKDIR /app
COPY --from=build /src/highscore . ❹
RUN mkdir /app/db ❺
RUN chgrp -R 0 /app/db && chmod -R g=u /app/db ❻
EXPOSE 8080 ❼
CMD ["/app/highscore"] ❽
```

❶ The base image used to build the binary of the highscore service.

❷ This command runs the compilation of the web service binary.

❸ The base image used to run the highscore service.

❹ Extracting the binary from the build image and copying it to the destination in the runtime container image.

❺ Creating a folder needed to store the highscores.

❻ The folder needs to be owned by the root group, so the user that runs the container (which is not known at build time) can access it. See also the Container Guidelines in the OpenShift documentation (*https://oreil.ly/gtANa*).

❼ The port the service is running on.

❽ On container startup, the binary will be started.

To build the application locally, a developer can check out the latest version of the repository and run docker build in the corresponding folder to get an image ready to run. That's essentially what OpenShift does as well, despite not using Docker to build the image.

After building the container image, OpenShift will push it to the built-in container registry. Any pod referencing this container image can pull it from the container registry.

If you haven't already, run the following command to build and deploy the highscore application:

```
$ oc new-app https://github.com/OperatingOpenShift/s3e \
  --context-dir=highscore --name=highscore
```

This will start a new build and deploy the service.

The command can be run by a developer or sysadmin to deploy the application once. However, the team wants to have a new build whenever they merge a change in version control. How does OpenShift know when the source code has changed and it should build a new version of the application container?

To see the different possibilities to trigger a new build, inspect the build configuration that OpenShift created for the highscore service.

To see the configuration, run the following command to get the BuildConfig of the highscore service:

```
$ oc describe buildconfig highscore
Name:    highscore
Namespace: arcade
Created: 53 seconds ago
Labels: app=highscore
    app.kubernetes.io/component=highscore
    app.kubernetes.io/instance=highscore
Annotations:    openshift.io/generated-by=OpenShiftNewApp
Latest Version: 1

Strategy:       Docker ❶
URL:            https://github.com/OperatingOpenShift/s3e
ContextDir:     highscore ❷
From Image:     ImageStreamTag alpine:latest ❸
Output to:      ImageStreamTag highscore:latest

Build Run Policy:       Serial
Triggered by:           Config, ImageChange ❹
Webhook Generic:
  URL:      https://api.crc.testing[...]/webhooks/<secret>/generic ❺
  AllowEnv:     false
Webhook GitHub:
  URL: https://api.crc.testing[...]/webhooks/<secret>/github ❻
Builds History Limit:
  Successful:   5
  Failed:               5

Build          Status  Duration          Creation Time
highscore-1    running running for 51s  2021-05-09 13:23:29 +0200 CEST
```

❶ The strategy of the build. OpenShift automatically detected the Dockerfile and selected the Docker build strategy.

❷ The context directory you passed via the new-app command to tell OpenShift to use the highscore folder in the Git repository.

❸ The image the Dockerfile is based on.

❹ A new change will be triggered by a new base image or a change to the config.

❺ A new build can also be triggered by requests to this generic webhook URL.

❻ A new build can also be triggered with requests to the GitHub-specific webhook URL.

By looking at the BuildConfig object you can see the different triggers for building a new version of the container image:

- *Base image changes:* When the base image changes, OpenShift will automatically create a new version of the application. This can happen, for example, after some bugs or vulnerabilities have been fixed in the base image.
- *Application code changes:* In addition, when the application code itself changes, you can trigger a new build using one of the webhook URLs. The generic webhook URL can be triggered, for example, using curl from the command line, so you can integrate it in any automation system. The GitHub-specific URL is designed to work with GitHub repositories. You can configure your GitHub repository, for example, to trigger a new build whenever a new change is merged to the main branch.

The <secret> parts in the webhook URLs need to be filled out with values from the BuildConfig. Their purpose is to make the URLs harder to guess, so nobody can flood your cluster with unnecessary builds without knowing the secrets.

You can get them by getting the whole BuildConfig object:

```
$ oc get buildconfig highscore -o yaml
apiVersion: build.openshift.io/v1
kind: BuildConfig
[...]
spec:
  [...]
  triggers:
 - github:
      secret: Bj7fzzVDVkoMY9729Rq8
    type: GitHub
  - generic:
      secret: D_88867wY9rjOtvd1vgA
    type: Generic
[...]
```

In this example, the generic webhook URL would be

https://api.crc.testing:6443/apis/build.openshift.io/v1/namespaces/arcade/build-configs/highscore/webhooks/D_88867wY9rjOtvd1vgA/generic and the GitHub webhook URL

> *https://api.crc.testing:6443/apis/build.openshift.io/v1/namespaces/arcade/build-configs/highscore/webhooks/Bj7fzzVDVkoMY9729Rq8/github.*

Triggering a build with the generic webhook

To trigger a build using the generic webhook URL from the BuildConfig, completed with the generated secret, send a POST http request:

```
$ curl -k -X POST https://api.crc.testing:6443/apis/build.openshift.io/v1/\
   namespaces/arcade/buildconfigs/highscore/webhooks/D_88867wY9rjOtvd1vgA/generic
[...]
   "status": "Success",
   "message": "invalid Content-Type on payload,
               ignoring payload and continuing with build",
   "code": 200
```

The webhook allows you to optionally send data in the POST request and will trigger a new build instantly.

Run the following command to see past and current builds:

```
$ oc get builds
NAME          TYPE     FROM          STATUS      STARTED         DURATION
highscore-1   Docker   Git@c7c9e95   Complete    4 minutes ago   1m10s  ❶
highscore-2   Docker   Git@c7c9e95   Running     7 seconds ago          ❷
```

❶ This build has been triggered by the oc `new-app` command. It already completed some minutes ago.

❷ This build has been triggered by the webhook.

To configure the behavior of the build, the POST request used to trigger the build needs to contain a body of the following format:

```
git:
  [...]
env:
- name: <name of the environment variable>
  value: <value of the variable>
```

For example, you may want to override the default environment when running the build for a staging or development environment. For that, your build can receive specific environment variables that differ from the configured defaults.

To allow overriding environment variables, the webhook configuration must be adjusted. Otherwise, the build system will take only the variables from the BuildConfig. Edit the BuildConfig resource and set the `allowEnv` option to enable passing environment variables:

```
$ oc edit buildconfig -n arcade highscore

[...]
    triggers:
    - generic:
        allowEnv: true
```

To send the data from the command line or a script, use a command like the following:

```
$ curl -H 'Content-Type: application/json' -k \
-d '{"env":[{"name":"MY_VAR","value":"MY_VALUE"}]}' \
https://api.crc.testing:6443/apis/build.openshift.io/v1/namespaces/arcade/\
buildconfigs/highscore/webhooks/D_88867wY9rjOtvd1vgA/generic
```

OpenShift supports a few more options to configure the behavior of a build that is triggered by a generic webhook. The OpenShift documentation (*https://oreil.ly/ vKhKG*) can give you a detailed explanation of all the supported options.

Triggering a build with the GitHub webhook

The GitHub webhook can be used to trigger a build automatically whenever a change is merged to a Git repository on GitHub.

To follow this exercise, create a fork of the repository (*https://github.com/OperatingO penShift/s3e*) used in this chapter on GitHub. In the repository settings, you will find the option to add a webhook as shown in Figure 5-1.

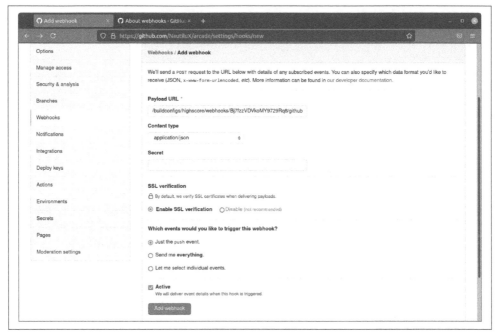

Figure 5-1. Adding a GitHub webhook in repository settings

In the field Payload URL, paste the GitHub webhook URL of your BuildConfig with the secret. The Secret field in the GitHub UI can be left empty.

 Triggering a build from a GitHub repository requires a cluster with a public-accessible domain name. Using OpenShift Local for it may be possible but difficult, so to practice this part you need to deploy a cluster that is publicly accessible using one of the methods described in Chapter 2.

More build triggers

The GitHub and generic webhooks are two of the most commonly used webhooks to trigger builds in OpenShift. However, OpenShift supports many more webhook configurations, including GitLab and Bitbucket, which can be configured similarly. In addition to webhooks, builds can be triggered by other events like configuration changes and image updates.

For a detailed explanation of all possible triggers, take a look at the OpenShift documentation (*https://oreil.ly/8G9hJ*), which describes how to configure all of them. However, the procedure is similar to the webhooks discussed in this chapter.

To enable an additional webhook, run a command like the following example, which enables a Bitbucket webhook:

```
$ oc set triggers buildconfig highscore --from-bitbucket
buildconfig.build.openshift.io/highscore triggers updated
```

You will find a new trigger added to the BuildConfig:

```
$ oc get bc highscore -o yaml
[...]
  successfulBuildsHistoryLimit: 5
  triggers:
  [...]
  - bitbucket:
      secret: gjuBrmqrDJLVcJlfX3tH
    type: Bitbucket
```

You can now use the information from this trigger to configure a webhook in Bitbucket, similarly to how you configured it in GitHub.

Source to Image (S2I) Build

OpenShift aims to make building and deploying the code produced by software developers as easy as possible.

The scenario OpenShift tries to achieve with Source to Image (S2I) is the following: the developer writes source code and doesn't need to care at all about how it'll be built into an image and run on the OpenShift cluster. No knowledge of how to write a Dockerfile for an application is required to use S2I.

That means OpenShift automatically detects which language the developer used in their project and chooses a base image to build the application container on. As of OpenShift 4.8, the following languages can be detected automatically:

- C#
- Java
- JavaScript
- Perl
- PHP
- Python
- Ruby
- Scala
- Go

The language detection also can be overridden to use a specific builder image. You can even create your own custom image to build an application, which you will learn about later in this chapter.

Automatic language detection

To demonstrate the language detection feature, the arcade project contains a second folder for the highscore service, */highscore-s2i/*. This folder doesn't contain a Docker-file, so when building this application, OpenShift will not choose the Docker strategy but will build it from the source code based on the language it detects.

To build the application from this folder, you only need to swap out the context directory in the `oc new-app` command given earlier:

```
$ oc new-app https://github.com/OperatingOpenShift/s3e \
  --context-dir=highscore-s2i --name=highscore

--> Found image [...] in image stream "openshift/golang" [...] for "golang"

[...]

    * The source repository appears to match: golang
```

 Remember: you may need to clean up the build artifacts from earlier with the following command:

```
$ oc delete all --selector app=highscore
```

As you can see from the output, OpenShift correctly detected that the application source code is using Go. In the automatically created BuildConfig, you can also see which image has been used for the application and which output image will be produced:

```
$ oc get buildconfig highscore -o yaml

[...]
output:
    to:
      kind: ImageStreamTag
      name: highscore:latest
[...]
source:
    contextDir: highscore-s2i
    git:
      uri: https://github.com/OperatingOpenShift/s3e
    type: Git
  strategy:
    sourceStrategy:
      from:
        kind: ImageStreamTag
        name: golang:1.13.4-ubi8
        namespace: openshift
    type: Source
```

You can inspect the build process by viewing the logs of the build pod:

```
$ oc logs highscore-1-build

[...]
Generating dockerfile with builder image image-registry.openshift-[...]
STEP 1: FROM image-registry.openshift-image-registry.svc:5000/openshift/golang
STEP 2: LABEL [...]
STEP 3: ENV OPENSHIFT_BUILD_NAME="highscore-1"
        OPENSHIFT_BUILD_NAMESPACE="arcade"
        OPENSHIFT_BUILD_SOURCE="https://github.com/OperatingOpenShift/s3e"
        OPENSHIFT_BUILD_COMMIT="37af2129de863ced37c75677eadd72b820407d9e"
STEP 4: USER root
STEP 5: COPY upload/src /tmp/src
STEP 6: RUN chown -R 1001:0 /tmp/src
STEP 7: USER 1001
STEP 8: RUN /usr/libexec/s2i/assemble
/tmp/src ~
go: downloading github.com/sdomino/scribble v0.0.0-20200707180004-3cc68461d505
go: extracting github.com/sdomino/scribble v0.0.0-20200707180004-3cc68461d505
go: downloading github.com/jcelliott/lumber v0.0.0-20160324203708-dd349441af25
go: extracting github.com/jcelliott/lumber v0.0.0-20160324203708-dd349441af25
go: finding github.com/sdomino/scribble v0.0.0-20200707180004-3cc68461d505
go: finding github.com/jcelliott/lumber v0.0.0-20160324203708-dd349441af25
~
STEP 9: CMD /usr/libexec/s2i/run
STEP 10: COMMIT temp.builder.openshift.io/arcade/highscore-1:6bda1705
[...]
Pushing image image-registry.[...].svc:5000/arcade/highscore:latest ...
[...]
Writing manifest to image destination
Storing signatures
Successfully pushed image-registry.openshift-image-registry.svc:5000/[...]
Push successful
```

In the output you can see that it first generates a Dockerfile based on the OpenShift builder image, and afterward uses it to build a container image. Step 8 of the Dockerfile is building the binary from the Go source code. When the build finishes successfully, the resulting container image is pushed to the internal container registry of the cluster. After finishing the build, the application is deployed to the cluster, referencing the newly built container image.

Expose the service to be able to access it and verify it's working as expected:

```
$ oc expose deploy highscore --port=8080
service/highscore exposed

$ oc expose svc highscore --hostname=arcade.apps-crc.testing
route.route.openshift.io/highscore exposed

$ curl arcade.apps-crc.testing/highscore
<html><body><h1>Highscores</h1></html>
```

Custom S2I Images

In some cases, you may want to provide a custom S2I builder image to the developers using OpenShift as a build platform. This may be a specific configuration you want to use to build the image, for example when you want to use a different runtime to run the service. Or it may be a language that is not supported by default.

The latter is the case for the custom image this section uses to show how a custom builder image can be created and used. The first game implemented by the arcade game publisher is implemented using the open source Godot engine (*https://godoten gine.org*). The company plans to use this as the default engine for future games and wants to provide an easy-to-use way of building and deploying games to the gaming platform, which is running OpenShift.

However, game developers do not necessarily have a lot of insight into what it means to run a game they build. On the other hand, they are probably experts at creating a game with the Godot editor (see Figure 5-2).

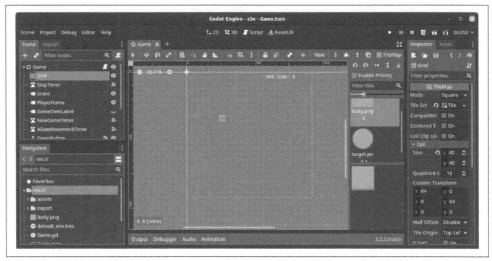

Figure 5-2. The Godot development environment

So the platform team decided to use a custom builder image to build Godot-based HTML5 games. That way, game developers wouldn't need to care about how a game is built and deployed but would focus on developing it, and building it would be a matter of running oc new-app. All files needed to build the S2I builder image can be found in GitHub (*https://oreil.ly/vilkO*).

The concept of S2I is to create a new image that is based on a builder image. Before committing the application image, the assemble script is executed that compiles the output artifacts needed to run the application. In the case of the Godot builder, the base image contains the Godot binary and everything it needs to compile an HTML5 file out of the Godot project it gets as input. To run the application, the builder image (and thus the output image) contains a run script that will be executed on container start. You can find more details about the requirements of a S2I builder image in the S2I documentation (*https://oreil.ly/Aguoq*).

This means that the output image contains everything needed to build as well as run the application. If you want to avoid that, there is a more complex process called runtime image (*https://oreil.ly/py5Sj*) but that requires developers to know the internals of the build process, so in that case, you're probably better off creating a multistage Dockerfile as described in "Docker Build" on page 74.

The builder image for Godot games can be built with the following Dockerfile:

```
FROM quay.io/buildah/stable
```

```
LABEL io.openshift.s2i.scripts-url="image:///usr/libexec/s2i"
COPY bin /usr/libexec/s2i
```

```
RUN dnf install -y unzip nginx
RUN mkdir -p /usr/share/nginx/html/
RUN chown 1001:0 /usr/share/nginx/html
RUN mkdir -p /var/cache/nginx
RUN chown 1001:0 /var/cache/nginx
COPY nginx.conf /etc/nginx/nginx.conf
```

❸
```
RUN curl -L https://[...]/Godot_[...]_headless.64.zip -o /tmp/godot.zip
RUN unzip /tmp/godot.zip
RUN curl -L https://[...]export_templates.tpz -o /tmp/export_templates.zip
RUN mv Godot_* /usr/bin/godot
RUN mkdir -p /tmp/godothome/.local/share/godot/templates/3.3.3.stable/
RUN chown -R 1001:0 /tmp/godothome/
USER 1001
WORKDIR /tmp/godothome/.local/share/godot/templates/3.3.3.stable/
RUN unzip -j /tmp/export_templates.zip templates/webassembly_release.zip \
templates/webassembly_debug.zip
```

❹
```
EXPOSE 8080
```

❶ Tell S2I where to find the assemble and run scripts and copy the provided scripts to the directory.

❷ Install NGINX, which is used as runtime.

❸ Install Godot, which is used to compile the game to HTML.

❹ During the build, no port needs to be exposed. Since the output image will be based on the builder image, the EXPOSE statement will allow OpenShift to detect which ports should be exposed as a service.

To build your own custom S2I builder image, you basically need to build a container image that is able to build and run your application using scripts with predefined names. When you label the image, S2I knows where to look for those scripts.

The minimal scripts you need are assemble, which builds the application, and run, which starts it. In the Godot case, build assembles the game to HTML5 and puts it in the directory where NGINX expects it:

```bash
#!/bin/bash

set -euxo pipefail

GAMENAME="$(cat /tmp/src/game.name| tr -d '\n')"
# assemble the game
mkdir -p "/usr/share/nginx/html/$GAMENAME"
mkdir -p "/tmp/godothome"
export HOME="/tmp/godothome"
/usr/bin/godot --export HTML5 /tmp/src/project.godot \
"/usr/share/nginx/html/$GAMENAME/index.html"

chmod -R a+rw "/usr/share/nginx/html/$GAMENAME"
```

The run script serves as entrypoint to the container, so all it does is start NGINX:

```bash
#!/bin/bash

exec /usr/sbin/nginx -g "daemon off;"
```

You can build the builder image locally and try to build an application using the s2i CLI tool from GitHub (*https://oreil.ly/rALIk*). However, since the build is slightly different in OpenShift than locally, we advise using the OpenShift build process right away.

To build the S2I builder image on OpenShift, run the following commands from within the directory containing the Dockerfile of the builder image:

```
$ oc new-build --binary --strategy=docker --name=godot-builder-image
```

```
$ oc start-build godot-builder-image --from-dir . -F
```

When that process is completed, you can use it to build and deploy the game application:

```
$ oc new-app --context-dir=game \
godot-builder-image:latest~https://github.com/OperatingOpenShift/s3e --name=s3e
```

Wait for the build and deploy to complete, expose the service as route, and you should be able to access the game:

```
$ oc expose svc s3e --hostname=arcade.apps-crc.testing

route.route.openshift.io/s3e exposed

$ curl arcade.apps-crc.testing/s3e
<html>
[...]
```

As you can see, building an S2I builder image is a bit more complex than just creating a Dockerfile. However, a baseline Docker image that needs to be distributed to development teams can get stale quickly, whereas updating an S2I builder image can even trigger a rebuild of all depending applications. So, if you want to provide an image for many others to use without worrying about how to build an application, S2I may be a more scalable approach.

Selecting a Build Strategy

As discussed in "Docker Build" on page 74, a Dockerfile might be a good choice as a quick-start solution, similar to using existing S2I builder images if they already fit your needs. Building custom S2I images is not a trivial task and should be considered only when they are expected to provide a clear benefit.

Red Hat OpenShift Pipelines

The OpenShift build infrastructure lets you easily build and deploy an application to an OpenShift cluster, as long as it fits one of the default S2I images or a Dockerfile is all it needs.

However, sometimes your deployment strategy requires you to run a more complex series of execution steps between the time a change hits version control and when the updated application begins running in production. These steps depend heavily on your organizational structure and strategy: do you want to automatically run unit and integration tests to verify that the code works as expected? Do you want to deploy to different stages before production or do canary deployments?

There are many different options to consider when it comes to how best to deploy your application. Such a series of executed steps is usually referred to as a *deployment pipeline*.

An example pipeline for a service like the highscore service could include the following steps:

1. Check out main

2. Run unit tests

3. Build container image

4. Publish container image

5. Run integration tests

6. Deploy service

OpenShift comes with a CI/CD solution called Red Hat OpenShift Pipelines (*https://oreil.ly/bi7mg*) that easily can be installed and used to build pipelines like this. Continuous integration usually means whatever is currently checked into version control will automatically be validated and deployed to some kind of environment, whether a test environment or production.

Overview

Red Hat OpenShift Pipelines is based on the Tekton (*https://tekton.dev*) CI/CD project. It can be used to build all kinds of pipelines using its generic data model that utilizes the Kubernetes infrastructure, which means managing a pipeline is just another interaction with the Kubernetes API, similar to managing deployments, services, or pods.

A pipeline can be triggered by various events, like a scheduler that triggers a nightly build or an HTTP listener that's triggered whenever a new change is merged to the main branch in GitHub.

It can be used, not only after a change has been merged to mainline, but also to verify a change before it is merged. When using GitHub, for example, where changes usually reach the main branch as a pull request, a pipeline can run to verify unit tests are green and the container can be built successfully before the code is even merged.

The following steps could make a pull request validation pipeline for the highscore service:

1. Run unit tests

2. Build container

3. Report success/failure

As you can see, different kinds of pipelines may exist in your CI for all kinds of purposes. Those different pipelines can consist of distinct steps, but they can also have some shared requirements. When you compare the pull request validation pipeline and the deployment pipeline above, you can see that the first two steps can be shared between the pipelines.

Figure 5-3 shows a rough overview of all the different resources that are usually involved in a pipeline when using Tekton. Some resources can be embedded in others so you don't necessarily need to create a single custom resource for everything. For example, a Task resource can be defined inline in a Pipeline resource.

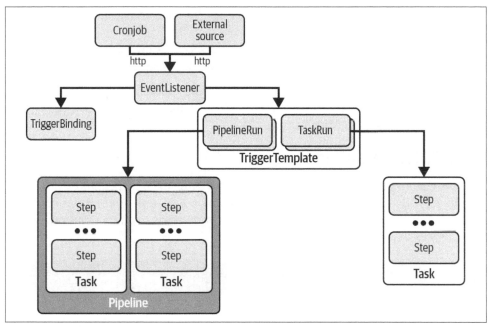

Figure 5-3. Overview of Red Hat OpenShift Pipelines components and resources

In Tekton, each pipeline is composed of *tasks*, which are objects that can be shared between pipelines to achieve reusability.

A pipeline can be triggered by an EventListener that will be exposed as a service in the OpenShift cluster. It can be triggered externally, manually, or from other components such as a CronJob running in OpenShift, for example, for rolling nightly builds.

The EventListener contains templates for PipelineRuns, which are concrete invocations of a pipeline. Whenever a PipelineRun object is created, the tasks that make up the pipeline will be executed. For simpler setups, an EventListener can also trigger tasks right away by specifying TaskRuns in the EventListener.

Each PipelineRun references a pipeline resource that defines which tasks it should run.

In Tekton, task resources can consist of one or multiple *steps*. Each step of a task will be executed sequentially within the same pod on the cluster, which means they will have access to the same file systems and run on the same node.

For our example build pipeline, this means the commands to check out the source code will need to be run only once, as long as steps 1–4 all run in the same task. After step 4, the application image will be present in some kind of container registry, so the local artifacts from the previous steps are not necessary anymore for steps 5 and 6.

A TriggerBinding is a separate resource that can be used to extract fields from an event and bind them to specific input parameters in the templates. For example, the HTTP request to the EventListener service could specify which branch to build, and the TriggerBinding would know which input parameter needs that information.

The following sections will guide you through installing Red Hat OpenShift Pipelines on your OpenShift cluster to create a first pipeline that will build and deploy the highscore service for the arcade gaming platform.

Install Red Hat OpenShift Pipelines

Red Hat OpenShift Pipelines is most easily installed from the OpenShift Console by installing the Red Hat OpenShift Pipelines Operator. Log in to your cluster and click your way to OperatorHub. You should see an overview of operators you can install into your cluster, as shown in Figure 5-4.

Figure 5-4. List of operators that can be installed to your cluster from OperatorHub

Chapter 8 talks more about operators and how they can help you operate your OpenShift cluster. For now, think of them as installers for arbitrary software for your cluster. In OperatorHub, you can select which software you want to install. They take configuration as input and make sure the software, in this case, Red Hat OpenShift Pipelines, is installed and running.

To install, select Red Hat OpenShift Pipelines, which will bring you to a version selection and configuration. For the pipelines in this chapter, the default parameters should work just fine. When the operator has finished installing, click View Operator.

Tekton comes with its own command-line interface that can be used to interact with your pipelines. You can use it to view logs of pipeline runs, start new runs, and so on. Scroll down on this page to download the CLI version that fits the Tekton version you just installed for your operating system as shown in Figure 5-5. Extract it and put it in a location that is listed in your PATH environment variable so you can run tkn commands.

Figure 5-5. Downloading the Tekton CLI

After successfully installing Red Hat OpenShift Pipelines, the OpenShift Console will get a new section to navigate to, called Pipelines, as you can see in Figure 5-6. On this page, you can view, create, and delete Tekton objects like pipelines and tasks.

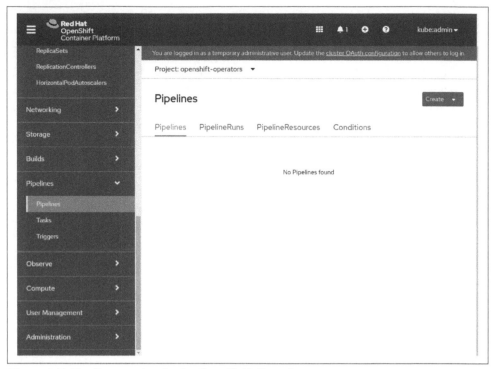

Figure 5-6. Pipelines section in the OpenShift Console

Right after the installation, no objects will exist. The next section will change that and help you create your first Tekton pipeline.

Setting Up the Pipeline

As you already know, Tekton pipelines are composed of tasks. Tasks are independent Kubernetes resources that you can create in the OpenShift cluster. They also can be invoked on their own and don't necessarily need a pipeline object. This is very useful for smaller tasks that don't need a full-blown pipeline, as well as for testing single tasks in the pipeline.

Implementing the tasks

When implementing a pipeline, it is best to have an idea of how the pipeline will look, and then start with the pieces that make up the pipeline. With Tekton, this is made easy, as tasks can be designed and issued independent of a pipeline.

The pipeline you will set up in this section is a simplified version of the pipeline described at the beginning of this chapter. It will consist of the following tasks and steps:

- Task 1

  — Step 1: Clone Git repository

  — Step 2: Run unit tests

- Task 2

  — Step 1: Configure project

  — Step 2: Build application

  — Step 3: Deploy and expose the application

The pipeline will verify that the code works as expected with unit tests, build and deploy the application with the OpenShift build infrastructure, and verify the necessary route exists. All of this will happen on the same cluster the application will be running on eventually. In a real-world scenario, you could also think of a cluster that runs the CI/CD for all applications and deploys them to different clusters, for example a staging and a production cluster.

First, create a task that checks out the arcade gaming platform highscore service and runs unit tests. The following commands need to be executed in that task:

```
$ git clone github.com/OperatingOpenShift/s3e
$ cd s3e/highscore
$ go test ./...
```

To embed these commands in a Tekton task, create a yaml file (for example, *task-unit.yaml*) that executes the preceding commands in two steps:

```
---
apiVersion: tekton.dev/v1beta1
kind: Task
metadata:
  name: verify-unit-tests
  namespace: arcade
spec:
  steps:
    - name: clone
      image: golang
      script: |
        #!/bin/bash

        git clone https://github.com/OperatingOpenShift/s3e /workspace/src
    - name: test-unit
      image: golang
      script: |
        #!/bin/bash

        cd /workspace/src/highscore
        go test ./...
```

Create the task resource in your cluster, then start the pipelines with the tkn CLI:

```
$ oc apply -f task-unit.yaml
task.tekton.dev/verify-unit-tests created

$ tkn task start verify-unit-tests --showlog
TaskRun started: verify-unit-tests-run-wzmhx
Waiting for logs to be available...
[clone] Cloning into '/workspace/src'...

[test-unit] go: downloading github.com/sdomino/scribble v0.0.0-[...]
[test-unit] go: downloading github.com/jcelliott/lumber v0.0.0-[...]
[test-unit] ok          github.com/OperatingOpenShift/s3e/highscore      0.060s
```

The output of the TaskRun is divided into the two steps of the task: clone and test-unit. As you can see, iterating over the implementation of a task is made easy with the Tekton CLI. The complexity of TaskRun objects and pods being created on the cluster is hidden from the developer. Nevertheless, it is useful to know about their existence since for some debugging issues, it may be necessary to look at the pods and containers Tekton created.

> You can find all files of the pipeline in the GitHub repository (*https://oreil.ly/jYlME*), so you can apply them either by checking it out locally or from the raw URL with this command:
>
> ```
> $ oc apply -f \
> https://raw.githubusercontent.com/OperatingOpenShift/\
> s3e/main/highscore/ci/task-unit.yaml
> ```

The second task mostly represents what you did manually in Chapter 3:

```
$ oc new-project arcade
$ oc new-build https://github.com/OperatingOpenShift/s3e --context-dir=highscore \
--name=highscore
$ oc start-build highscore
$ oc create deployment highscore \
--image=image-registry.openshift-image-registry.svc:5000/arcade/highscore
$ oc expose deployment highscore
$ oc expose service highscore \
--hostname=arcade.apps-crc.testing --path=/highscore
```

However, since the idea of a pipeline is that it will run more than once, you need to make sure that the pipeline is *idempotent*. That means, independent of how often the pipeline is started, the OpenShift cluster will, in the end, get the latest version of the application deployed. When the pipeline runs the first time, it'll create the project and deploy the resources. If it runs the second time, those resources already exist. If it runs again and everything is up-to-date already, the pipeline doesn't change anything.

To achieve this, you can use the declarative way of defining the resources the pipeline needs to apply. Instead of running oc create deployment highscore, create a *deployment.yaml,* and run `oc apply -f deployment.yaml` as this command will update existing deployments to match the definition.

Here's what the full task could look like:

```
---
apiVersion: tekton.dev/v1beta1
kind: Task
metadata:
  name: build-deploy
  namespace: arcade
spec:
  steps:
    - name: clone
      image: golang
      script: |
        #!/bin/bash

        git clone https://github.com/OperatingOpenShift/s3e /workspace/src
    - name: configure-project
      image: image-registry.openshift-image-registry.svc:5000/openshift/cli ❶
      script: |
        #!/bin/bash

        set -euo pipefail ❷

        cd /workspace/src/highscore/ci
        oc apply -f imagestream.yaml ❸
        oc apply -f buildconfig.yaml ❹
    - name: build
      image: image-registry.openshift-image-registry.svc:5000/openshift/cli
      script: |
        #!/bin/bash

        set -euo pipefail

        oc start-build -F highscore -n arcade ❺
    - name: deploy
      image: image-registry.openshift-image-registry.svc:5000/openshift/cli
      script: |
        #!/bin/bash

        set -euxo pipefail

        cd /workspace/src/highscore/ci
        oc apply -f deployment.yaml ❻

        BUILDDATE=$(date +%Y-%m-%d-%H%M%S)
        oc patch deployment highscore -p \
        "{\"spec\":{\"template\":{\"metadata\":{\"labels\":\
        {\"last-build\":\"$BUILDDATE\"}}}}" ❼
```

```
oc apply -f service.yaml ❽

# Generate and apply route
HOSTNAME="arcade.$(oc get ingresses.config.openshift.io \
cluster -o jsonpath='{.spec.domain}')" ❾

oc apply -f <(cat <<-EOF
  apiVersion: route.openshift.io/v1
  kind: Route
  metadata:
    labels:
      app: highscore
    name: highscore
    namespace: arcade
  spec:
    host: $HOSTNAME
    path: /highscore
    port:
      targetPort: 8080
    to:
      kind: Service
      name: highscore
EOF
)
```

❶ This step will use the openshift/cli container image from the cluster-internal registry. It is a simple base image that you can use for scripts that interact with your cluster.

❷ Make sure the pipeline fails whenever one of the commands fails. This will help debugging issues as a single failing command can be hidden by all subsequent commands that run successfully. Additionally, it'll make sure the pipeline doesn't run dangerous commands under the false assumption that the previous commands succeeded.

❸ The ImageStream resource is created or updated in a declarative way.

❹ The BuildConfig resource is created or updated. These objects are the output of running oc new-build commands. We get the same results as with running the iterative commands by applying those files to the cluster. To get to the example files, the resources have first been created with oc new-build and then exported and committed to the Git repository with oc get buildconfig -o yaml.

❺ This will start a build based on the BuildConfig. The -F flag ensures the build is failed or completed after running this command. Also, the build output will be visible in the logs of the TaskRun.

❻ Create or update the deployment.

❼ Label the pods of the deployment with the current timestamp. This is a simple trick to force rolling out the new image. A more advanced way would be to tag the image with a commit hash and use the new tag in the deployment.

❽ Ensure the service is exposed as a route, again using the declarative way.

❾ The route contains the hostname as a dynamic part so it can be deployed to any kind of OpenShift cluster, not just OpenShift Local. It is determined using the `cluster` ingress resource to create a cluster domain name.

For the dynamic generation of a hostname for the route, the following RBAC resources need to be created in the cluster, as the default pipeline user doesn't have permission to read the ingress resource:

```
- - -
apiVersion: rbac.authorization.k8s.io/v1
kind: ClusterRole
metadata:
  name: hostnamereader
rules:
- apiGroups:
  - config.openshift.io
  resources:
  - ingresses
  verbs:
  - get

- - -
apiVersion: rbac.authorization.k8s.io/v1
kind: ClusterRoleBinding
metadata:
  name: pipeline-hostname
roleRef:
  apiGroup: rbac.authorization.k8s.io
  kind: ClusterRole
  name: hostnamereader
subjects:
- kind: ServiceAccount
  name: pipeline
  namespace: arcade
```

To test the task, apply the resources to your OpenShift cluster and run the task with tkn:

```
$ oc apply -f task-deploy.yaml
task.tekton.dev/build-deploy created

$ oc apply -f rbac.yaml
clusterrole.rbac.authorization.k8s.io/hostnamereader created
clusterrolebinding.rbac.authorization.k8s.io/pipeline-hostname created

$ tkn task start build-deploy --showlog
TaskRun started: build-deploy-run-xpwbb
Waiting for logs to be available...
[clone] Cloning into '/workspace/src'...

[configure-project] namespace/arcade unchanged
[configure-project] imagestream.image.openshift.io/highscore created
[configure-project] buildconfig.build.openshift.io/highscore created

[build] build.build.openshift.io/highscore-1 started
[build] [...]
[build] Push successful

[deploy] deployment.apps/highscore created
[deploy] service/highscore created
[deploy] route.route.openshift.io/highscore created
```

When running the first time, the task will create all objects the application needs and you will be able to access the application as usual to verify:

```
$ curl arcade.apps-crc.testing/highscore
<html><body><h1>Highscores</h1></html>
```

When you start the task a second time by running tkn start again, you will notice that the output of the oc apply commands changes:

```
[deploy] deployment.apps/highscore unchanged
[deploy] service/highscore unchanged
[deploy] route.route.openshift.io/highscore unchanged
```

This means the content of the applied files didn't change, so nothing had to be done. This is the idempotent behavior we expect, and it's why we're using the declarative commands to create the objects.

To get to those files, you can first run the iterative commands to create deployments, services, and routes once again. Then export the objects with oc get -o yaml. After some cleanup work in the YAML, you get to the files that can set up your application.

Composing the pipeline

Now that you've implemented all the tasks that make up the pipeline, you need to define the pipeline itself. A pipeline in the sense of Tekton is a Kubernetes resource, similar to a task. A minimal pipeline that will be composed of the two tasks defined in the previous section can look like the following:

```
---
apiVersion: tekton.dev/v1beta1
kind: Pipeline
metadata:
  name: build-pipeline
  namespace: arcade
spec:
  tasks:
    - name: verify-unit-tests    ❶
      taskRef:
        name: verify-unit-tests  ❷
    - name: build-deploy
      taskRef:
        name: build-deploy
      runAfter:
        - verify-unit-tests       ❸
```

❶ The name of the task specified. This can be different from the task referenced.

❷ The name of the task object to run.

❸ Define that `build-deploy` should run after `verify-unit-tests`

As you can see, the pipeline is not just a list of tasks to run, but each task has a name that can be different from the task it references. Pipelines can parameterize the tasks they reference. For example, a task that clones a repository and builds an image could be reused in multiple services. In this example case, you may want to give the task a more concrete name, like `build-deploy-highscore`.

With the `runAfter` property, you can define whether a given task depends on a previous step to finish. In some cases, the tasks can be independent of each other and can run in parallel. For example, when building multiple coupled services in the same pipeline, each service could run independently. Integration tests would wait for all builds to finish, and only then the deployment to production would be triggered. Figure 5-7 visualizes this example.

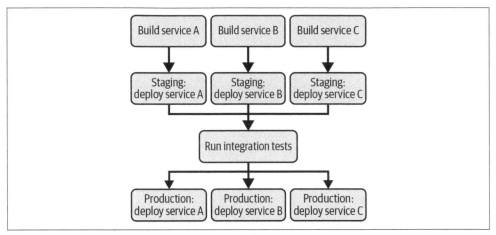

Figure 5-7. Pipeline running builds in parallel

As shown in Figure 5-7, each task that deploys to the staging environment would depend on the build of the given service using a `runAfter` property. The task running the integration tests would list all the stage deployments in the `runAfter` property. When the integration tests succeed, the deployment tasks to production are triggered in parallel again. They depend only on the integration tests. However, this is only an example rather than a recommended pattern. When building multiple services, you should try to make them deployable independent of each other.

For this chapter, the simpler pipeline will be sufficient to show the overall concept. For a more detailed explanation of how a pipeline can be composed, using input and output resources, shared volumes, and more advanced features, take a look at the Tekton documentation (*https://oreil.ly/GDxo9*).

Apply the pipeline to the cluster and start the pipeline with `tkn start`, similar to how you started the standalone tasks before:

```
$ oc apply -f pipeline.yaml
pipeline.tekton.dev/build-pipeline created

$ tkn pipeline start build-pipeline --showlog
PipelineRun started: build-pipeline-run-l6tp4
Waiting for logs to be available...
[verify-unit-tests : clone] Cloning into '/workspace/src'...

[verify-unit-tests : test-unit] [...]
[verify-unit-tests : test-unit] ok
github.com/OperatingOpenShift/s3e/highscore      0.003s

[build-deploy : clone] Cloning into '/workspace/src'...

[build-deploy : configure-project] namespace/arcade unchanged
```

```
[build-deploy : configure-project] [...]

[build-deploy : build] build.build.openshift.io/highscore-3 started
[build-deploy : build] Cloning "https://github.com/OperatingOpenShift/s3e" ...
[build-deploy : build] [...]
[build-deploy : build] Push successful

[build-deploy : deploy] deployment.apps/highscore configured
[build-deploy : deploy] service/highscore unchanged
[build-deploy : deploy] route.route.openshift.io/highscore unchanged
```

To get an overview of the pipelines you have deployed to the cluster and their last status, run the following command:

```
$ tkn pipelines list
NAME            AGE             LAST RUN                  DURATION   STATUS
build-pipeline  52 minutes ago  build-pipeline-run-l6tp4  1 minute   Succeeded
```

The Tekton CLI can also give you an overview of any given pipeline with the tkn pipeline describe command:

```
$ tkn pipeline describe build-pipeline
Name:       build-pipeline
Namespace:  arcade

* Resources

 No resources

* Params

 No params

* Results

 No results

* Workspaces

 No workspaces

* Tasks

NAME                TASKREF            RUNAFTER            TIMEOUT
· verify-unit-tests verify-unit-tests                      ---
· build-deploy       build-deploy       verify-unit-tests   ---

* PipelineRuns

NAME                       STARTED         DURATION   STATUS
· build-pipeline-run-l6tp4 49 minutes ago  1 minute   Succeeded
· build-pipeline-run-7z44j 53 minutes ago  2 minutes  Succeeded
```

In the output of this command, you get an overview of the tasks and the most recent runs of the pipeline. In addition, it shows you the resources, parameters, results, and workspaces of the pipeline. As you can see, there is much more in pipeline definitions than we can cover in this chapter.

You also can get a good overview of the existing pipelines and their overall health in the OpenShift Console. Navigate to the Pipelines section again, and you should see all pipelines existing on the cluster. Click the pipeline you created to get an overview of it, as shown in Figure 5-8, including the tasks and the steps of each task.

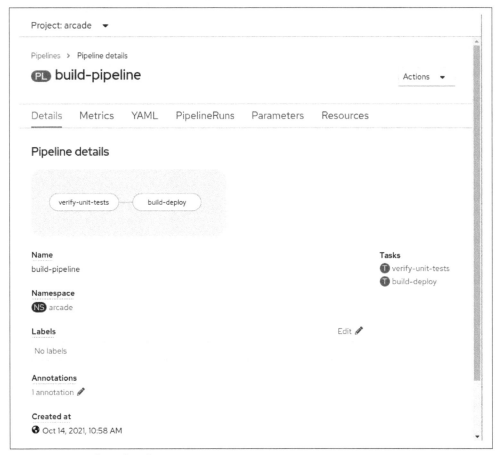

Figure 5-8. Pipeline details

Navigate to the PipelineRuns tab to get an overview of the last runs of the pipeline. This page, shown in Figure 5-9, is useful for looking at the overall health of the pipeline and detecting flaky behavior.

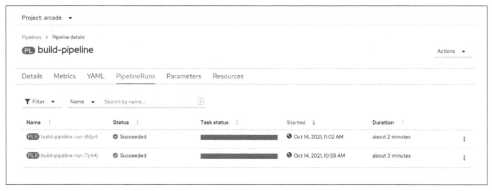

Figure 5-9. Last runs of the pipeline

To dig deeper, you can select one of the PipelineRuns to get a detailed overview of the tasks and steps in Figure 5-10. If the run failed, you will see the exact step that made it fail, and you can even look into the logs right from the OpenShift Console.

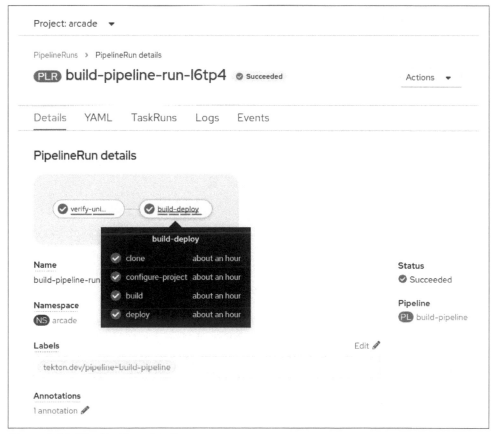

Figure 5-10. PipelineRun details

Once a pipeline is defined and works as expected, you probably wouldn't trigger it from the command line but have it run automatically. Using the OpenShift Console you can observe the behavior, start debugging, and even trigger new runs. However, for investigating concrete problems, the Tekton CLI is a helpful tool.

Turning the Pipeline into Continuous Integration

To run the pipeline automatically, we need to create two more resources that come with Tekton: an EventListener and a Trigger. Both resources can be created as stand-alone objects, or they can be embedded in the same resource. This is a general concept in Tekton to allow reusing objects in different places.

For readability, we will embed the Trigger resource in the EventListener in this example:

```
---
apiVersion: triggers.tekton.dev/v1alpha1
kind: EventListener
metadata:
  name: build-pipeline-listener
  namespace: arcade
spec:
  serviceAccountName: pipeline ❶
  triggers:
    - name: build-pipeline-trigger
      template:
        spec:
          resourceTemplates: ❷
          - apiVersion: "tekton.dev/v1beta1"
            kind: PipelineRun
            metadata:
              generateName: build-pipeline- ❸
            spec:
              pipelineRef:
                name: build-pipeline ❹
```

❶ The name of the service account to use for objects that will be created. This needs to be specified; otherwise, the default will be used. The Red Hat OpenShift Pipelines Operator will create the `pipeline` service account.

❷ The list of resources, which will be created when this EventListener receives an event.

❸ A prefix for the PipelineRun resources this EventListener will create.

❹ Reference to the pipeline this PipelineRun should start.

When creating this EventListener object, Tekton will start a web service that's waiting for incoming requests. Those requests will then start a new pipeline run by creating the PipelineRun resources inside the cluster as specified by the template.

Create the EventListener resource as usual:

```
$ oc apply -f eventlistener.yaml
eventlistener.triggers.tekton.dev/build-pipeline-listener created
```

List services to see the service that is created by Tekton:

```
$ oc get services
NAME                         TYPE       CLUSTER-IP     EXTERNAL-IP   PORT(S)
el-build-pipeline-listener   ClusterIP  10.217.4.192   <none>        8080/TCP
highscore                    ClusterIP  10.217.5.217   <none>        8080/TCP
```

To test the EventListener, create a curl pod and send an empty JSON via POST to the service:

```
$ oc run curl --image=curlimages/curl --command sleep 30h
pod/curl created

$ oc exec curl -- curl -s el-build-pipeline-listener:8080 -X POST --data '{}'
{"eventListener":"build-pipeline-listener","namespace":"arcade",
"eventListenerUID":"aecac3b4-a865-44df-92f0-4ac470a4bae4",
"eventID":"a1bb9392-5f58-47fb-bdfa-c68736fd690c"}
```

When you look back at Tekton CLI or the pipelines section in OpenShift Console, you should see a new PipelineRun showing up, running the defined pipeline with a name that starts with `build-pipeline-` as defined in the template. Figure 5-11 shows what this will look like in the OpenShift Console.

Figure 5-11. Pipeline triggered by EventListener

The team responsible for building and deploying the highscore application decided that, to start with, a nightly build and deployment will be good enough. To trigger that pipeline automatically every night, we can now create a CronJob resource, which will do exactly what we did manually from the cron pod before:

```
---
apiVersion: batch/v1beta1
kind: CronJob
metadata:
  name: highscore-nightly-build
  namespace: arcade
spec:
  serviceAccountName: pipeline
  schedule: "0 1 * * *" ❶
  jobTemplate:
    spec:
      template:
        spec:
          containers:
          - name: trigger
            image: curlimages/curl
            args: ["curl", "-s", "-XPOST", "--data", "{}",
              "http://el-build-pipeline-listener:8080"] ❷
          restartPolicy: Never
```

❶ This schedule will spawn a new job every day at 1 A.M.

❷ The curl command will be executed in the job and trigger a new run via the EventListener.

Apply the CronJob to the cluster:

```
$ oc apply -f cronjob.yaml
cronjob.batch/highscore-nightly-build created
```

Nightly builds are a common pattern often used when many components are supposed to work together and a reproducible version is needed. It's also often applied for products that have long-running build pipelines. However, for a distributed system with smaller standalone components, a single release strategy for each component is preferred.

As the team grows, many commits are created every day and the highscore team wants to deploy the service as soon as the automation verifies a new change. Instead of the CronJob, they decide that they want to trigger the pipeline each time a new commit is merged to the main branch on GitHub.

 For this section to work, you will need a cluster that is accessible from the internet.

Similar to how builds can be triggered from GitHub using a webhook, the Tekton EventListener supports GitHub events. For that to work, the EventListener service needs to be exposed to the internet via an OpenShift route. To verify that only events from GitHub trigger a new build, generate a secret token that will be shared with GitHub. Tekton will then verify that each request contains the right token before starting the pipeline.

The first step is to generate the token and store it in a secret on the OpenShift cluster:

```
$ oc create secret generic --from-literal=secret=my-secret github-secret
secret/github-secret created
```

For this example, the secret token is my-secret. As you may have guessed already, you should instead generate a longer and more secure token to avoid unintended builds.

Next, create a separate EventListener that will be responsible for requests only from GitHub:

```
---
apiVersion: triggers.tekton.dev/v1alpha1
kind: EventListener
metadata:
  name: github-listener
  namespace: arcade
spec:
  serviceAccountName: pipeline
  triggers:
    - name: github-push-trigger
      interceptors:
        - ref:
            name: "github"
          params:
            - name: "secretRef"
              value:
                secretName: github-secret ❶
                secretKey: secret ❷
            - name: "eventTypes"
              value: ["push"] ❸
      template:
        spec:
          resourceTemplates:
          - apiVersion: "tekton.dev/v1beta1"
            kind: PipelineRun
            metadata:
              generateName: gh-build-pipeline-
            spec:
              pipelineRef:
                name: build-pipeline
```

❶ The name of the secret that contains the token.

❷ A secret can contain multiple key/value pairs, and this is the key you specified for the token.

❸ Tekton can filter requests by events that GitHub emits. The push event is fired when a commit is merged.

The template part is similar to the template of the EventListener you created earlier. Only the name generation part is different so it'll be easier to distinguish builds triggered from GitHub from pipelines triggered from inside the cluster, for example via a CronJob.

Apply the EventListener to the cluster and expose it to the internet so GitHub can trigger it:

```
$ oc apply -f github-event-listener.yaml
eventlistener.triggers.tekton.dev/github-listener created

$ oc expose svc el-github-listener
route.route.openshift.io/el-github-listener exposed
```

Extract the URL from the route:

```
$ oc get route
NAME                HOST/PORT
el-github-listener  el-github-listener-arcade.apps.myclusterdomain.com
```

Navigate to the GitHub project where you want to enable the webhook, for example your fork of the example repository. Head to the settings tab and open the Webhooks section, for example *https://github.com/<your-user>/s3e/settings/hooks*.

Enter the URL to the webhook EventListener in the payload URL field, set the content type to `application/json`, and enter the token you stored in the secret, as shown in Figure 5-12.

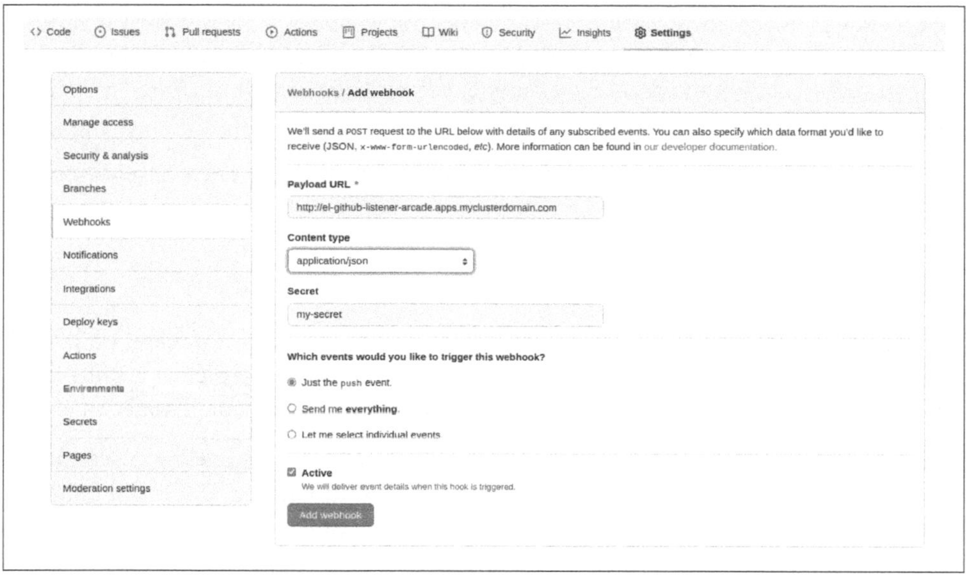

Figure 5-12. Webhook configuration in GitHub

You can choose which events the webhook should receive. Since our webhook filters for push events anyway, this option makes sense for us. Click Add webhook to enable the webhook.

GitHub will send a test event to your webhook right after enabling it. Head to the OpenShift Console to verify that it is working as expected. You should see a new PipelineRun with the prefix specified by the GitHub EventListener, as shown in Figure 5-13.

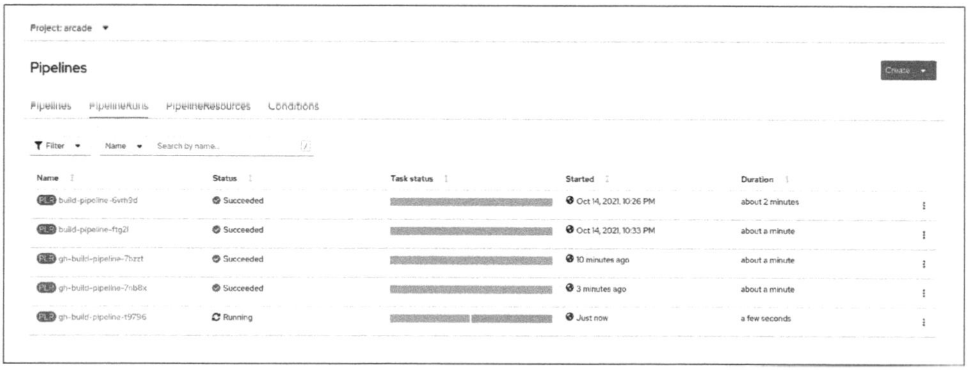

Figure 5-13. Pipeline triggered by GitHub push event

To see a full list of the events you can subscribe your pipeline to, see the GitHub documentation (*https://oreil.ly/v5vFe*). The next step could be to subscribe to `pull_request` events to verify unit tests when a pull request is opened for the repository and approve or deny it based on the result. There are even predefined tasks that you can reuse for this purpose, for example, the pull request (*https://oreil.ly/bBTlU*) task.

The Tekton documentation (*https://tekton.dev/docs/triggers*) is a good resource for such advanced topics.

Summary

OpenShift comes with a large toolset to help you get your software built and deployed. From simply rebuilding the image based on a Dockerfile, to a full-blown deploy pipeline, all the necessary tools are included or can be installed easily.

In this chapter, you learned about many of the different options to achieve seemingly the same result: deploy an application to your OpenShift Cluster. Understanding the different options and which one is the best fit for your application is important.

For a simple one-image app, a build whenever a change is merged with S2I may be sufficient. In contrast, if you're planning to create a bigger application consisting of many different services, it makes sense to think about creating a pipeline or even preparing pieces that can be reused as more applications are added to the landscape. Tekton makes sharing parts of a pipeline to reuse across projects very easy.

Depending on the scale of the application, you may want to use a dedicated cluster to host your pipelines, while the application itself can be deployed to a separate cluster. This is useful to separate the workloads. The requirements for an internal development cluster may be different from a capacity and security standpoint than the ones running your software in production.

In addition, separating the build system from production helps to make sure the development environment doesn't consume the resources of your production system. The resources a pipeline system like Tekton needs should not be underestimated. With a growing team and service landscape, you will quickly reach a point where the build system fully utilizes your OpenShift cluster.

Understanding the utilization of your clusters is important to make good choices about the resources used as well as to understand the health of your workloads. The next chapter will help you understand how OpenShift can provide insights into your resources and workloads.

## CHAPTER 6

In-Cluster Monitoring Stack

Rick Rackow

The best platform is of no use if it is not fully functional. To make sure a platform is running at its best, there are mechanisms that can be utilized (i.e., software or instrumentation), to perform "self-healing." However, there are occasions where these mechanisms fail or still need manual intervention for a variety of reasons. Additionally, it is important to collect various signals from the platform to get a good overview of it; this is called "observability."

In this chapter, we discuss OpenShift's built-in mechanisms and functionality for monitoring and observability. We detail each component that generates signals within the mechanisms and instruct you on how to work with them, before we dive deeper into strategies and best practices for monitoring, alerting, and observability in Chapter 7.

Cluster Monitoring Operator

The Cluster Monitoring Operator is at the heart of the monitoring platform. Chapter 9 discusses operators in depth, but we briefly touch on them here.

An operator ensures that a given state is always present on the cluster in a control loop. In the case of the Cluster Monitoring Operator, this means that all parts of the monitoring platform are present on the cluster, up-to-date, configured as specified, and running. The Cluster Monitoring Operator is managed by the Cluster Version Operator, which takes cares of all *cluster operators*. You can get a full list of all cluster operators by executing the following:

```
$ oc get clusteroperators
NAME                                          VERSION
authentication                                4.9.18
config-operator                               4.9.18
console                                       4.9.18
dns                                           4.9.18
etcd                                          4.9.18
image-registry                                4.9.18
ingress                                       4.9.18
kube-apiserver                                4.9.18
kube-controller-manager                       4.9.18
kube-scheduler                                4.9.18
machine-api                                   4.9.18
machine-approver                              4.9.18
machine-config                                4.9.18
marketplace                                   4.9.18
monitoring                                    4.9.18
network                                       4.9.18
node-tuning                                   4.9.18
openshift-apiserver                           4.9.18
openshift-controller-manager                  4.9.18
openshift-samples                             4.9.18
operator-lifecycle-manager                    4.9.18
operator-lifecycle-manager-catalog            4.9.18
operator-lifecycle-manager-packageserver      4.9.18
service-ca                                    4.9.18
```

The Cluster Monitoring Operator is registered here as *monitoring*. Because the Cluster Monitoring Operator is included as one of the cluster operators, it will get updated as part of a cluster update. This update is where it can change its configuration and the base configuration for any of the components it manages. While this means that monitoring is prioritized in the cluster, it also requires frequent updating to your cluster.

> We are focusing on the bigger picture, meaning that we are going to leave anything that touches RBAC out, where it is not explicitly needed. You can find information on RBAC in Chapter 4.

The Cluster Monitoring Operator is to a certain degree an opinionated version of kube-prometheus (*https://oreil.ly/xMgCx*). This reflects the general approach to many things in and around Openshift, which itself is an opinionated approach to Kubernetes. The Cluster Monitoring Operator does not deny its roots, which becomes particularly obvious looking at the code. The configuration and generation of the required manifests uses jsonnet (*https://jsonnet.org*). It's not a problem if you are not familiar with jsonnet. *jsonnet* is essentially a templating language that has is the ability to make imports. You can import other jsonnet dependencies and then use them in your own jsonnet code accordingly. Reviewing the jsonnet imports of Cluster Monitoring Operator reveals its heritage:

```json
{
  "version": 1,
  "dependencies": [
    {
      "source": {
        "git": {
          "remote": "https://github.com/etcd-io/etcd",
          "subdir": "contrib/mixin"
        }
      },
      "version": "main"
    },
    {
      "source": {
        "git": {
          "remote": "https://github.com/prometheus-operator/kube-prometheus",
          "subdir": "jsonnet/kube-prometheus"
        }
      },
      "version": "main"
    },
    {
      "source": {
        "git": {
          "remote": "https://github.com/prometheus-operator/prometheus-operator",
          "subdir": "jsonnet/prometheus-operator"
        }
      },
      "version": "main"
    },
    {
      "source": {
        "git": {
          "remote": "https://github.com/openshift/openshift-state-metrics",
          "subdir": "jsonnet"
        }
      },
      "version": "master",
      "name": "openshift-state-metrics"
    },
    {
      "source": {
        "git": {
          "remote": "https://github.com/openshift/telemeter",
          "subdir": "jsonnet/telemeter"
        }
      },
      "version": "master",
      "name": "telemeter-client"
```

```
    },
    {
      "source": {
        "git": {
          "remote": "https://github.com/thanos-io/kube-thanos",
          "subdir": "jsonnet/kube-thanos"
        }
      },
      "version": "main"
    },
    {
      "source": {
        "git": {
          "remote": "https://github.com/thanos-io/thanos",
          "subdir": "mixin"
        }
      },
      "version": "main"
    }
  ],
  "legacyImports": true
}
```

jsonnet imports kube-prometheus directly as a dependency along with some other *mixins*. Every dependency is essentially the upstream of Cluster Monitoring Operator. Not everything is consumed from those upstream resources, but a good portion is, including the kubernetes-mixin (*https://oreil.ly/ORG51*), which provides a large set of the alerting definitions that will land on your cluster. Having those upstream dependencies enables OpenShift to stay engaged with what's happening in the Kubernetes community and benefit from new ideas and experiences directly. This is especially true for components that have large communities, like the Prometheus Operator.

On the other hand, having upstream dependencies can add a layer that potentially slows changes, as they first have to land in upstream projects before they trickle down into Cluster Monitor Operator. Additionally, in most cases those upstream projects mainly cater to Kubernetes users and not OpenShift in particular, which can become an issue in areas that need a high level of fine-tuning like SLO-related alerts.

Prometheus Operator

It's common to see comments on GitHub complaining that Prometheus Operator doesn't do X according to how operator-sdk says in the docs. The simple answer is that Prometheus Operator long predates Operator SDK and anything similar. It was created near the end of 2016 to simplify the complex deployment of Prometheus on Kubernetes and Prometheus Operator. It is one of the first operators ever created. In fact, this is where the term operator was first coined.

> All we want to really do, is monitor those services that we have in Kubernetes that are some Pods, so that's exactly why at CoreOS we built the Prometheus Operator.
>
> —Frederic Branczyk at CoreOS Fest 2017

Prometheus Operator allows you to leverage what you need from Kubernetes to configure your monitoring tool. Ultimately, Prometheus Operator serves as an abstraction layer to Prometheus configuration, which can be achieved by utilizing control loops.

The desired state is a full piece of Prometheus configuration. To define this state you have to extend the Kubernetes, or in this case, OpenShift, cluster using additional resources. These additional resources are called *custom resources*. In order to use them, you first need to define them using *custom resources definitions*. Each operator usually comes with its own set of custom resources, and Prometheus Operator is no different. The Prometheus Operator watches the following set of custom resources:

- Prometheus
- PrometheusRule
- Alertmanager
- ServiceMonitor
- AlertmanagerConfig

Each of them plays an integral part in the stack, and we are going to look into each of them separately. Keep in mind that the Cluster Monitoring Operator is caring for all of these on your OpenShift cluster.

Prometheus

The *Prometheus* custom resource allows you to define everything around the deployment of the actual Prometheus instances that are on your cluster.

In short, Prometheus is a monitoring tool with enormous capabilities.

Prometheus's architecture is built around scraping metrics from `targets`. To function correctly, these targets need to offer an HTTP endpoint that exposes metrics in the correct format (*https://oreil.ly/Tn4Ys*). Once a metric is scraped it is stored in Prometheus's Time Series Database (TSDB).

Persisting Your Metrics.   Out of the box, the storage for Prometheus on OpenShift is ephemeral. By default, there are two instances and thus redundancy, but you might want to persist your metrics, especially in environments where pods can frequently be restarted due to node replacements.

As an example, you may decide to use spot instances for cost savings. In order to persist your metrics, you need to tell the Cluster Monitoring stack where to do that and for how long. You do that by adding the information to a configmap. First, you'll need to create the configmap:

```
apiVersion: v1
kind: ConfigMap
metadata:
  name: user-workload-monitoring-config
  namespace: openshift-user-workload-monitoring
data:
  config.yaml: |
```

After this header you can start to add information about retention, the amount of storage you want to allocate, and the type of storage to use.

```
apiVersion: v1
kind: ConfigMap
metadata:
  name: cluster-monitoring-config
  namespace: openshift-monitoring
data:
  config.yaml: |
    prometheusK8s:
      retention: 10d
      volumeClaimTemplate:
        spec:
          storageClassName: local-storage
          resources:
            requests:
              storage: 40Gi
```

The storageClassName and the volumeMode depend on the environment that your cluster is living in, meaning which cloud provider or bare metal solution you have deployed your cluster to. The amount of storage and the corresponding retention depend on the nodes in your cluster and also how many pods you are running.

Once you have applied the above, the Cluster Monitoring stack will take care of all the rest:

```
$ oc apply -f monitoringPersistence.yaml
configmap/cluster-monitoring-config created

$ oc get pvc
NAME                                  STATUS    STORAGECLASS    AGE
prometheus-k8s-db-prometheus-k8s-0    Pending   local-storage   96s
```

You have to be absolutely sure that the storage you are trying to use is available; otherwise, your whole monitoring stack will fail to launch.

In that case, you can delete the configmap or the storage-related sections. After some time, fresh and running Prometheus pods without persistent storage attached to them will appear.

Query using PromQL. If you have done everything correctly, Prometheus with a persistent storage and predefined retention is up and ready to be queried using PromQL, the Prometheus Query Language. PromQL is also used to build alerts based on the aforementioned metrics. See Example 6-1 for an example of the up metric. It follows the format of `name{ label="labelValue" }:value`. It describes the status of a given target in an OpenShift cluster, in this case, the apiserver. Additionally, some labels are added to the metric that can be queried similarly to the actual metrics name.

Example 6-1. Metric

```
up{apiserver="kube-apiserver",
    endpoint="https",
    instance="192.168.126.11:6443",
    job="apiserver",
    namespace="default",
    service="kubernetes"}:1
```

There are multiple ways to access the metrics stored in Prometheus. The most common one with a bare Prometheus instance is just Prometheus's GUI, where you type in any PromQL query and then receive the result. Figure 6-1 shows an example Prometheus query executed to receive all up metrics.

Figure 6-1. Example Prometheus query using the GUI

The Prometheus instance that the Prometheus Operator places on your OpenShift cluster is exposed directly via a route. You can identify it with the following command:

```
$ oc get route prometheus-k8s -n openshift-monitoring
NAME             HOST/PORT
prometheus-k8s   prometheus-k8s-openshift-monitoring.apps-crc.testing
```

However, OpenShift also has a built-in abstraction for the native Prometheus user interface that you can find under the monitoring tab in the OpenShift console as seen in Figure 6-2.

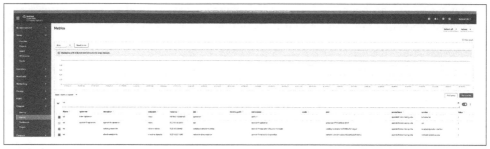

Figure 6-2. Monitoring tab in the OpenShift console

Given how complex queries can become, it is important to utilize *PrometheusRules*. *PrometheusRules* is another custom resource brought to the cluster as part of the Prometheus Operator, and it allows you to define two different kind of rules in the Prometheus instance. Rules themselves are persisted and constantly evaluated instructions for Prometheus in the form of PromQL with a small set of extra instructions. The two options you have at hand are *Recording Rules* and *Alerting Rules*. We will look at each of these and then build an example alert using the up metric we examined earlier.

> Recording rules allow you to precompute frequently needed or computationally expensive expressions and save their result as a new set of time series.
>
> —Prometheus documentation

Recording Rules increase access speed because they are precomputed. They also give your predefined query a name that you can access it by. Let's build an example recording rule and look at its components:

```
rules:
- record: services:up:sum
    expr: sum by (service) (up)
```

Note that the recording rule is defined under the `rules` section of Prometheus. Though Prometheus Operators' `PrometheusRule` is abstracting the configuration away when it is actually applied to the cluster, it is helpful to understand how the actual configuration of Prometheus works.

The `record` is the canonical name that you can access the query by from now on.

The `expr` is the actual query that you want to precompute. In this case `sum by (service) (up)`.

As mentioned earlier, Prometheus Operator takes care of abstracting the actual Prometheus configuration away from you, so you can use a `PrometheusRule` and put it onto the cluster. Example 6-2 shows the `PrometheusRule` version of the recording rule. You can see that, in addition to the bare Prometheus Instructions, you also need to define the apiVersion, the kind, and a name.

Example 6-2. PrometheusRule

```
apiVersion: monitoring.coreos.com/v1
kind: PrometheusRule
metadata:
  name: up
spec:
  groups:
  - name: up.rules
    rules:
    - expr: sum by (service) (up)
      record: services:up:sum
```

Once applied using `oc apply -f ourRule.yaml` you can access your recording rule from Prometheus, just like every built-in rule as shown in Figure 6-3.

Figure 6-3. Querying Prometheus recording rule

Using precomputed rules doesn't seem like a big win for a small query like this, but the more expensive the query becomes, the more use you can get out of it. We discuss how to determine the cost of a query in the Add-Ons section.

Alerting Rules. Alerting Rules give you the chance to build alerts by making Prometheus evaluate certain conditions using PromQL. To access your Recording Rule in an Alerting Rule, start with:

```
    rules:
    - alert: notUp
      expr: sum by (service) (up) < 1
      for: 10m
      labels:
        severity: critical
      annotations:
        summary: Service is  not up
```

Be sure to give those alerting rules meaningful names that make sense to you. For this example, we chose the name notUp. expr is where you put the query that is being evaluated. We added a condition to it at the end. In this case, we want to check if the result of your query is less than 1. The next line, for:, adds a timer. The result of our query needs to be less than 1 for 10m. If that is the case, Prometheus will create an alert. The alert will get a label/value pair severity: "critical" and an annotation. The annotation is commonly used to give a human-readable explanation for what is going wrong.

Deploy Your Rules.   Now your Alerting Rule needs to find its way to the on-cluster Prometheus instance. You will use a PrometheusRule again but with a slightly modified expression. In fact, you'll want to use your Recording Rule and put both of those rules in one file so that your final PrometheusRule looks like this:

```
apiVersion: monitoring.coreos.com/v1
kind: PrometheusRule
metadata:
  name: up
spec:
  groups:
  - name: up.rules
    rules:
    - expr: sum by (service) (up)
      record: services:up:sum
    - expr: services:up:sum < 1
      alert: notUp
      for: 10m
      labels:
        severity: critical
      annotations:
        summary: Service is  not up
```

You can go ahead and deploy to your cluster as follows:

```
$ oc apply -f ourAlert.yaml
prometheusrule.monitoring.coreos.com/up configured
```

It takes a while for Prometheus Operator to rewrite the Prometheus configuration and to reload. As soon as that is done, you can find your shiny new rules under the rules tab as seen in Figure 6-4.

Figure 6-4. Rules tab

Additionally, since one of the rules is an Alerting Rule, it will also show up under the alerts tab, shown in Figure 6-5. This allows you to determine if an alert for it is firing.

Figure 6-5. Alerts tab

Alertmanager

While Prometheus does all the work related to metrics scraping, storing, and evaluation, Alertmanager takes care of everything related to alerting, once an alert is generated by Prometheus as the result of a query evaluation. This includes deciding where an alert should go, modifying it, and storing all silences for alerts that aren't currently relevant.

In a self-managed scenario you would need to deploy an Alertmanager in some way and then link it to your Prometheus instance so that the Prometheus-generated alerts could actually land with Alertmanager. On OpenShift, the Cluster Monitoring Operator takes care of all of that for you. Your cluster will start off with an `Alertmanager` custom resource present in the *openshift-monitoring* namespace. This will cause the Prometheus Operator to deploy an Alertmanager instance ready and waiting for you to configure. It is likely that the deployment will not need to be configured here because both the Prometheus instance deployment and the Alertmanager instance are configured by the monitoring stack, according to the value in the *cluster-monitoring-config* configmap.

The interesting bits are done via the *AlertmanagerConfig* and a secret. Configuring Alertmanager via a secret is the legacy way of doing it that was created before the *AlertmanagerConfig* custom resource was introduced to Prometheus Operator. While it is legacy to Prometheus Operator, it is still the standard way in OpenShift's Cluster Monitoring.

Configure Alertmanager via a Secret. When you get started with your fresh cluster, you will see a console error message similar to Figure 6-6 that invites you to configure Alertmanager.

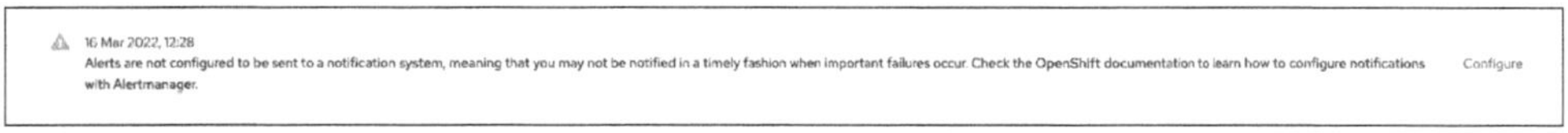

Figure 6-6. Console error message

To do so, you must adjust a secret in the openshift-monitoring namespace. The downsides to configuring via a secret are that you're not managing a resource native to Prometheus Operator and that the configuration is base64 encoded:

```
$ oc get secrets alertmanager-main -o yaml
apiVersion: v1
data:
  alertmanager.yaml: U2hvcnRlciBzdHJpbmcgdG8gZml0IHRoZSBib29r
kind: Secret
metadata:
  creationTimestamp: "2022-03-15T22:11:43Z"
  labels:
    app.kubernetes.io/component: alert-router
    app.kubernetes.io/instance: main
    app.kubernetes.io/name: alertmanager
    app.kubernetes.io/part-of: openshift-monitoring
    app.kubernetes.io/version: 0.23.0
  name: alertmanager-main
  namespace: openshift-monitoring
  resourceVersion: "35824"
  uid: 8adb7fee-3650-47d7-9ffa-5b7ba1e299a1
type: Opaque
```

After decoding the base64 encoded string, you'll get the actual configuration yaml. With the following command, you can get the secret, access part you are interested in, decode the base64 encoded string, show the output in your terminal, and pipe it to a file:

```
$ oc -n openshift-monitoring get secret \
alertmanager-main \
--template='{{index .data "alertmanager.yaml" }}' | base64 --decode \
| tee alertmanager.yaml
"global":
  "resolve_timeout": "5m"
"inhibit_rules":
- "equal":
  - "namespace"
  - "alertname"
  "source_matchers":
  - "severity = critical"
  "target_matchers":
  - "severity =~ warning|info"
- "equal":
  - "namespace"
  - "alertname"
  "source_matchers":
  - "severity = warning"
  "target_matchers":
  - "severity = info"
"receivers":
- "name": "Default"
- "name": "Watchdog"
- "name": "Critical"
"route":
  "group_by":
  - "namespace"
  "group_interval": "5m"
  "group_wait": "30s"
  "receiver": "Default"
  "repeat_interval": "12h"
  "routes":
  - "matchers":
    - "alertname = Watchdog"
    "receiver": "Watchdog"
  - "matchers":
    - "severity = critical"
    "receiver": "Critical"
```

Now you can edit the configuration to meet your needs.

Practice Alert Routing. While we don't know your exact configuration needs, let's review the possibilities. To do so, we selected the following example: routing an Alert from the Prometheus part to a PagerDuty receiver, should it fire. All other possible receivers are configured fairly similarly. You can sign up for a free trial on PagerDuty if you do not have an account already.

To get started, log in to your account and either create a service or pick an existing service to which you want to send notifications from OpenShift. You should then be able to move to the settings of that service and a Prometheus integration. Once that is done you can retrieve the key as shown in Figure 6-7.

Figure 6-7. PagerDuty Prometheus integration

You can now start to add your new receiver to the Alertmanager Config along with the other receivers:

```
"receivers":
- "name": "Default"
- "name": "Watchdog"
- "name": "Critical"
- "name": "OpenShiftDefault"
  "pagerduty_configs":
  - "service_key": "e000deee1a214406c15931b99a9b812c"
    "url": " events.eu.pagerduty.com/generic/2010-04-15/create_event.json "
```

Next, match your exact alert's name and route that to PagerDuty:

```
"route":
  "group_by":
  - "namespace"
  "group_interval": "5m"
  "group_wait": "30s"
  "receiver": "Default"
  "repeat_interval": "12h"
  "routes":
  - "matchers":
    - "alertname = Watchdog"
    "receiver": "Watchdog"
```

```
  - "matchers":
    - "severity = critical"
    "receiver": "Critical"
  - "receiver": "OpenShiftDefault"
    "match":
      "alertname": "notUp"
```

Your whole alertmanager.yaml should now look similar to Example 6-3.

Example 6-3. alertmanager.yaml

```
"global":
  "resolve_timeout": "5m"
"inhibit_rules":
- "equal":
  - "namespace"
  - "alertname"
  "source_matchers":
  - "severity = critical"
  "target_matchers":
  - "severity =~ warning|info"
- "equal":
  - "namespace"
  - "alertname"
  "source_matchers":
  - "severity = warning"
  "target_matchers":
  - "severity = info"
"receivers":
- "name": "Default"
- "name": "Watchdog"
- "name": "Critical"
- "name": "OpenShiftDefault"
  "pagerduty_configs":
  - "service_key": "e000deee1a214406c15931b99a9b812c"
    "url": "https://events.eu.pagerduty.com/generic/2010-04-5/create_event.json"
"route":
  "group_by":
  - "namespace"
  "group_interval": "5m"
  "group_wait": "30s"
  "receiver": "Default"
  "repeat_interval": "12h"
  "routes":
  - "matchers":
    - "alertname = Watchdog"
    "receiver": "Watchdog"
  - "matchers":
    - "severity = critical"
    "receiver": "Critical"
  - "receiver": "OpenShiftDefault"
```

```
"match":
  "alertname": "notUp"
```

As a final step, replace the currently existing secret on cluster with your new *alert-manager.yaml*. You can do this with the following command:

```
$ oc -n openshift-monitoring create secret generic alertmanager-main \
--from-file=alertmanager.yaml \
--dry-run=client -o=yaml |  oc -n openshift-monitoring replace secret \
--filename=-
```

Double-check that everything worked as expected by browsing to the console: under Cluster Settings → Configuration → Alertmanager you can find all existing receivers, including your newly created PagerDuty receiver as shown in Figure 6-8.

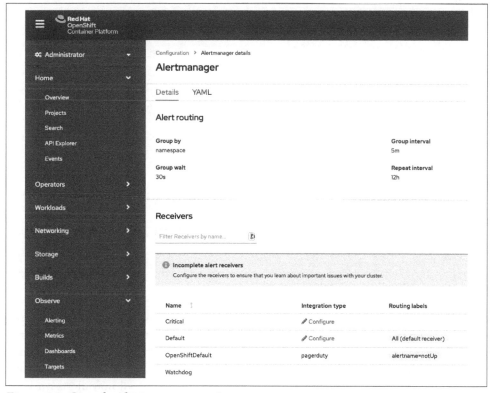

Figure 6-8. Console Alertmanager receivers

Configure Alertmanager from the UI.   You can configure an Alertmanager from the console UI.

In Figure 6-8 you can see that the default receiver and the watchdog receiver already exist, but they are not configured. You can go ahead and click the Configure button for the default receiver. From the dropdown menu select *PagerDuty* as the receiver type. Select the integration type, which in this case is *Prometheus* and then complete the remaining fields as shown in Figure 6-9.

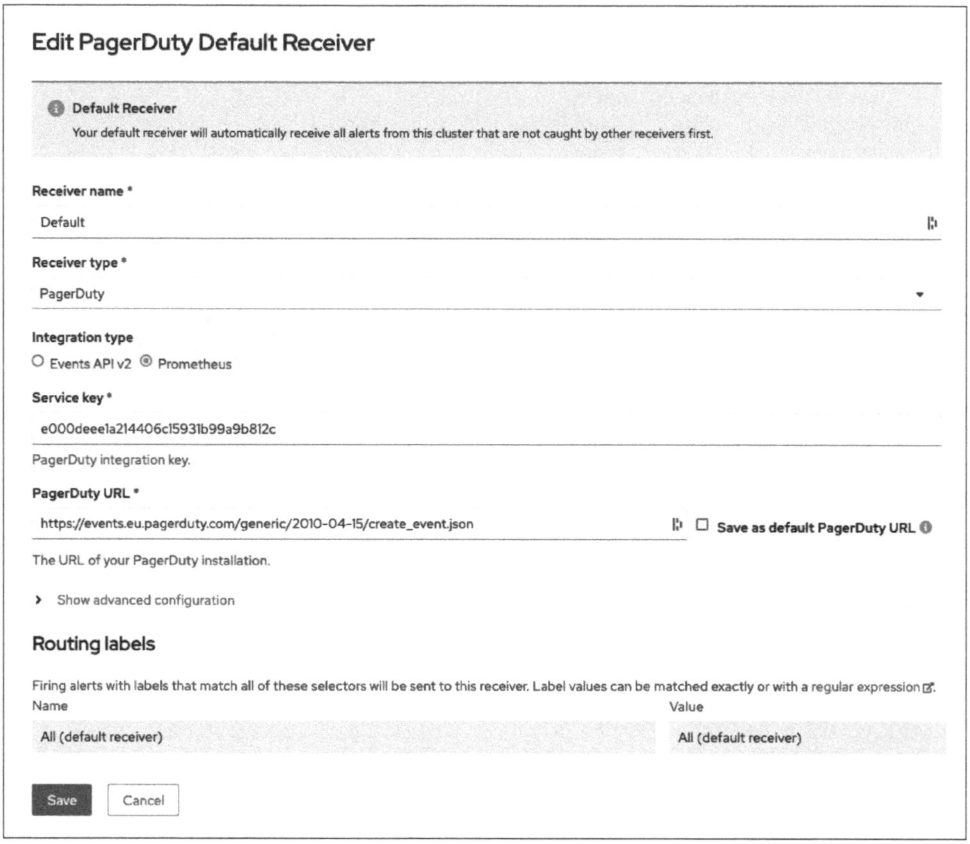

Edit PagerDuty Default Receiver

ⓘ **Default Receiver**
Your default receiver will automatically receive all alerts from this cluster that are not caught by other receivers first.

Receiver name *

Default

Receiver type *

PagerDuty

Integration type
○ Events API v2 ◉ Prometheus

Service key *

e000deee1a214406c15931b99a9b812c

PagerDuty integration key.

PagerDuty URL *

https://events.eu.pagerduty.com/generic/2010-04-15/create_event.json ☐ **Save as default PagerDuty URL** ⓘ

The URL of your PagerDuty installation.

> Show advanced configuration

Routing labels

Firing alerts with labels that match all of these selectors will be sent to this receiver. Label values can be matched exactly or with a regular expression ⧉.

Name	Value
All (default receiver)	All (default receiver)

Save   Cancel

Figure 6-9. Console Alertmanager default receiver

Upon saving your settings, you'll be returned to the overview page where you can see that the receiver, Critical, is preinstalled. As was seen in Example 6-3 this receiver is responsible for forwarding all alerts with a critical severity to a given endpoint. Since you can configure the routing based on severity in PagerDuty itself, you can remove that receiver by clicking the three red dots on the side. Now, all new alerts on your cluster will start to flow to PagerDuty as shown in Figure 6-10.

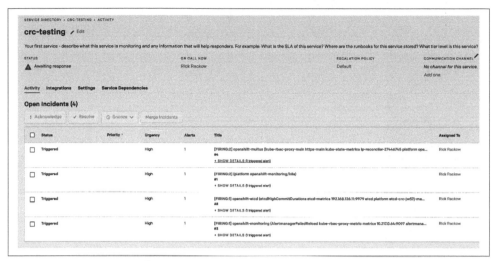

Figure 6-10. PagerDuty alerts

By default, Alertmanager will also resolve alerts in your external tool, if the alert is no longer present on the cluster. You can silence alerts directly through the OpenShift console or using the Alertmanager UI. It's advantageous to use the console to set up silence alerts, as there's always the possibility that the Alertmanager UI will be removed at some point in the future.

To set up a silence for an alert, go to Observe → Alerting in the console. Find the active alert you want to silence and click the three dots on the right and pick Silence Alert. As you can see in figure Figure 6-11, a silence matches the labels and values of a given alert. OpenShift prefills these fields to ensure that only this exact alert is receiving a silence. If you want to define your silence more loosely, for example, like you want to silence *ClusterNotUpgradeable* regardless of its severity, remove the severity label and its value. To complete the silence, add a timeframe at the top and a specific reason this alert is silenced (e.g., "We cannot currently upgrade, because we are not ready for a breaking change in the next OpenShift release").

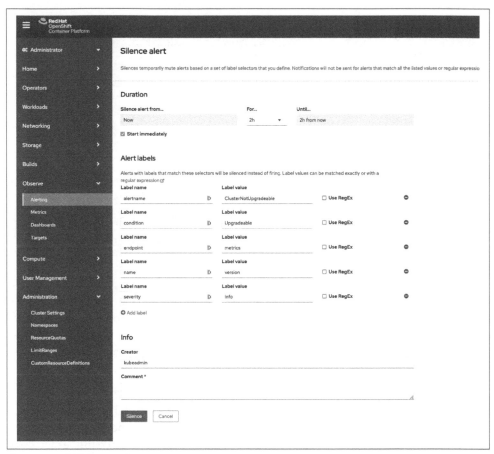

Figure 6-11. Silence alert

User Workload Monitoring

To use your cluster to deploy many services, you will need User Workload Monitoring to create separation between the cluster's monitoring and your own workload by providing limited tenant isolation.

To turn on User Workload Monitoring, you will need to edit the `configmap`:

```
apiVersion: v1
kind: ConfigMap
metadata:
  name: cluster-monitoring-config
  namespace: openshift-monitoring
data:
  config.yaml: |
    enableUserWorkload: true
```

`enableUserWorkload: true` ensures that the Cluster Monitoring stack deploys the User Workload Monitoring. Once you have edited the `ConfigMap` you can observe the stack being deployed:

```
$ oc -n openshift-user-workload-monitoring get pod
NAME                                  READY  STATUS   RESTARTS  AGE
prometheus-operator-b55fdf657-zmlt5   2/2    Running  0         49s
prometheus-user-workload-0            5/5    Running  0         34s
thanos-ruler-user-workload-0          3/3    Running  0         34s
```

Now you will be able to monitor all your services. The next section walks you through an example to get you familiar with this part of Cluster Monitoring.

Though it's possible to use `PodMonitors` to discover your target, we like the Service-Monitor model, as it's the more scalable option.

First, you'll need to start an app to be scraped. To make sure that you can experiment freely, create a new namespace:

```
apiVersion: v1
kind: Namespace
metadata:
  name: ns1
```

Into this namespace, you can now deploy an example app:

```
apiVersion: apps/v1
kind: Deployment
metadata:
  labels:
    app: prometheus-example-app
  name: prometheus-example-app
  namespace: ns1
spec:
  replicas: 1
  selector:
    matchLabels:
      app: prometheus-example-app
  template:
    metadata:
      labels:
        app: prometheus-example-app
    spec:
      containers:
      - image: ghcr.io/rhobs/prometheus-example-app:0.4.0
        imagePullPolicy: IfNotPresent
        name: prometheus-example-app
```

You will also need a service in front of the app:

```
apiVersion: v1
kind: Service
metadata:
```

```
    labels:
      app: prometheus-example-app
    name: prometheus-example-app
    namespace: ns1
  spec:
    ports:
    - port: 8080
      protocol: TCP
      targetPort: 8080
      name: web
    selector:
      app: prometheus-example-app
    type: ClusterIP
```

Apply the above YAML and watch your pods being created in your new namespace:

```
$ oc apply -f  deploy.yaml
namespace/ns1 created
deployment.apps/prometheus-example-app created
service/prometheus-example-app created

$ oc get all -n ns1
NAME                                              READY    STATUS     RESTARTS
pod/prometheus-example-app-676776dcb9-tc98c       1/1      Running    0

NAME                               TYPE        CLUSTER-IP    EXTERNAL-IP   PORT(S)
service/prometheus-example-app     ClusterIP   10.217.5.38   <none>        8080/TCP

NAME                                      READY   UP-TO-DATE   AVAILABLE
deployment.apps/prometheus-example-app    1/1     1            1

NAME                                                DESIRED   CURRENT   READY
replicaset.apps/prometheus-example-app-676776dcb9   1         1         1
```

To actually deploy the monitoring-specific component, start with the
ServiceMonitor:

```
apiVersion: monitoring.coreos.com/v1
kind: ServiceMonitor
metadata:
  labels:
    k8s-app: prometheus-example-monitor
  name: prometheus-example-monitor
  namespace: ns1
spec:
  endpoints:
  - interval: 30s
    port: web
    scheme: http
  selector:
    matchLabels:
      app: prometheus-example-app
```

The `serviceMonitor` requires certain information: which port to target and how often Prometheus should later scrape that service. To make sure that the ServiceMonitor targets the right service, the label and value in the `selector` section of the specification need to match.

After you have applied the above YAML you can find your service under the targets, either in the Prometheus UI or in the OpenShift console under Observe → Target_. Filter to see User targets only, as shown in Figure 6-12.

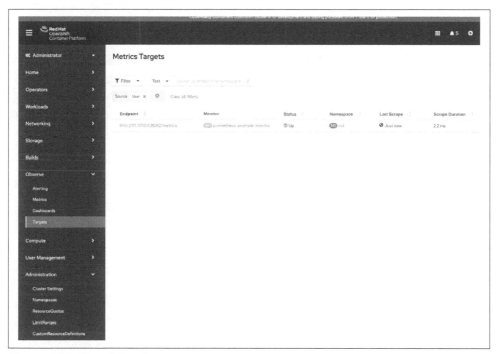

Figure 6-12. User-defined targets

Next you'll need to create an alerting rule to ensure you'll know if the service goes down. For this example, you'll use the recording and alerting rules as shown in Example 6-4. Notice that you are explicitly selecting the metrics for your service by specifying `job="prometheus-example-app"` when accessing the up metrics.

Example 6-4. User workload alerting rule

```
apiVersion: monitoring.coreos.com/v1
kind: PrometheusRule
metadata:
  name: up
  namespace: ns1
spec:
```

```
groups:
- name: up.rules
  rules:
  - expr: sum by (service) (up{job="prometheus-example-app"})
    record: example:services:up:sum
  - expr: example:services:up:sum < 1
    alert: exampleNotUp
    for: 10m
    labels:
      severity: critical
    annotations:
      summary: Service is  not up
```

At this point, the only way to find information about your application is to manually look for it in the alerts tab. To route your alert somewhere, you can use `Alertmanager Config` for your workloads. To route your alert using the example we provided above, you'll first need to go back to the Cluster Monitoring configuration, as shown in Example 6-5.

Example 6-5. User workload with alerting enabled

```
apiVersion: v1
kind: ConfigMap
metadata:
  name: cluster-monitoring-config
  namespace: openshift-monitoring
data:
  config.yaml: |
    enableUserWorkload: true
    alertmanagerMain:
      enableUserAlertmanagerConfig: true
```

After you apply the YAML, deploy your routing rules. Normally we would recommend creating a separate service in PagerDuty to differentiate between workloads and clusters in a multitenant environment; even workloads on a single cluster should be separated so that you can push alerts to different services. For this example, however, you will use the same PagerDuty service as you did for your cluster, for ease of reproduction.

Unlike cluster alerts, you can leverage the `AlertmanagerConfig`. To create your alert, you'll need to create an alertmanagerconfig.yaml locally and then apply that to the cluster. To start, specify some information about the resource itself: what kind of resource it is, which API it belongs to, and the namespace in which it should live. In this case, it will be deployed to `ns1`:

```
apiVersion: monitoring.coreos.com/v1alpha1
kind: AlertmanagerConfig
metadata:
```

```
  name: example-routing
  namespace: ns1
```

Then you'll need to define which alert to route where by specifying the receiver to be used under `receiver`:

```
spec:
  route:
    receiver: default
    groupBy: [job]
```

The last step is to create the receiver that you want to leverage. For certain types of receivers you will need to store the `serviceKey` in a secret. To create the secret, base64 encode your service key and put it in the YAML so that it appears as follows:

```
apiVersion: v1
kind: Secret
type: Opaque
metadata:
  name: pagerduty-config
  namespace: ns1
data:
  serviceKey: ZTAwMGRlZWUxYTIxNDQwNmMxNTkzMWI5OWE5YjgxMmM=
```

Now you can access the service key.

```
receivers:
- name: default
  pagerdutyConfigs:
    - url: 'https://events.eu.pagerduty.com/generic/20-4-5/create_event.json'
      serviceKey:
        name: 'pagerduty-config'
        key: 'serviceKey'
```

You also can now define multiple receivers and, respectively, multiple routes. This will not be necessary, however, if you follow the separation of uses cases by namespace or project. AlertmanagerConfigs are namespace scoped, meaning that for every new namespace, you will need to define a new AlertmanagerConfig and apply it. For `ns1` you can now apply the full example as shown in Example 6-6. For convenience, we put the secret creation and the AlertmanagerConfig in a single file.

Example 6-6. UWM AlertmanagerConfig

```
apiVersion: monitoring.coreos.com/v1alpha1
kind: AlertmanagerConfig
metadata:
  name: example-routing
  namespace: ns1
spec:
  route:
    receiver: default
    groupBy: [job]
```

```
    receivers:
    - name: default
      pagerdutyConfigs:
        - url: 'https://events.eu.pagerduty.com/generic/20-4-5/create_event.json'
          serviceKey:
            name: 'pagerduty-config'
            key: 'serviceKey'
---
apiVersion: v1
kind: Secret
type: Opaque
metadata:
  name: pagerduty-config
  namespace: ns1
data:
  serviceKey: ZTAwMGRlZWUxYTIxNDQwNmMxNTkzMWI5OWE5YjgxMmM=
```

You will now have alerts sent to your PagerDuty service if your example application is
not up.

Visualizing Metrics

While monitoring and alerting is crucial to keep your platform and services up
and running, sometimes it's helpful to get a visual impression of how your cluster
is doing. For this purpose, OpenShift provides an embedded Grafana instance and
dashboards embedded into the console UI.

Console Dashboards

Red Hat generally recommends using the dashboards via the console UI to visualize
your cluster. We believe that any solution that is proven to be best in class for graph-
ing and dashboarding is the preferred option as long as it's still part of OpenShift.

To find all the dashboards that are shipped as part of OpenShift, go to Observe →
Dashboards. These dashboards are split into different categories that you can choose
from (top left), as shown in Figure 6-13.

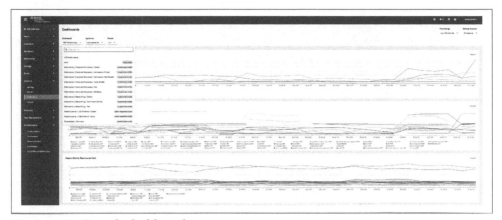

Figure 6-13. Console dashboards

Select the dashboard you want, choose a timeframe to view, and set how often you would like to see the page refreshed.

Using Grafana

To develop your own dashboard, we recommend using Grafana. Find the route to your cluster's instance using the following command:

```
$ oc get route grafana -n openshift-monitoring
NAME       HOST/PORT
grafana    grafana-openshift-monitoring.apps-crc.testing
```

Pull up the given URL in your browser and log in. There you will be prompted with Grafana's starting screen. Access your dashboards by clicking General/Home at the top left. Here you will see a folder that contains all the dashboards, as shown in Figure 6-14. These are the same dashboards you located previously in the console UI.

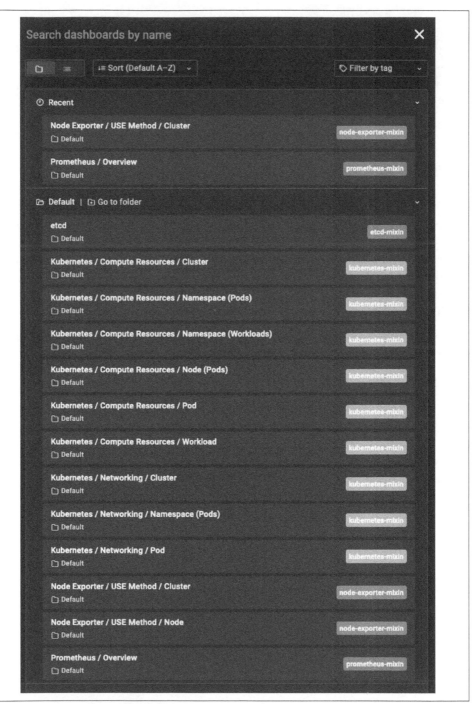

Figure 6-14. Grafana dashboards folder

To explore metrics or create dashboards, you will need to elevate yourself to admin.

Grafana's core configuration is defined in a secret that you can get with a one-liner:

```
$ oc -n openshift-monitoring get secret grafana-config \
  --template='{{ index .data "grafana.ini" }}' | base64 -d | tee grafana.ini
[analytics]
check_for_updates = false
reporting_enabled = false
[auth]
disable_login_form = true
disable_signout_menu = true
[auth.basic]
enabled = false
[auth.proxy]
auto_sign_up = true
enabled = true
header_name = X-Forwarded-User
[paths]
data = /var/lib/grafana
logs = /var/lib/grafana/logs
plugins = /var/lib/grafana/plugins
provisioning = /etc/grafana/provisioning
[security]
admin_user = WHAT_YOU_ARE_DOING_IS_VOIDING_SUPPORT_00000000000
cookie_secure = true
[server]
http_addr = 127.0.0.1
http_port = 3001
```

Please take note of the remark under `admin_user`. You will not have support for Grafana if you proceed with your changes, but you will continue to have support if you choose to roll back.

To make your changes, replace the string in `admin_user` with the user that you would like to use or are using. In the example below, we used `kubeadmin`:

```
[analytics]
check_for_updates = false
reporting_enabled = false
[auth]
disable_login_form = true
disable_signout_menu = true
[auth.basic]
enabled = false
[auth.proxy]
auto_sign_up = true
enabled = true
header_name = X-Forwarded-User
[paths]
data = /var/lib/grafana
logs = /var/lib/grafana/logs
plugins = /var/lib/grafana/plugins
```

```
provisioning = /etc/grafana/provisioning
[security]
admin_user = kubeadmin
cookie_secure = true
[server]
http_addr = 127.0.0.1
http_port = 3001
```

Next, you'll need to apply that configuration and reroll the Grafana pod to use your new configuration. Base64 encode everything again in a one-liner:

```
$ oc -n openshift-monitoring create secret generic grafana-config \
--from-file=grafana.ini \
--dry-run=client -o=yaml |  oc -n openshift-monitoring replace secret \
--filename=- && oc delete pod $(oc get pods | grep grafana | awk '{print $1}')
```

You should now find yourself with admin privileges, as shown in the Grafana UI in Figure 6-15.

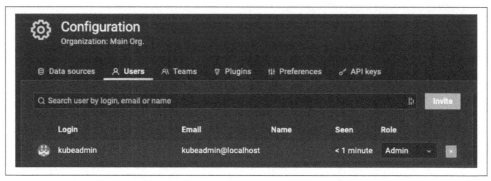

Figure 6-15. Grafana admin

Your elevated privileges will persist only until the Grafana container is restarted again.

You can now develop dashboards right on the cluster that you can use later. Click the + icon and choose Dashboard. From here you can create dashboards customized to your needs, as shown in Figure 6-16.

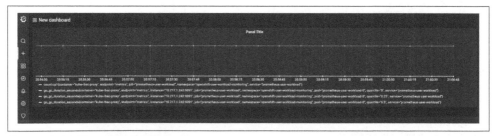

Figure 6-16. Example dashboard

Summary

In this chapter, we discussed the tools that come with OpenShift that help you make your cluster run smoothly. You have learned how to interact with the Cluster Monitoring stacks and how to customize with and beyond support. In the next chapter, we talk about advanced monitoring and observability strategies.

## CHAPTER 7

Advanced Monitoring and Observability Strategies

Rick Rackow

In Chapter 6 you got to know OpenShift's monitoring stack and the basics of monitoring, alerting, and observability. This chapter looks further into this topic and covers more advanced strategies to monitor your services.

Service Oriented Monitoring

Just as infrastructure and services have changed over time, so has the approach to monitoring, and not just since the publishing of *Site Reliability Engineering* (*https:// oreil.ly/2cN73*) by Betsy Beyer and colleagues have engineers sought better ways of monitoring their stack. With the shift to containerized workloads in particular, there are significantly more moving pieces of infrastructure, and it is not feasible to treat each of them with minute care. Think of it as cattle vs. pet. Each of your pets has a name, and you know exactly how it is doing and what it possibly needs. In cattle, each animal is part of the herd, and they're more than merely a number to their owner. However, what matters is not so much the feeling of each individual animal but much rather that the results add up, like the amount of milk received in a day from the cattle. In practice, that means instead of checking the health of underlying nodes, or even worse, individual containers, you shift your focus to the health of your services. Though that might feel strange at the beginning, the benefits become more obvious the more your infrastructure and service landscape grows.

If you consider a basic OpenShift installation with three master nodes and three worker nodes, you can easily deploy hundreds of pods with multiple containers each to said cluster. Do you really care about each of those containers, or do you rather care about the health of the service they provide? Most likely the latter, and this is where Service Level Objectives, or SLOs, come into play. They provide the technical abstraction of what is important to the users of a given service and what level of performance and reliability is required.

Service Level Indicators

Let's walk through a practical example: you deploy a golang application to your OpenShift cluster, maybe similar to the example application from Chapter 6, and you start off with a single instance, so one pod, with a single container. The expectation is that it keeps delivering a 200 response status code every time and within a reasonable timeframe. When you monitor this service implementation, you can assume that high CPU usage or unusually high memory usage means there is an issue with the pod, and the service doesn't respond as expected. However, there are two big problems with this: there's no guarantee that the service isn't responding if it's consuming more resources, and what happens if you scale?

The scaled-out scenario would be that you have five pods behind a service that is exposed via a route, as shown in Figure 7-1.

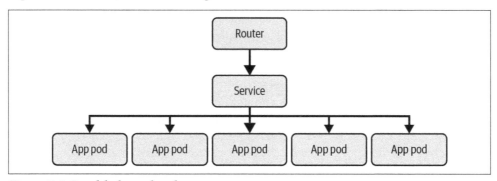

Figure 7-1. Load-balanced pods

If you attempt to monitor them the same way as a single pod, you start to run into issues quickly. Your service may still be functioning as expected even with a single pod that has issues.

This is where monitoring for the services' quality comes into play: instead of focussing on the resources or other metrics called *core vitals* as the primary indicator, you instead shift focus to the service itself.

We mentioned how the service's quality and reliability are defined by its reliability to deliver 200 response codes and to do so in a timely manner. If you now only monitor for successful requests, though, you will you have to start guessing what is happening if you see a drop in requests. Did you just have fewer users or in fact an issue? Hence, you would much rather watch how many errors your service is producing along with how long the requests are taking. Those two signals indicate how well your service is doing. It makes sense that they are called *Service Level Indicators*.

Service Level Objectives

The definition of SLIs was the staircase to the next question: how well do you expect your service to behave or, asked differently, how much misbehavior is tolerated?

A common pitfall when answering this question is to strive for perfection, but that is, in most cases at least, not required and not possible, either.

> While it's tempting to ask for a system that can scale its load "infinitely" without any latency increase and that is "always" available, this requirement is unrealistic. Even a system that approaches such ideals will probably take a long time to design and build, and will be expensive to operate—and probably turn out to be unnecessarily better than what users would be happy (or even delighted) to have.
>
> —*Site Reliability Engineering* by Betsy Beyer and colleagues

Setting those objectives for your service is a complex process. If you want to deep dive into the topic, we recommend Alex Hidalgo's Implementing Service Level Objectives (*https://oreil.ly/jCk03*). But we don't want to widely target the process of setting the *Service Level Objective* itself in too much depth, along with all its organizational challenges, but rather focus on how to monitor a service after you have determined your SLO. So let's assume your example service requires 99% of requests to succeed. That will be its Service Level Objective. Now come up with a plan to get paged accordingly. The question is when to page. There are a couple of different approaches that basically reflect the maturity level of your alerting. Let's walk through the different stages using the *apiserver_request_total* metrics. This will work nicely because you need only this one metric to determine the basic error-focused SLO of the OpenShift API, which is essential to cluster usability.

Stage 1

In the base stage you only monitor your error rate. Looking at the metric, you can get all requests that do not succeed by querying with a label selector like this:

```
apiserver_request_total{code=~"5..",job="apiserver"}
```

In this example, you use the *apiserver_request_total* metric and with the label selectors get only requests that have a 5xx status code. Since the API server's behavior is outside your control, it doesn't make much sense to include 4xx as error as well. With a regular workload, however, it totally makes sense to treat 2xx and 3xx as successful requests, as you should assume that a user would never receive a 4xx status code. In any case where that happens, you should have a catch-all kind of mechanism in place to make sure they get redirected to an existing resource using a 3xx status, hence when a user *does* receive a 4xx code, there's a misbehavior that should be accounted for.

With this out of the way, you can move ahead and start to build a query. You want to start with a request rate:

```
rate(apiserver_request_total{job="apiserver"}[5m])
```

This will get you the per-second rate of HTTP requests as measured over the last 5 minutes. Add an aggregation to the query to strip all the labels away and return the aggregated sum:

```
sum(rate(apiserver_request_total{job="apiserver"}[5m]))
```

Next, you want to get the rate of total requests to the burn rate. To achieve that, you divide the error rate by the total request rate:

```
sum(rate(apiserver_request_total{code=~"5..", job="apiserver"}[5m])) /
sum(rate(apiserver_request_total{job="apiserver"}[5m]))
```

Time to think about a threshold. If your SLO is 99%, as we said, with this type of query you *must* fire an alert at the latest when you have an error rate that is 1% or higher for some time, five minutes in this example, as otherwise you won't have guarantees to detect threats to your SLO. However, you will also get alerts for spikes in the error rate that might not actually be a threat to your SLO.

Stage 2

This second level of maturity is basically playing around with the time windows. The first option here is to increase the alert window. Instead of watching the last five minutes, as we did in stage 1, you are now watching a longer timeframe, for example 24 hours. This means you sacrifice a bit more error budget before you fire your alert, but you also don't get ultrasensitive alerts. However, this comes at a price, which is that you have to calculate way more data points, which takes more resources on your Prometheus instance and also takes significantly longer, as you can see in Figure 7-2.

Figure 7-2. 24h vs 5m window

Additionally, you might have alerts lingering for a very long time and potentially even the full 36 hours.

The other knob you can turn here is the alert duration, like this:

```
- alert: HighErrorRate
  expr: sum(rate(apiserver_request_total{code=~"5..", job="apiserver"}[5m])) /
      sum(rate(apiserver_request_total{job="apiserver"}[5m])) > 0.01
  for: 1h
```

Using an extra `for` condition in your alert definition means that the alert-worthy condition needs to persist, in this example for one hour. You vastly improve the signal-to-noise ratio of your alert significantly, but in turn, you impacted your time to detection. Any issue will be detected only after one hour. It doesn't matter if there is a 100% outage or if you are just slightly bleeding error budget away at an error rate of 1% for an hour.

Stage 3

The next best idea is to monitor for what actually matters: the error budget, so the amount of time or request, that your SLO allows you to have errors. In our scenario of a 99% SLO, that means you can have a full outage for 7 hours and 12 minutes in a 30-day window.

> If you want to calculate your own error budget without doing the math yourself, you can use SLOs with Prometheus (*https://prom tools.dev*).

To monitor for our error budget, we want to know how fast we are burning it. This is called the *burn rate*. At a burn rate of 1, we will have used all our error budget at the end of our rolling window. At this point, you have to ask yourself how fast you and your team can fix any given issue after its detection, to determine how much budget you allow to be burned before you alert.

Let's assume that it's a good idea to fire an alert and let someone know that something is wrong if 5% of the error budget has been burnt in an hour. Everything here is variable, so you could adjust this as you determine what works best for your team and situation. Let's take a peek at the math before we continue.

A burn rate of 1 means that all budget is burned exactly at the end of the window, so 30 days. This means that permanently having a 1% error rate for our 99% SLO, we get a burn rate of 1. An error rate of 2% would result in a burn rate of 2, and so on. To find out how fast our budget is burned, we do the following calculation:

$$\frac{window}{burn\ rate} = time\ until\ budget\ used$$

To find out which burn rate we need, to have 5% of the budget burnt after one hour, we need to adjust the equation a tiny bit. We first convert our 30 days to hours, so it gets a little easier to juggle. We multiply by 24 and get 720 hours as the result. Next, we calculate how long it would take for all our budget to be used, if 5% is burnt in an hour:

$$5\% = 1h$$

Multiply this by 20 to get to 100%:

$$100\% = 20h$$

We now know that we need a burn rate, with which all budget is burnt, after 20 hours, so we can adjust our base equation as follows:

$$\frac{720h}{burn\ rate} = 20h$$

Now we can solve for *burn rate*:

$$\frac{720h}{burn\ rate} = 20h$$

$$720h = 20h * burn\ rate$$

$$\frac{720h}{20h} = \text{burn rate}$$

$$36 = \text{burn rate}$$

With that burn rate of 36, we now get to build our burn rate-based alert:

```
- alert: HighErrorRate
    expr: sum(rate(apiserver_request_total{code=~"5..",job="apiserver"}[1h])) /
          sum(rate(apiserver_request_total{job="apiserver"}[1h])) > 36 * 0.01
```

As you can see, we have adjusted the timeframe for the `rate` to one hour and added the burn rate of 36.

The interesting and also problematic bit here is that this is not a *catch-all* kind of situation. For example, if you have errors that cause burn rate of 5, you will still run out of budget before the end of the window but never notice. To mitigate this, you could add multiple burn rate-based alerts:

```
- alert: HighErrorRate
    expr: (
            sum(rate(apiserver_request_total{code=~"5..",job="apiserver"}[1h])) /
            sum(rate(apiserver_request_total{job="apiserver"}[1h])) > 14.4 * 0.01s
            or
            sum(rate(apiserver_request_total{code=~"5..",job="apiserver"}[6h])) /
            sum(rate(apiserver_request_total{job="apiserver"}[6h])) > 6 * 0.01s
            )
```

This is a better solution, but you still have issues. Either you add a set of alerts for slow bleeding, and then you have a possible alert overlap and multiple alerts firing for the same issue, or you have blind spots for slow bleeding or very slow recovery times.

Final Stage

The current best solution to this: multiwindow, multi-burn-rate alerts. They look something like the following:

```
expr: (
        job:slo_errors_per_request:ratio_rate1h{job="myjob"} > (14.4*0.001)
      and
        job:slo_errors_per_request:ratio_rate5m{job="myjob"} > (14.4*0.001)
      )
    or
      (
        job:slo_errors_per_request:ratio_rate6h{job="myjob"} > (6*0.001)
      and
        job:slo_errors_per_request:ratio_rate30m{job="myjob"} > (6*0.001)
      )
severity: page

expr: (
```

```
    job:slo_errors_per_request:ratio_rate24h{job="myjob"} > (3*0.001)
  and
    job:slo_errors_per_request:ratio_rate2h{job="myjob"} > (3*0.001)
  )
or
  (
    job:slo_errors_per_request:ratio_rate3d{job="myjob"} > 0.001
  and
    job:slo_errors_per_request:ratio_rate6h{job="myjob"} > 0.001
  )
severity: ticket
```

The idea here is that you have the window that you want to monitor, so one hour, and then you add a shorter window—five minutes in this case—to check if you are still burning budget currently. This allows for the same precision when getting notified, but you can also recover quickly and won't have stale alerts.

A clear downside to a sophisticated and precise solution like this is there are a lot of parameters to specify, manage, and understand. This can make alerting hard and raises the bar for newcomers.

Tools

As you can see, the whole process of creating alerts, understanding them, and eventually managing them can become very complicated. We don't want that. To make life easier, there are some tools that greatly help in the process of creating alerts or help with service-based monitoring in general. In this section, you will get to know some of them.

Route Monitor Operator

Red Hat offers managed OpenShift and has a whole team of SREs to manage those clusters. This also means that certain challenges at scale are not an issue in smaller environments, but in turn they can be solved because the engineering resources exist. One of those cases is closed-box monitoring. Closed-box monitoring treats the system that is to be monitored as unknown and assumes you don't get any insight into it, so you have to send requests to probe it. This allows you to discover error patterns that might otherwise have stayed undetected, as the problematic requests never would have reached the part of your stack that produces metrics. Consider DNS issues or expired certificates. You would never uncover those on your edge, because there's no completed HTTP request.

There are service providers that offer closed-box monitoring, such as Pingdom or Statuscake, as well as Grafana Cloud and others, but they obviously come at a price and that can get out of hand quickly. Luckily, the Prometheus community has created the *BlackBox exporter*, which facilitates closed-box monitoring by creating a synthetic request every time it is scraped by Prometheus. Route Monitor Operator uses that but on top adds multiwindow multi-burn-rate alerts for each of the probed objects. So all you need to get a full set of alerts for your SLO is to create a `RouteMonitor` and add your desired SLO to it.

Pyrra

Pyrra is a new open-source tool initially designed by Matthias Loibl and Nadine Vehling. It's basically a one-stop shop for all things SLO, which can hardly surprise anyone, given Matthias' extensive past in OpenShift's monitoring team and contributions to the kubernetes-mixin (*https://oreil.ly/eaFAE*). Pyrra gives you a dashboard for a visual overview of how you are doing in terms of your SLO, but more importantly it autogenerates all required alerts for any service you give it.

Installation. The repository comes with everything required to get a running Pyrra deployment. First, clone the repository:

```
$ git clone https://github.com/pyrra-dev/pyrra.git
```

```
$ cd pyrra
```

Pyrra needs to be able to authenticate against OpenShift. Create a `ServiceAccount` and get its bearer token. Instead of manually getting a `serviceAccountToken`, we use *projected volumes* to automount the token into the pod and be able to use it. This holds the big advantage of automatically rotated tokens, plus the token never has to leave the cluster. To deploy Pyrra including the ServiceAccount, run the following commands:

```
$ oc apply -f examples/openshift/deploy/openshift.yaml
```

```
$ oc apply -f examples/openshift/deploy/role.yaml
```

```
$ oc apply -f examples/openshift/deploy/api.yaml
```

To Pyrra, you can leverage OpenShift's router and create a route with the following command:

```
$ oc expose service pyrra-api -n openshift-monitoring
```

To reach the Pyrra UI, execute the following command to receive the URL of the route that you created with the preceding command:

```
$ oc get route pyrra-api -n openshift-monitoring
```

Example. Pyrra is now ready and running, so it's time to deploy an example, but before you do, let's take a look:

```
apiVersion: pyrra.dev/v1alpha1
kind: ServiceLevelObjective
metadata:
  labels:
    prometheus: k8s
    role: alert-rules
  name: apiserver-read-response-errors
  namespace: openshift-monitoring
spec:
  description: "My cool API alerts"
  indicator:
    ratio:
      errors:
        metric: apiserver_request_total{job="apiserver",code=~"5.."}
      total:
        metric: apiserver_request_total{job="apiserver"}
  target: "99.00"
  window: 2w
```

Since Pyrra is using existing metrics, you need to let it know what the total is and what the failures are. This is so you can get exactly the same queries out that were discussed earlier in this chapter. Additionally, Pyrra needs a target, which is your SLO.

Once you apply the above, you can see that Pyrra created all the required `Prometheus` `Rules` with the following command:

```
$ oc get prometheusrules -n openshift-monitoring| grep apiserver
apiserver-read-response-errors              27d
apiserver-write-response-errors             27d
```

Now you can also view the SLOs and their error budget via the Pyrra UI as shown in Figure 7-3.

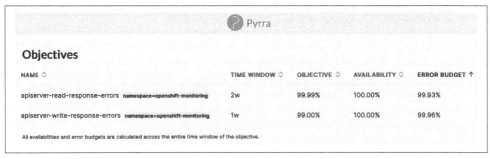

Figure 7-3. Pyrra SLO overview

You can also check each of the SLOs separately for a further breakdown as seen in Figure 7-4.

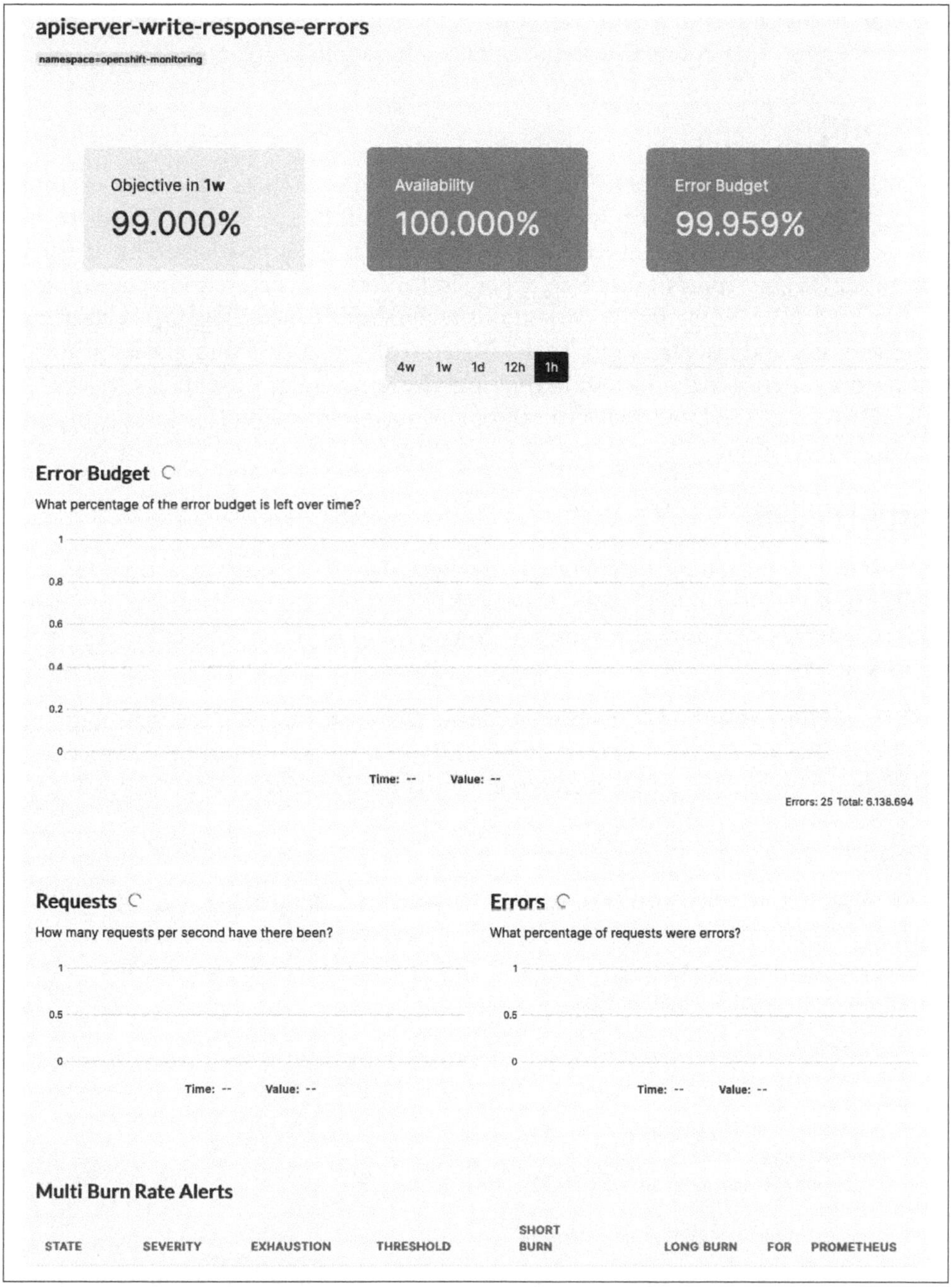

apiserver-write-response-errors

namespace=openshift-monitoring

Objective in **1w**	Availability	Error Budget
99.000%	**100.000%**	**99.959%**

4w   1w   1d   12h   **1h**

Error Budget ↻

What percentage of the error budget is left over time?

Time: --   Value: --

Errors: 25 Total: 6.138.694

Requests ↻

How many requests per second have there been?

Time: --   Value: --

Errors ↻

What percentage of requests were errors?

Time: --   Value: --

Multi Burn Rate Alerts

STATE	SEVERITY	EXHAUSTION	THRESHOLD	SHORT BURN	LONG BURN	FOR	PROMETHEUS

Figure 7-4. Pyrra SLO breakdown

With that you get a great overview at a glance and have a nice package together with the Prometheus Alerts.

You can do the same thing for every other namespace if you enabled User Workload Monitoring, as explained in Chapter 6, and use your application's metrics.

Logging

So far, our discussion has been very focused on metrics. That's because everything for metrics collection and access comes with OpenShift out of the box. But there will be a point at which you want to check the logs and not tail pod logs. This is where structured logging comes into place. OpenShift offers a structured logging solution by installing *ClusterLogging*. The beauty of OpenShift's ClusterLogging is clearly in the ease of use and installation for small cluster deployments. If your cluster grows or you need to aggregate the logs from multiple clusters, you can use its *log forwarding* capability. The next section walks you through your options with ClusterLogging and a sample installation.

ClusterLogging

ClusterLogging, made and maintained by Red Hat, is in essence a branded and opinionated Elasticsearch, Fluentd, Kibana (EFK) stack. The fact that it's opinionated is in your favor here, as that means you don't have to be a subject-matter expert for the EFK stack.

ClusterLogging deploys a pod to every node via a `DaemonSet` and scrapes all container logs from that node as well as from journals. Logs then get sent to the Elasticsearch instances where you can access them via either API or Kibana.

Installation

ClusterLogging consists of two main components: `openshift-logging` and an `elasticsearch-operator`. They live in separate namespaces, and it is very important to be careful with the naming. First, you will create the namespace for the Elasticsearch operator that looks like this:

```
apiVersion: v1
kind: Namespace
metadata:
  name: openshift-operators-redhat
  annotations:
    openshift.io/node-selector: ""
  labels:
    openshift.io/cluster-monitoring: "true"
```

Make sure to have the `openshift.io/cluster-monitoring` label on the namespace, so it's automatically monitored by the in-cluster monitoring stack.

Next create the second namespace, in which the openshift-logging part lives:

```
apiVersion: v1
kind: Namespace
metadata:
  name: openshift-logging
  annotations:
    openshift.io/node-selector: ""
  labels:
    openshift.io/cluster-monitoring: "true"
```

Here again, the label openshift.io/cluster-monitoring is important to automatically get monitoring.

The next step is for you to create an operatorGroup. An operatorGroup helps the operator lifecycle manager deploy operators in that it specifies in which namespaces RBAC rules have to be created.

The following enables that for the openshift-operators-redhat namespaces:

```
apiVersion: operators.coreos.com/v1
kind: OperatorGroup
metadata:
  name: openshift-operators-redhat
  namespace: openshift-operators-redhat
spec: {}
```

Now, to make the operator lifecycle manager aware that you want to install the elasticsearch-operator, you need to add a subscription to the cluster. The following subscription does that. You can change the channel if you desire, but the stable channel is a good first choice:

```
apiVersion: operators.coreos.com/v1alpha1
kind: Subscription
metadata:
  name: "elasticsearch-operator"
  namespace: "openshift-operators-redhat"
spec:
  channel: "stable"
  installPlanApproval: "Automatic"
  source: "redhat-operators"
  sourceNamespace: "openshift-marketplace"
  name: "elasticsearch-operator"
```

With the preceding setting of installPlanApproval: "Automatic" your Elasticsearch stack will also upgrade automatically, which *usually* works best for most use cases, but it might need a change depending on your needs.

After you have applied all of that to your cluster, verify that it worked by checking whether a cluster service version (CSV) got placed in your namespaces:

```
$ oc get csv --all-namespaces
NAMESPACE                              NAME
default                                elasticsearch-operator.5.4.0-152
kube-node-lease                        elasticsearch-operator.5.4.0-152
kube-public                            elasticsearch-operator.5.4.0-152
kube-system                            elasticsearch-operator.5.4.0-152
ns1                                    elasticsearch-operator.5.4.0-152
openshift-apiserver-operator           elasticsearch-operator.5.4.0-152
openshift-apiserver                    elasticsearch-operator.5.4.0-152
openshift-authentication-operator      elasticsearch-operator.5.4.0-152
```

Now your cluster is ready for openshift-logging, and for that you will need an operator group again. However, as opposed to the first operator group, you want this to target only a specific namespace, as follows:

```
apiVersion: operators.coreos.com/v1
kind: OperatorGroup
metadata:
  name: cluster-logging
  namespace: openshift-logging
spec:
  targetNamespaces:
  - openshift-logging
```

The last part of the installation is to subscribe to the cluster logging operator channel like so:

```
apiVersion: operators.coreos.com/v1alpha1
kind: Subscription
metadata:
  name: cluster-logging
  namespace: openshift-logging
spec:
  channel: "stable"
  name: cluster-logging
  source: redhat-operators
  sourceNamespace: openshift-marketplace
```

Since this time we target only a single namespace, you can verify whether everything went as expected with the following command:

```
$ oc get csv -n openshift-logging
NAME                              DISPLAY
cluster-logging.5.4.0-138         Red Hat OpenShift Logging
elasticsearch-operator.5.4.0-152  OpenShift Elasticsearch Operator
```

You'll find all of the above to copy or work with on our GitHub repository (*https://oreil.ly/XP2TQ*). To perform all of the above steps in one go, execute the following:

```
$ git clone git@github.com:OperatingOpenShift/openshift-logging-example.git

$ oc apply -f openshift-logging-example/deploy/
```

Configuration

The two operators together take care of deploying your whole logging stack, but they can and, in fact, have to be configured. That is done via a custom resource. Here's an example:

```
apiVersion: "logging.openshift.io/v1"
kind: "ClusterLogging"
metadata:
  name: "instance"
  namespace: "openshift-logging"
spec:
  managementState: "Managed"
  logStore:
    type: "elasticsearch"
    retentionPolicy:
      application:
        maxAge: 1d
      infra:
        maxAge: 7d
      audit:
        maxAge: 7d
    elasticsearch:
      nodeCount: 3
      storage:
        storageClassName: "gp2" # CHANGE THIS ACCORDINGLY
        size: 200G
      resources:
        limits:
          memory: "16Gi"
        requests:
          memory: "16Gi"
      proxy:
        resources:
          limits:
            memory: 256Mi
          requests:
            memory: 256Mi
      redundancyPolicy: "SingleRedundancy"
  visualization:
    type: "kibana"
    kibana:
      replicas: 1
  collection:
    logs:
      type: "fluentd"
      fluentd: {}
```

The preceding example deploys three Elasticsearch nodes, provisions 200GB persistent storage for each of them, and takes care of all the cluster syncing. Apart from that, it also deploys Fluentd and a Kibana instance for visualization.

The resources, mainly memory, are close to the absolute minimum, so there is a chance this might not work on a CodeReadyContainers installation.

Once the above is applied and the resources are created, collect all logs from your OpenShift cluster.

Log Forwarding

The alternative to storing your logs on the cluster is to send them somewhere. This is a good idea if you use any kind of SaaS provider for all your other logs or just generally if you want to aggregate logs from multiple clusters or sources. ClusterLogging provides this capability out of the box. You can also configure a subset of metrics to be forwarded:

```
apiVersion: "logging.openshift.io/v1"
kind: ClusterLogForwarder
metadata:
  name: instance
  namespace: openshift-logging
spec:
  outputs:
    - name: loki-insecure
      type: "loki"
      url: http://clouder:3100/loki/api/v1/push
  pipelines:
    - name: application-logs
      inputRefs:
      - application
      - audit
      outputRefs:
      - loki-insecure
```

Here you can see that cluster logging uses a resource called *ClusterLogForwarder* in which you can describe its configuration. There are various types available, like Loki in the example, but also Kafka or just another Elasticsearch instance. The configuration varies a little depending on which system you want to forward to. For Loki, you only need a URL and to define which logs to ship.

Loki

ClusterLogging aside, one option mentioned at the end of the last section is gaining popularity: Loki. Loki is a set of logging tools from Grafana. The idea is to be able to query logs similarly to metrics, except using LogQL instead of PromQL. It ties in well with Grafana for dashboards, but at the time of writing, it is too unstable and poorly documented to be a viable option.

Visualization

You have learned how to get metrics and to alert on them, as well as how to get logs. However, sometimes it is helpful to get a visual impression of what is happening. Chapter 6 mentioned the built-in Grafana and how to work around the authentication. The more viable and long-lived alternative is to deploy your own Grafana, which you can control any way you want.

The next sections will walk you through how to install Grafana Operator, get an instance up and running, and deploy a sample dashboard.

Installation

While installing ClusterLogging, you learned how to install an operator from OperatorHub via the command line. This time, you will leverage the OpenShift UI instead. You also can do this via the CLI, but getting to know both possible ways is good practice.

The first step is to log in to the OpenShift web console with your credentials and then click Operators → OperatorHub on the navigation on the left-hand side.

Now you are at the OperatorHub, the marketplace that you used in Chapter 5 to install the pipelines Operator. Type *Grafana Operator* in the search field as shown in Figure 7-5.

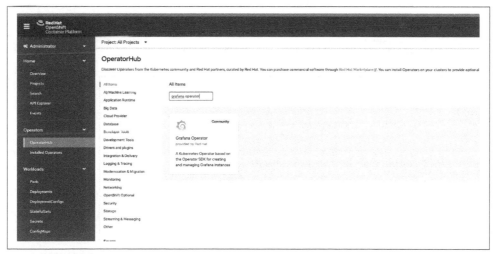

Figure 7-5. OperatorHub search

After you click the Grafana Operator tile, you get a little warning pop-up that reminds you that this operator is not maintained or provided by Red Hat. Acknowledge and proceed to the installation dialog, which will be similar to Figure 7-6.

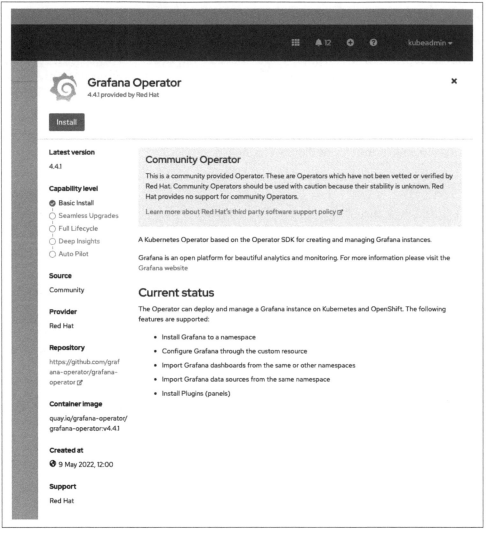

Figure 7-6. Grafana Operator installation dialog

In the follow-up to this dialog, pick and choose a namespace to install into and your upgrade method. Here you should choose create project so that the Grafana Operator nicely lives in its own project. Fill out the dialog similar to Figure 7-7.

Once this is done, click the *Create* button and a screen message will encourage you to have patience, and the process may take a few minutes. You will get status updates taken from the log messages about what is currently happening under the hood.

After everything is done and ready, click View Operator and start to deploy dashboards and data sources.

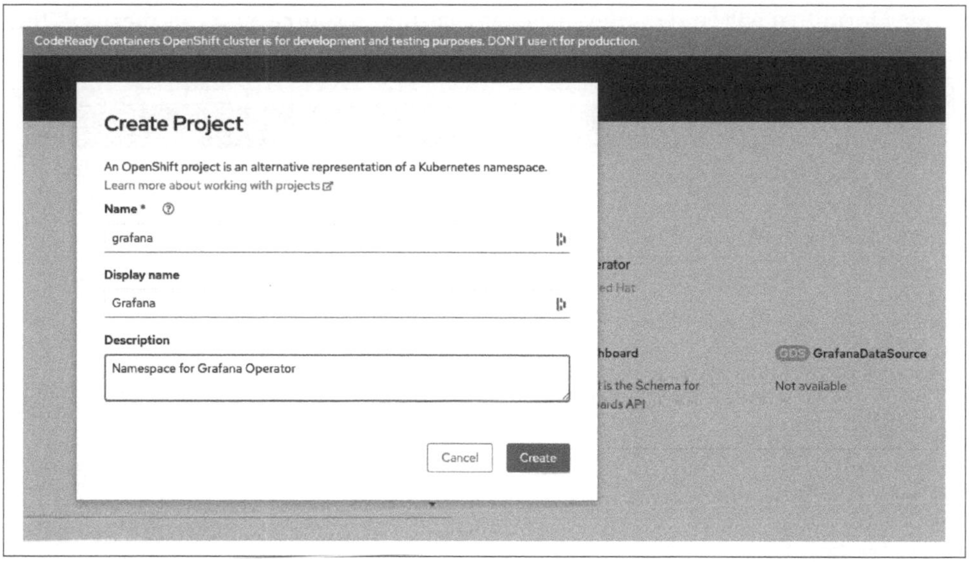

Figure 7-7. Grafana Operator project

Creating a Grafana Instance

The first step is to create a Grafana instance because without that, neither the data source nor anything else is very useful.

Go to the Grafana operator's page by clicking Operators → Installed Operators → Grafana Operator on the navigation bar. Click Grafana and create an instance. If you don't fill out anything, that will do just fine and will create an instance with default values.

Data Source

Grafana is just a tool for visualizing in this context, which means it also needs something to actually visualize. There are a lot of supported options, but the first step in an OpenShift cluster is to connect to potential data sources that are inside the cluster, in other words the Cluster Monitoring stack.

As explained in Chapter 6, Cluster Monitoring stands on top of a Prometheus Operator stack, so you can safely assume that you will work with a Prometheus-style endpoint.

To create the data source, go once again to the Grafana Operator's page. To get there click Operators → Installed Operators → Grafana Operator on the navigation bar. Now click *GrafanaDataSource*.

Things are a little complicated with all the different options here, because of all the various options you have after you create GrafanaDataSource. In essence, you are filling a form that will land on the cluster as a custom resource, and this means in this form you can also specify all options. Figure 7-8 shows a full working example.

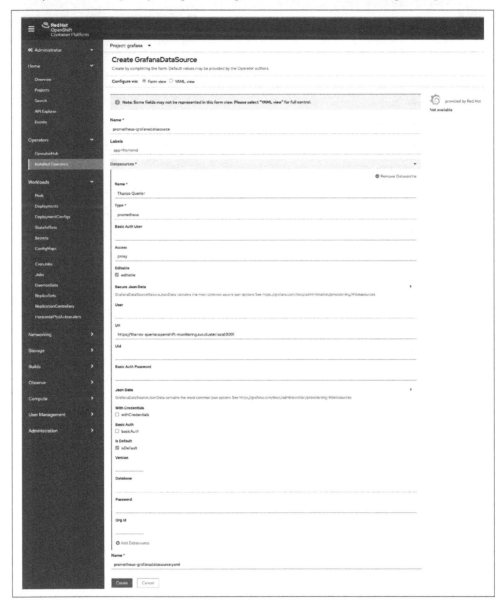

Figure 7-8. GrafanaDataSource Thanos querier

Alternatively, you can also write the YAML, by clicking the YAML view button. The practical thing is that everything gets replicated accordingly. This means if you started to fill the form but YAML is easier for some other bits, you can switch views, and the information you provided so far will be present in the YAML and vice-versa. The respective YAML for our form example would look something like the following:

```yaml
apiVersion: integreatly.org/v1alpha1
kind: GrafanaDataSource
metadata:
  name: prometheus-grafanadatasource
  namespace: grafana
spec:
  datasources:
    - secureJsonData:
        httpHeaderValue1: 'Bearer ${BEARER_TOKEN}'
      jsonData:
        httpHeaderName1: Authorization
        timeInterval: 5s
        tlsSkipVerify: true
      access: proxy
      editable: true
      isDefault: true
      name: Thanos Querier
      type: prometheus
      url: 'https://thanos-querier.openshift-monitoring.svc.cluster.local:9091'
    name: prometheus-grafanadatasource.yaml
```

If you read that closely, you noticed that it uses a bearer token to authenticate against the Thanos Querier. To get this bearer token, either use your own user token or create a service account. Creating a ServiceAccount and using that token is the recommended way and is also a better practice in terms of security, as you learned in Chapter 4.

To create the token, execute the following commands. The account has been created as part of creating a Grafana instance, so you now need to add it to the groups with the following commands and get the token:

```
$ oc adm policy add-cluster-role-to-user \
cluster-monitoring-view -z grafana-serviceaccount \
clusterrole.rbac.authorization.k8s.io/cluster-monitoring-view

added: "grafana-serviceaccount"

$ oc serviceaccounts get-token grafana-serviceaccount -n grafana
```

Now that you have the token, you can adjust the above YAML (or form) and replace ${BEARER_TOKEN} with your token.

Dashboards

To make sure everything works so far, expose the Grafana instance. To do so, execute the following command:

```
$ oc expose svc grafana-service -n grafana
route.route.openshift.io/grafana-service exposed
```

After that you can use `oc get route -n grafana` to get the URL. If you type or copy that into your browser, you will be prompted with a login screen. Unless you changed something in the defaults, the credentials are stored in a secret in the `grafana` namespace, and you can get them like so:

```
$ oc get secret grafana-admin-credentials -o yaml
apiVersion: v1
data:
  GF_SECURITY_ADMIN_PASSWORD: MXRZRGtGY1I0Ymh5enc9PQ==
  GF_SECURITY_ADMIN_USER: YWRtaW4=
kind: Secret
```

Values in Kubernetes secrets are base64 encoded. Be sure to decode them before you use them.

Once you're logged in, click Settings → Data Sources and select your data sources. Don't change anything, just click Save & Test, and if everything went well, you should see a green status letting you know that it's working, similar to Figure 7-9.

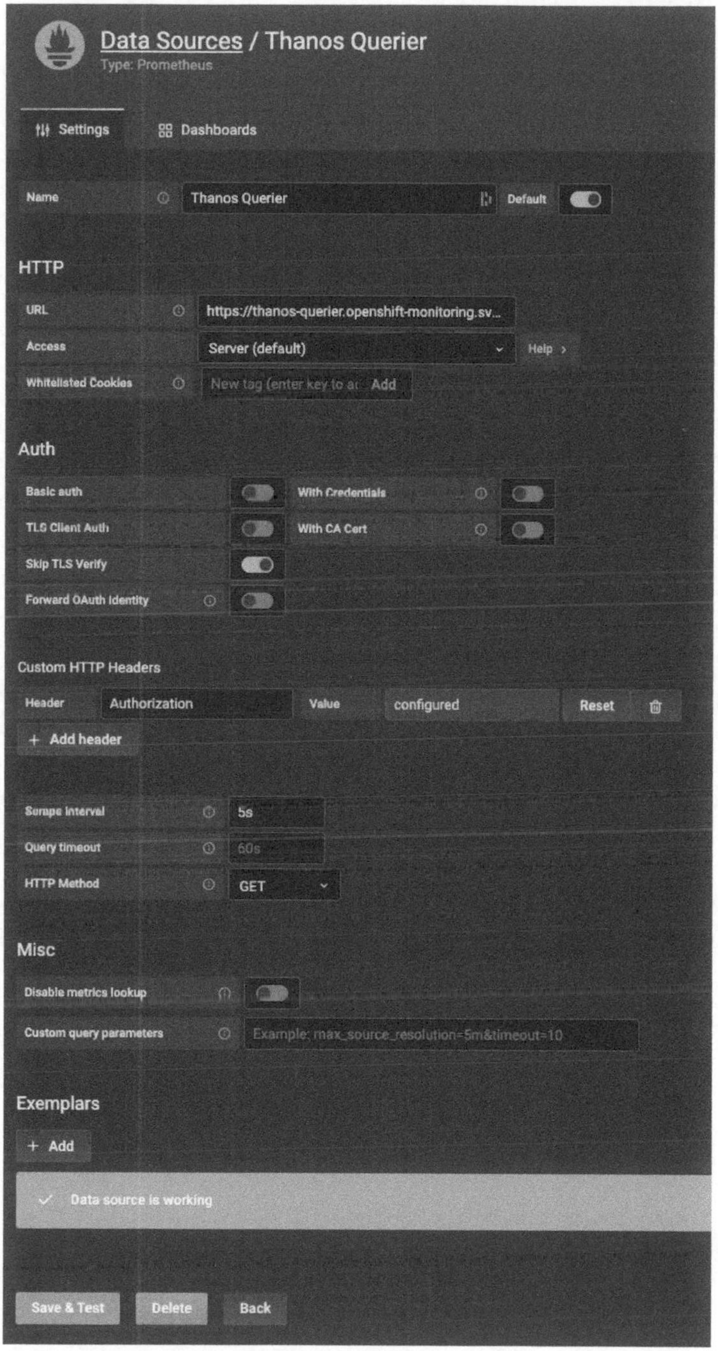

Figure 7-9. Grafana working datasource

From here you can now start to build your own dashboards. After you are done, click Share and copy the JSON. Head back to the Grafana Operator page in the OpenShift console by clicking Operators → Installed Operators → Grafana Operator and click GrafanaDashboard to create a new one. In the form field, paste the JSON data and hit *create*. This will persist your changes.

Summary

In this chapter you have learned how to create alerts for your SLOs, how to visualize them, and how to collect logs and visualize basically anything with Grafana. Now it's up to you to make the best use of it. The best results are achieved if you combine the different sources of information instead of treating them as isolated silos.

An example: if you start to receive alerts for an SLO budget burn, make sure to check all remaining alerts for this service, but just like that, you can also view your dashboards and see if you can spot obvious outliers. Once you have found something, you can check the logs for anything that stands out during that timeframe.

As an SRE you need to use your experience together with the data you have instead of relying on your gut feeling. Chapter 10 talks about further strategies for larger cluster deployments and multicluster.

The evolution of tools is moving at a rapid pace, and the focus moves more and more to *shift left*. That means, on a virtual timeline, you want to move to the left, so you detect issues earlier. Part of achieving this is to have the proper follow-up actions after an alert is triggered: if you burned your error budget, especially more than you had available, you *must* investigate the root cause and fix it, instead of putting mitigations in place. If alerts are creating too much noise, fix those too instead of just covering up or putting mitigations like time-based silencing in place. The current generation of tools allows for all sorts of customization.

That aside, other tools can help you with the detection during your test. That should cover whether alerts are firing during your E2E tests or other tools like Parca that help you detect performance and resources issues long before they start to impact your production workload.

## CHAPTER 8

Automating OpenShift Cluster Operations

Manuel Dewald

What does it mean to operate an OpenShift cluster?

Typically, operating software is divided into two distinct kinds of work:

Firefighting work
> Something stopped working so the pager of an operations team goes off and somebody starts looking into the problem immediately until the problem is solved.

Execution of maintenance tasks that are often repetitive
> This includes installing new software or software updates, updating configuration, refreshing certificates, or cleanup tasks.

This is not much different for OpenShift clusters. After setting up Cluster Monitoring as described in Chapter 7, your cluster should reach out to you, your operations, or the SRE team when it needs attention: Often the alerts issued by OpenShift will even give you hints on how to mitigate the problem that just occurred.

An OpenShift cluster itself should not need much attention if nothing goes wrong. That means repetitive tasks such as renewing the certificates that OpenShift needs to run should be mostly automated.

An exception to that is installing updates. Installing updates to the next minor or major version should be nondisruptive to the workload of your cluster, but installing the update is a maintenance task you need to care for.

That means most remaining maintenance tasks left specific to your deployment of the OpenShift cluster. How you want to handle cluster updates is up to you. What kind of SSL certificate you're using for your web applications and how they get installed and renewed are your responsibility. How users of the cluster will log in and which permissions they get depend on your organization.

Installing the cluster is itself an operations task you need to care for, as this depends on the infrastructure you want to use for it. Depending on how many clusters you're planning to operate and the planned cluster lifecycle, installation can be a significant source of operations effort. If you operate small clusters per team, you'll find yourself creating more and more OpenShift clusters as soon as adoption increases. You'll need to care for their health and ultimately their deprovisioning when they're not needed anymore.

OpenShift provides many tools you can use to ease the operations of the clusters, like smooth cluster updates and installers for all different kinds of infrastructure, but it's your responsibility to adjust the cluster to your needs.

Site Reliability Engineering (SRE) is all about automating software operations.

The software an SRE team manages can be OpenShift as well. All the different operations tasks, from installing and configuring a cluster to analyzing and reacting to problems that occur regularly, should be automated with software.

To achieve that goal, operations are handed to a software engineering team that has no other job than writing and running software that operates the cluster. An SRE team usually is a DevOps team, as it will run the software it produces (the automation software) that is responsible for operating one or more OpenShift clusters.

In addition, the SRE team acts as operations team and gets alerted when something goes wrong with the software under their responsibility, such as OpenShift. If a problem occurs repeatedly, the SRE team acts by eliminating the problem or automating the remediation.

SRE team members typically will find themselves doing an additional kind of work: maintenance of the software they built to automate cluster operations. Just like any kind of software, there will be new features to implement, bugs to be fixed, dependencies to be updated, and so on.

Recurring Operations Tasks

So far, this chapter has discussed that one part of keeping a cluster up and running consists of running some kinds of repetitive tasks, although OpenShift itself doesn't need that much attention when it's installed and running. This means many of the things you might need to run depend on your workloads. This section covers some of the most common examples.

Application Updates

Application updates can mean installing new versions of an application that you are using to support your workloads or your developers, for example, an application like Tekton that you use to run the continuous integration system for the applications running on the cluster.

On the other hand, these also can be updates of your in-house developments, the workloads that you want to run on your OpenShift cluster to support your business. You've seen examples of how to automate the update of your apps in Chapter 5: using a CI pipeline built on Tekton or using the OpenShift built-in build system.

Certificate Renewals

Another example of a recurring task when operating an OpenShift cluster is the renewal of SSL certificates. These recurring operations tasks you successfully automated using an OpenShift operator in Chapter 3. If the existing operator doesn't fit your needs or you want to use self-signed certificates, for example because your cluster is not exposed to the internet, managing those certificates is up to you.

OpenShift Updates

Installing updates of OpenShift itself is an important operations task as well. Every few weeks, there is a new release of OpenShift. When running Red Hat OpenShift Container Platform, the support is limited to a few minor versions below the latest version, so you will want to stay as close to the latest release as possible. Installing those updates can be done via the oc CLI, or using the OpenShift Console, as shown in Figure 8-1.

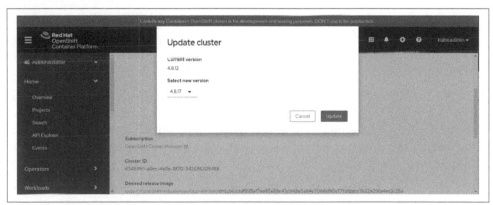

Figure 8-1. Upgrading an OpenShift cluster from the OpenShift Console

However, when you're running more than one cluster, you might want to automate those updates and schedule when those updates are installed. That way you don't have to visit every cluster to install the update according to your schedule.

Backups

For every workload you run that contains data critical for your business, you should have a backup plan. For OpenShift, you may want to create backups of etcd, the database backing the OpenShift control plane.

Not only does the cluster database need backups, but you also want to create backups of your workloads that are deployed to the cluster, like the applications that are running on it. The next section examines this example. Think about the backups of the highscore system. Currently whenever the pod is restarted, all scores of players will be lost. But you may want to preserve the data that is pushed to the highscore service, so it's kept after a pod restart. You will also need to create backups so that you can restore an old version in an event that caused data to be lost or corrupted.

Automating Recurring Operations Tasks

Now that you've seen a few examples of operations tasks that are recurring and can be automated, you will be able to identify more such tasks when they come your way. The next step after identifying an automatable operations task of your OpenShift cluster is to automate it. The automation can be done within the cluster or outside of it, for example on a dedicated OpenShift cluster for automation tasks.

This section takes two example operations tasks and automates them within the cluster: application backups and OpenShift version updates.

Persistence

Until this point, all services of the arcade gaming publisher have been handled as if they were stateless applications.

However, the highscore service is not stateless. The state, being the player scores, will be lost whenever the highscore pod is restarted. That means whenever a new version is rolled out, the pod may be moved to a different node, and all scores will be removed. That doesn't sound like a good player experience, so the first thing you should do is persist that data.

This section doesn't go into much of the details of handling persistent storage with OpenShift, as this is only a prerequisite to showcase a scenario you can use as a blueprint to automate all kinds of operations tasks.

First, if you haven't already done so, install the highscore service, as well as the game service, which will be used to generate some scores to persist:

```
$ oc new-project arcade

$ oc new-app --name=game --context-dir=game \
  https://github.com/OperatingOpenShift/s3e
--> Found container image f0b8a9a ...
[...]
--> Creating resources ...
[...]
--> Success
[...]

$ oc new-app --name=highscore --context-dir=highscore \
  https://github.com/OperatingOpenShift/s3e
--> Found container image c059bfa
[...]
--> Creating resources ...
[...]
--> Success
[...]

$ DOMAIN=$(oc get ingresses.config.openshift.io  cluster \
  -o jsonpath='{.spec.domain}')

$ oc expose svc game --path=/s3e --hostname=arcade.$DOMAIN
route.route.openshift.io/game exposed

$ oc expose svc highscore --path=/highscore --hostname=arcade.$DOMAIN
route.route.openshift.io/highscore exposed
```

To make the data of the highscore service database persist after a restart of the pod, you can create a PersistentVolumeClaim and mount it into the pod at the location where the application stores the data.

If the cluster is configured with a Container Storage Interface (CSI) that supports dynamic provisioning, a PersistentVolume will be automatically provisioned to back the PersistentVolumeClaim. In this section, an OpenShift cluster on GCP is used with a default CSI driver that allows dynamic provisioning: `pd.csi.storage.gke.io`. You can see the existing configurations by listing the StorageClasses of the cluster:

```
$ oc get storageclasses
NAME                PROVISIONER            VOLUMEBINDINGMODE       AGE
standard (default)  pd.csi.storage.gke.io  WaitForFirstConsumer    31m
```

Any other CSI driver with dynamic provisioning support will work; just make sure it's set as the default so the example YAML files in this section will work. The first part of attaching persistent storage will also work with manually provisioned PersistentVolumes, but at the latest, the use of VolumeSnapshots requires dynamic provisioning.

In addition, handling persistent storage is much easier with dynamically provisioned PersistentVolumes: the CSI driver will interact with the infrastructure (in this example GCP) to generate the necessary storage objects that will be represented by a PersistentVolume in OpenShift. Without dynamic provisioning, you will have to care for all the handling of the storage and the in-cluster representation.

 All files used in this chapter can be found in the Git repository (*https://github.com/OperatingOpenShift/s3e*) to follow along, so you don't need to type them. You can find all resources in the *highscore/ backup* folder (*https://oreil.ly/zyrBy*) and apply them directly using a URL with a command like the following, which will create a PersistentVolumeClaim:

```
$ oc apply -f https://raw.githubusercontent.com/\
OperatingOpenShift/s3e/main/highscore/backup/\
02-persistentvolumeclaim.yaml
```

The PersistentVolumeClaim resource should be similar to the following yaml:

```
apiVersion: v1
kind: PersistentVolumeClaim
metadata:
  name: score
spec:
  accessModes:
    - ReadWriteOnce
  volumeMode: Filesystem
  resources:
    requests:
      storage: 1Gi
```

Apply the file to the OpenShift cluster using oc apply:

```
$ oc apply -f 02-persistentvolumeclaim.yaml
persistentvolumeclaim/score created
```

Next, modify the deployment of the highscore service to mount the PersistentVolumeClaim at the location */app/db*:

```
$ oc edit deployment highscore
[...]
kind: Deployment
metadata:
  name: highscore
  namespace: arcade
spec:
  [...]
  template:
    [...]
    spec:
      containers:
      - image: image-registry.openshift-image-registry.svc:5000/arcade/highscore
        name: highscore
        [...]
```

```
        volumeMounts:
        - mountPath: /app/db
          name: score-vol
        volumes:
        - name: score-vol
          persistentVolumeClaim:
            claimName: score
    [...]
```

 You can find the full deployment object as well in the Git repository (*https://oreil.ly/Md4SN*) and apply from there with the following command:

```
$ oc apply -f https://raw.githubusercontent.com/\
OperatingOpenShift/s3e/main/highscore/\
backup/03-deployment.yaml
```

You can now watch the PersistentVolume coming up as soon as it is provisioned by
the CSI driver:

```
$ oc get persistentvolumes
NAME                                        CAPACITY   CLAIM         STORAGECLASS
pvc-5e441a1c-5dda-4c9c-ac87-d70da507158d    1Gi        arcade/score  standard
pvc-60226480-121a-437d-85c1-a0dc19062ac3    10Gi       [...]         standard
pvc-d656739d-50ac-4c65-8400-167617a88d1a    10Gi       [...]         standard
```

Now comes the fun part! Get the URL of the game from the route, visit it in your
browser with a player name as parameter using a URL like *arcade.apps.<your-cluster-
domain>/s3e?player_name=Alice*, and generate some scores.

When you have generated enough scores, you can come back and delete the highscore pod to verify the scores are really written to the persistent storage:

```
$ oc delete pod -l deployment=highscore
```

When a new highscore pod is created by OpenShift, get the route and visit it in the
browser, for example at *arcade.apps.<your-cluster-domain>/highscore*. You should still
see the scores you generated previously.

Creating Snapshots

Now that your service has some persistent data to back up, you can use VolumeSnapshots to create snapshots of the data. As with persistent storage, this section doesn't
cover the full topic, but it shows you the basics of how to create a snapshot. For
more information, take a look at the OpenShift documentation for VolumeSnapshots
(*https://oreil.ly/8Afhj*).

A snapshot can be created with a VolumeSnapshot object like the following, which
will create a backup of the data in the referenced PersistentVolumeClaim score. This

is the PersistentVolumeClaim you mounted at the highscore pod in the previous section:

```
apiVersion: snapshot.storage.k8s.io/v1
kind: VolumeSnapshot
metadata:
  name: score-backup
spec:
  source:
    persistentVolumeClaimName: score ❶
```

❶ The PersistentVolumeClaim for which a snapshot will be created.

To use the data of the backup, you can create another PersistentVolumeClaim based on the snapshot. The corresponding PersistentVolume will be populated with the data of the backup.

As mentioned earlier, you will need a CSI driver that supports dynamic provisioning of volumes to create a PersistentVolume that is populated with the snapshot data. Create the following PersistentVolumeClaim, which references your VolumeSnapshot:

```
apiVersion: v1
kind: PersistentVolumeClaim
metadata:
  name: score-backup
spec:
  dataSource:
    name: score-backup ❶
    kind: VolumeSnapshot
    apiGroup: snapshot.storage.k8s.io
  accessModes:
    - ReadWriteOnce
  resources:
    requests:
      storage: 1Gi
```

❶ The VolumeSnapshot can be used as a data source to populate a volume created for this PersistentVolumeClaim.

To inspect the snapshot data, create a pod that mounts the PersistentVolumeClaim:

```
apiVersion: v1
kind: Pod
metadata:
  name: score-backup
  namespace: arcade
spec:
  containers:
    - name: alpine
      image: alpine:latest
      command: ["sleep", "24h"]
```

```
      volumeMounts:
        - name: backup
          mountPath: /backup
  volumes:
    - name: backup
      persistentVolumeClaim:
        claimName: score-backup
```

Apply the YAML files for VolumeSnapshot, PersistentVolumeClaim, and the pod:

```
$ oc apply -f 04-volumesnapshot.yaml
volumesnapshot.snapshot.storage.k8s.io/score-backup created

$ oc apply -f 05-backup-pvc.yaml
persistentvolumeclaim/score-backup created

$ oc apply -f 06-pod.yaml
pod/score-backup created
```

Creating and populating the volume may take a few minutes. You can observe the
PersistentVolume being created for the backup:

```
$ oc get persistentvolumes
NAME                            CAPACITY   STATUS   CLAIM
pvc-5e441a1c-5dda-4c9c-[...]    1Gi        Bound    arcade/score
pvc-b78c1d9f-25c9-4a24-[...]    1Gi        Bound    arcade/score-backup
[...]
```

After the volume is created and bound to the pod, it should move from pending to
ready state. Execute a shell inside the pod to inspect the backup data:

```
$ oc get pods
NAME                          READY   STATUS      RESTARTS   AGE
game-1-build                  0/1     Completed   0          10m
game-755cfc5569-8rt6z         1/1     Running     0          9m27s
highscore-1-build             0/1     Completed   0          10m
highscore-5845f55bf8-wnh5t    1/1     Running     0          8m47s
score-backup                  1/1     Running     0          7m55s

$ oc rsh score-backup
/ # ls /backup
GameScores/  lost+found/
/ # cat /backup/GameScores/s3e.json
{
        "game": "s3e",
        "scores": [
                {
                        "game": "s3e",
                        "version": "0.9",
                        "player": "Alice",
                        "score": 5000
                }
        ]
}/ #
```

You are now able to create snapshots of the application data on demand. To restore the data when needed, you can create a PersistentVolumeClaim with backup data and mount it to an application pod.

Using CronJobs for Task Automation

As with all manual operations on your OpenShift cluster, the goal of the operations or SRE team should be to automate running the data backups. Besides the benefit that it doesn't consume a human's time, automating such tasks is less prone to errors than humans manually executing those steps.

To automate tasks on a cluster there are many different options. In Chapter 5 you learned about using Tekton to execute a build pipeline. You could also create pipelines that execute the backup task.

While this has many benefits like visibility in the OpenShift Pipelines user interface, in some cases you want to use simpler alternatives to execute your tasks. For example, when you're tasked with operating more than one cluster for application development teams, you may want to keep the footprint of your operations tools per cluster as small as possible. Installing an operator and an application like OpenShift Pipelines may be too much overhead. In addition, you may want to leave the management of such applications to your users, who can also use OpenShift Pipelines as CI for their own applications.

In such cases, it's often easier to not touch those tools to make sure you do not restrict what the cluster owners can and can't do with the cluster.

Fortunately, OpenShift by default supports running simple tasks, like bash scripts based on your specific schedule. If you followed Chapter 5 closely, you already used this option: To trigger a Tekton pipeline regularly, a CronJob has been used that sends a request to a webhook. This is done in a simple bash script. You can do the same to execute arbitrary scripts or start any container based on a defined schedule inside the OpenShift cluster.

Automated VolumeSnapshots

To automate the backup creation, you will need to access the OpenShift API from inside the CronJob. The easiest way to write a script that communicates with the OpenShift API is using the `openshift/cli` container image that is present in the OpenShift Image Registry of all clusters by default.

Within a container using this image, you can use the `oc` CLI, which will be connected to the OpenShift cluster the container is running on automatically. All you need to do is ensure that the service account used to run the script has all the permissions it needs to execute the commands to create a backup.

First, create a role with the necessary permissions:

```
kind: Role
apiVersion: rbac.authorization.k8s.io/v1
metadata:
  name: highscore-backup
  namespace: arcade
rules:
- apiGroups:
  - snapshot.storage.k8s.io
  resources:
  - volumesnapshots
  verbs:
  - create
  - get
- apiGroups:
  - ""
  resources:
  - persistentvolumeclaims
  verbs:
  - create
  - get
```

Every user or service account with this role will be able to create VolumeSnapshots and PersistentVolumeClaims, which are all you need to run the backup script from above.

Next, create a service account that you can use in the CronJob:

```
apiVersion: v1
kind: ServiceAccount
metadata:
  name: highscore-backup
  namespace: arcade
```

Finally, bind the role to the newly created service account with the following Role-Binding:

```
kind: RoleBinding
apiVersion: rbac.authorization.k8s.io/v1
metadata:
  name: highscore-backup
  namespace: arcade
subjects:
- kind: ServiceAccount
  name: highscore-backup
  namespace: arcade
roleRef:
  kind: Role
  name: highscore-backup
  group: rbac.authorization.k8s.io
```

After applying these three YAML files with `oc apply -f <file.yaml>`, you now have a service account that can create backups of the highscore service and not much more.

The following CronJob references this service account, so the container that will execute the script uses it to connect to your OpenShift cluster:

```
apiVersion: batch/v1
kind: CronJob
metadata:
  name: highscore-backup
  namespace: arcade
spec:
  schedule: "0 2 * * *" ❶
  jobTemplate:
    spec:
      template:
        spec:
          serviceAccountName: highscore-backup ❷
          containers:
          - name: backup
            image: |-
              image-registry.openshift-image-registry.svc:5000/openshift/cli ❸
            imagePullPolicy: IfNotPresent
            command: ❹
            - /bin/bash
            - -c
            - |
              #!/bin/bash

              set -xeuo pipefail ❺
              BASEURL=https://raw.githubusercontent.com/OperatingOpenShift/s3e/\
              main/highscore/backup

              curl $BASEURL/04-volumesnapshot.yaml | \
                sed s/score-backup/score-backup-$(date +%F-%H-%M-%S)/g | \
                oc apply -f - ❻

              curl $BASEURL/05-backup-pvc.yaml | \
                sed s/score-backup/score-backup-$(date +%F-%H-%M-%S)/g | \
                oc apply -f -
          restartPolicy: OnFailure
```

❶ The scheduling of the CronJob. The backup script will be executed every night at 2 A.M. To observe what it does, you may want to adjust the scheduling so it runs more often, for example every minute, by setting the `schedule` property to `* * * * *`.

❷ The name of the service account to use for running the job. Reference the service account you created above.

❸ The image to use for the container running the script. This CronJob uses the openshift/cli, which exists by default in the cluster internal registry.

❹ The command to execute in the container. This is an array, consisting of the command and its parameters. A common approach is to use the bash binary and pass the script using the -c argument.

❺ Set the -x flag for easier debugging of scripts. All commands will be printed to STDOUT so you can see what has been executed. The set -euo pipefail is useful to ensure the script fails when one of the commands fails. Especially when executing destructive actions like oc delete commands, you want to ensure all previous commands have been executed as expected, for example, to identify which objects you want to delete.

❻ Apply the VolumeSnapshot and PersistentVolumeClaim YAML files from the Git repository, but name them with the current timestamp.

Create the CronJob object and watch pods coming up that execute your script:

```
$ oc apply -f 08-cronjob.yaml
cronjob.batch/highscore-backup created
```

```
$ oc get pods
NAME                                READY   STATUS      RESTARTS   AGE
game-1-build                        0/1     Completed   0          18m
game-565df96b4b-fmfv4               1/1     Running     0          17m
highscore-1-build                   0/1     Completed   0          18m
highscore-868759b59-5gzz7           1/1     Running     0          16m
highscore-backup-27315110--1-2rxfd  0/1     Completed   0          60s
```

In the output of oc get pods you can see that the status of the CronJob's pod is "Completed," indicating the script has been executed successfully.

You can view the logs of this CronJob's pod like you do with any other pod using the oc logs command. The logs will help you understand if the script did what you expected:

```
$ oc logs highscore-backup-27315121--1-wzkts
+ BASEURL=https://raw.githubusercontent.com/OperatingOpenShift/
s3e/main/highscore/backup
+ curl https://raw.githubusercontent.com/[...]/backup/04-volumesnapshot.yaml
+ oc apply -f -
++ date +%F-%H-%M-%S
+ sed s/score-backup/score-backup-2021-12-07-20-01-02/g
volumesnapshot.snapshot.storage.k8s.io/score-backup-2021-12-07-20-01-02 created
+ curl https://raw.githubusercontent.com/[...]/backup/05-backup-pvc.yaml
+ oc apply -f -
++ date +%F-%H-%M-%S
+ sed s/score-backup/score-backup-2021-12-07-20-01-02/g
```

List the VolumeSnapshot and PersistentVolumeClaim created by the script:

```
$ oc get persistentvolumeclaims
NAME                              STATUS    STORAGECLASS    AGE
score                             Bound     standard        28m
score-backup-2021-12-07-20-01-02  Pending   standard        25s

$ oc get volumesnapshots
NAME                              READYTOUSE    SOURCEPVC    AGE
score-backup-2021-12-07-20-01-02                score        35s
```

It looks like the script does what you expected it to do. To make this backup process ready for your production cluster, it would probably need some additional thoughts, like how long those backups should be retained, how to restore them, and so on. However, this example showed you how to quickly automate arbitrary tasks to operate applications on your cluster.

Automated OpenShift updates

To show an example of operating the cluster itself, let's see how to automate updating the cluster to the latest version of OpenShift. This example uses the same tools as in the previous example.

First, create the RBAC necessary to install updates. This includes a service account, a ClusterRole, and a ClusterRoleBinding:

```
---
apiVersion: v1
kind: ServiceAccount
metadata:
  name: cluster-update
  namespace: default
---
kind: ClusterRole
apiVersion: rbac.authorization.k8s.io/v1
metadata:
  name: cluster-update
rules:
- apiGroups:
  - config.openshift.io
  resources:
  - clusterversions
  verbs:
  - get
  - update
---
kind: ClusterRoleBinding
apiVersion: rbac.authorization.k8s.io/v1
metadata:
  name: cluster-update
subjects:
```

```
  - kind: ServiceAccount
    name: cluster-update
    namespace: default
roleRef:
    kind: ClusterRole
    name: cluster-update
    apiGroup: ""
```

It's a common pattern to store all RBAC objects in a single file, as shown above, to make developing them easier.

After applying those objects, schedule the cluster updates using a CronJob:

```
apiVersion: batch/v1
kind: CronJob
metadata:
  name: cluster-update
  namespace: default
spec:
  schedule: "0 1 1 * *" ❶
  jobTemplate:
    spec:
      template:
        spec:
          serviceAccountName: cluster-update ❷
          containers:
          - name: update
            image: |-
              image-registry.openshift-image-registry.svc:5000/openshift/cli
            imagePullPolicy: IfNotPresent
            command:
            - /bin/bash
            - -c
            - |
              #!/bin/bash

              set -euxo pipefail
              oc adm upgrade --to-latest=true ❸
          restartPolicy: OnFailure
```

❶ The scheduling of this CronJob will run cluster updates on the first of each month.

❷ The service account to use for the container running the script.

❸ This command initiates the cluster update.

If an update is available, you should see an update being installed as soon as this CronJob is executed for the first time:

```
$ oc get pods -n default
NAME                          READY   STATUS      RESTARTS   AGE
cluster-update-27314948-rmjz6  0/1    Completed   0          50s

$ oc logs cluster-update-27314948-rmjz6
+ oc adm update --to-latest=true
Updating to latest version 4.8.22

$ oc get clusterversions
NAME      AVAILABLE   PROGRESSING   STATUS
version   True        True          Working towards 4.8.22: downloading update
```

The output of `oc get clusterversions` shows you that there is an update being installed. How often you want to install updates and when is good timing depend on the needs of your organization. Installing updates regularly is important to make sure your clusters are in a supported state and that security fixes are applied on time.

These are two common examples of cluster operations tasks and how to automate them. The resources needed for those tasks to run (i.e., CronJob and RBAC YAML files) are part of the configuration of your cluster.

Over time, more tasks will be automated, and you may even need to run those tasks on multiple clusters that you manage. The following section shows how to track what is applied to a cluster and how to ensure it's done on all your clusters.

Cluster Configuration

You have learned about the first part of operating OpenShift clusters: maintenance tasks that operations or SRE teams execute and automate. The second big piece of operating OpenShift clusters is configuring them to your needs. This means adjusting the clusters to make them fit what you expect from the cluster or what your customers, who run their workloads on the cluster, expect from it.

A simple but important example of this kind of configuration is that you need to make sure that the right people get access to the cluster.

To configure the access to an OpenShift cluster, you usually create an IdentityProvider (IDP) resource to connect an Identity Provider to the OpenShift cluster that your users can use to log in.

A common use case of IdentityProvider resources is to set up an external IDP to grant access to the cluster for a defined group of people. For example, you can connect your OpenShift cluster to a GCP Oauth provider. That will allow users to log in to the OpenShift cluster using their Google account. Alternatively, you can use a

GitHub IDP, which allows you to specify a group of people who are allowed to log in to the OpenShift cluster using their GitHub accounts.

In addition to accessing the cluster, you also need to make sure that all people who can access the cluster get the right permissions. In Chapter 4, you learned what it means to grant permissions to specific users using role-based access control. As role-based access control is also part of the Kubernetes control plane, it gets configured via Kubernetes resources.

Just as the developers use the cluster for tasks like deploying their applications, you need to configure the access for yourself. As an operator of the cluster, or as a site reliability engineer, you need to make sure that you have all the permissions that you need to administer the cluster. These might be a bit more extensive permissions than a typical application developer would get.

In addition to access and permission control, the configuration of monitoring, logging, and alerting is also an important part of the configuration of your cluster. As you explored in Chapter 6, whenever you create a new cluster, you want to make sure the cluster is alerting you when something goes wrong.

You typically don't want that configuration to be created manually; in the ideal case, you apply all those configurations automatically as soon as the cluster is installed. With automatic configuration, there is no way that someone can forget to enable the alerting on a cluster. You can start monitoring and operating the cluster right away.

Configuring an OpenShift cluster also means deploying the right applications to the cluster that you need to operate it. For example, if you are using Tekton to run the CI of certain applications, deploying Tekton is also part of the configuration that you want to apply to an OpenShift cluster you created.

All the repetitive tasks you need to execute on the OpenShift clusters that you want to automate are part of the configuration you need to apply as well. You explored examples of repetitive tasks and how they're represented in configuration files in "Using CronJobs for Task Automation" on page 176. Whether they are Tekton pipelines or CronJobs, you should treat them the same as any other configuration.

Other pieces of cluster configuration, depending on the use of the cluster, are the workload the cluster is supposed to run, including namespaces, service accounts, deployments, services, routes, and so on.

But how do you make sure all those pieces (mostly YAML files) are applied to every cluster you manage? The beginning of this chapter already touched on the topic of automatic configuration management. The next section shows you a very useful tool to automate how all your resources are created and updated on your cluster, which is a supported part of OpenShift.

Manage Cluster Configuration with OpenShift GitOps

In software development, it is a well-established default to have all changes that go to production come in from a version control system in a central repository. Every change is integrated into a single code-line, for example, a default branch on Git.

When you create a new Git repository on GitHub, a default branch called *main* will be created. It is expected to be where most development goes through. When a new version needs to be produced, a release is cut, which is reflected via a tag on a specific commit in the main branch. When debugging a problem, developers only need to know the version of the application in use, so they can check out the respective commit and investigate the exact code that's running on the system.

New changes usually go through some sort of review process before they reach main. In GitHub or GitLab, this is done via pull or merge requests that show the changes someone wants to apply. Reviewers can comment, ask for changes, or approve a request, so it can be merged and integrated into the next release. In addition to human reviewers, pipelines can observe and validate requests by running unit tests and integration tests to make sure the change doesn't introduce a regression.

This workflow has proven to be effective in software development and deployment. Git has proven to be an efficient tool to version application code, with a huge set of tools built around it to allow managing changes for both corporate teams and open source communities.

Leveraging this approach to manage everything related to operating a software deployment, like OpenShift clusters, is typically referred to as GitOps.

Everything you've seen so far in this chapter that is deployed to OpenShift to operate a cluster is a text file in the end—just like source code. This kind of specifying infrastructure is usually called Infrastructure as Code (IaC), although configuration files are not exactly code. They lag behind actual code first and foremost at the point of testability: Writing unit tests for a program written in Go is easy, but unit-testing a YAML file is not. There are testing frameworks, but they don't seem to have a wide acceptance yet.

The idea of GitOps is to manage those text files in the same way as the source code of software products to benefit in the same way. Applied to managing OpenShift clusters, that includes:

Traceability
    What's deployed to a given OpenShift cluster can be inspected by looking at a Git repository.

Review process

> Everything that's deployed has been reviewed by more than one human to minimize the risk of breaking things. If something breaks, a change can be reverted easily to bring back the last state that's known to work.

Automated testing

> Verifying that the file changes are valid and that they follow given constraints can be done via a CI pipeline. Although it may require more implementation effort and higher cost than for testing source code, it's also possible to automate integration testing proposed changes by deploying them to test clusters before or after they're merged.

Automated deployment

> When a change is merged or released, it is applied automatically to all target OpenShift clusters.

Building a GitOps workflow to manage your OpenShift cluster configuration is easy with OpenShift GitOps, which can be installed from OperatorHub using the OpenShift Console, similar to installing Tekton.

GitOps can be used to apply a set of files that are managed in a Git repository to an OpenShift cluster it is installed to.

However, if you're managing more than one OpenShift cluster and needed to deploy OpenShift GitOps to every single cluster, it would only shift the problem: how would you manage to install OpenShift GitOps to all the clusters you're managing? Luckily, OpenShift GitOps supports managing not only the cluster it's installed on but other clusters as well.

Installing OpenShift GitOps

OpenShift GitOps is based on Argo CD (*https://argoproj.github.io/cd*). This section covers only the basics of Argo CD and can't cover all the features it offers to users. If you want to learn more, see the Argo documentation (*https://argoproj.github.io/cd*), which explains its concepts in greater detail.

To install OpenShift GitOps using the OpenShift Console, visit the OperatorHub section in the OpenShift console, search for `OpenShift GitOps` and click Install as shown in Figure 8-2.

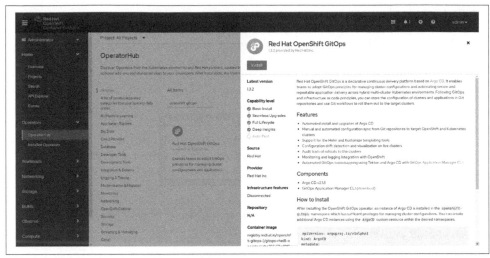

Figure 8-2. Installing OpenShift GitOps from OperatorHub

OpenShift will attempt to install the OpenShift GitOps operator, which will take a few minutes. As soon as the setup is done, you will be forwarded to the page shown in Figure 8-3, which gives you an overview of what kind of resources are managed by the operator.

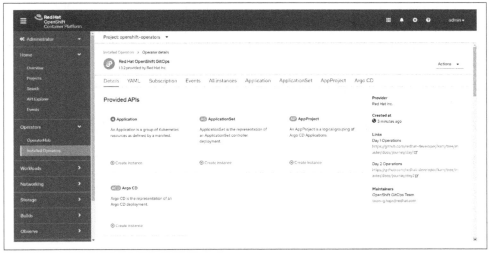

Figure 8-3. Overview page of the OpenShift GitOps operator

You've now successfully installed the OpenShift GitOps operator, which can be used to install and configure Argo CD deployments. You can install multiple Argo CD deployments on your cluster using the OpenShift GitOps operator, for example if you need specific configurations per namespace.

Click "Create instance" in the Argo CD box to create a new Argo CD deployment.

This will present you with a form you can use to customize the Argo CD deployment. You can stay with the defaults for now for most fields, except the namespace field, which is not visible in the form view.

Switch to the YAML view, shown in Figure 8-4, to update the namespace and set it to a namespace where you want the instance to be created, for example, `gitops`.

> The namespace needs to exist before you can install Argo CD into it. You can create the namespace using the command `oc new-project gitops`.

Figure 8-4. Customizing the Argo CD instance

> Changing the namespace is not strictly required, but additional permissions may need to be set up on some occasions if you want to deploy resources to a different namespace than the instance is installed to.

Click Create to create the Argo CD deployment. Again, it will take a few minutes to set up all the resources Argo CD needs to run, and until Argo CD itself is up and running.

After creating the Argo CD instance, you should see the list of Argo CD deployments the operator currently manages. At this point, this should be only the instance you just created. Click the name of the instance to see the list of resources the operator created for Argo CD, as shown in Figure 8-5.

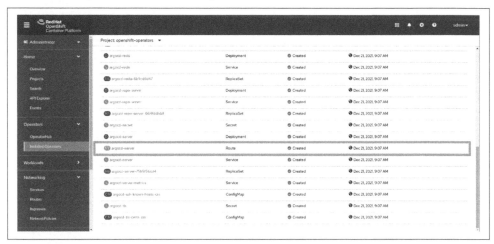

Figure 8-5. Resources associated with the Argo CD instance

One of those resources (marked with a box in Figure 8-5) is a route called `argocd-server`. Click its name to inspect the details of the route. On the details of the route, you should see the URL that has been created for Argo CD. Click that URL to open it in your browser, and you should see the Argo CD login screen shown in Figure 8-6.

Figure 8-6. A nice greeting from the Argo squid

Click "Log in via OpenShift" to use your OpenShift user to access Argo CD.

Managing Configuration with OpenShift GitOps

Argo CD uses the concept of applications that you can create and sync to one or more clusters. An application is usually backed by a Git repository, of which a specific path can be deployed. Argo CD will check out the repository and apply all files inside the specified folder.

Click the New App button in the upper left corner of the Argo CD user interface and fill in the form fields according to your needs (see Figure 8-7).

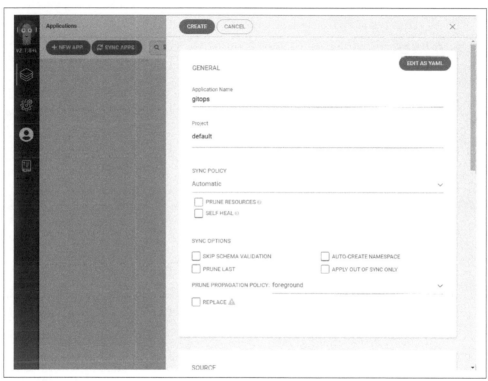

Figure 8-7. Configure the behavior of the application

You can decide if Argo CD should automatically sync changes from the Git repository to the cluster or if you want to initiate that manually. Enter the Git repository you want to sync, as well as the path in the repository that contains the objects you want to sync. To follow this example, you can use GitHub (*https://github.com/OperatingOpenShift/s3e*) and the *gitops* folder that contains the CronJob for creating backups of the highscore application.

Also, you can choose the namespace in which to create the resources. As mentioned previously, for now, it's easiest if you deploy everything into the namespace that Argo CD is running in.

Finally, select the cluster you want to deploy the application to. At this point, you have only one cluster, and that is the cluster running Argo CD itself. This cluster is automatically created with the name "in-cluster" that you can select from the pull-down menu as shown in Figure 8-8.

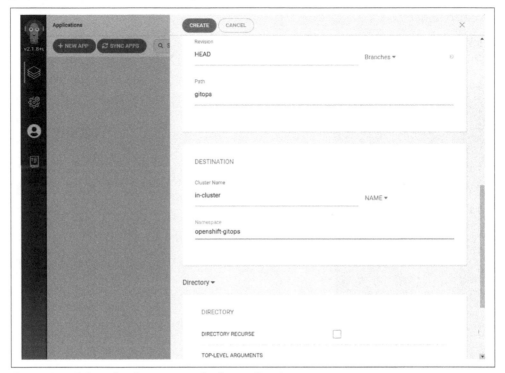

Figure 8-8. Select the cluster to apply the application resources to

Click Create to create the application.

In some cases, you may get a permission denied error or be unable to select the in-cluster destination, depending on the configuration of your cluster. If this happens, you will need to adjust the permissions in the Argo CD deployment. The easiest way is to relax the permissions in the Argo CD resource in the operator settings. To do this, navigate to the OpenShift GitOps page in the OpenShift Console and edit the Argo CD object, as shown in Figure 8-9. Set the default policy to `role:admin`, which will grant every user who doesn't have a different role assigned the admin role.

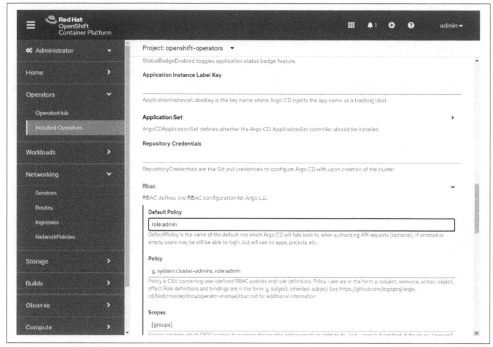

Figure 8-9. Updating the Argo CD settings to grant your user privileges in Argo CD

Afterward, you should be able to create the application.

Of course, you will not want to use this kind of setting in a production environment, but since this depends on which groups and users are set up, you will need to figure out a setting specific to your use case. Please see the Argo CD documentation (*https:// oreil.ly/mzl8t*) to learn more about setting up the Argo CD roles for your OpenShift users.

This example creates a service account and CronJob in the namespaces of Argo CD. To enable the pods created from the CronJob to create VolumeSnapshots and PersistentVolumeClaims in the `arcade` namespace, you need to bind the previously deployed role to the service account in the Argo CD namespace with a RoleBinding like the following:

```
kind: RoleBinding
apiVersion: rbac.authorization.k8s.io/v1
metadata:
  name: highscore-backup
  namespace: arcade
subjects:
- kind: ServiceAccount
  name: highscore-backup
  namespace: gitops
```

```
roleRef:
  kind: Role
  name: highscore-backup
  apiGroup: ""
```

You could also have this RoleBinding applied by Argo CD itself, but as mentioned, deploying resources to a different namespace in-cluster may require additional RBAC.

When the application is created, you should see a box for it on the Argo CD dashboard and its sync status, as shown in Figure 8-10.

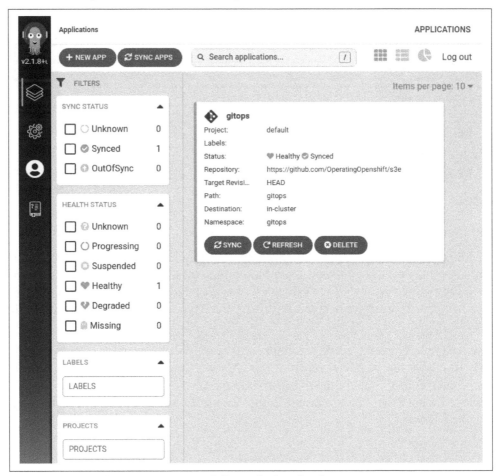

Figure 8-10. Configuration is successfully applied to the cluster

On the dashboard, click the box of the application you just created to view more details about the synchronization and the objects that have been created in the cluster. See Figure 8-11 for how this looks in the example of the highscore backup.

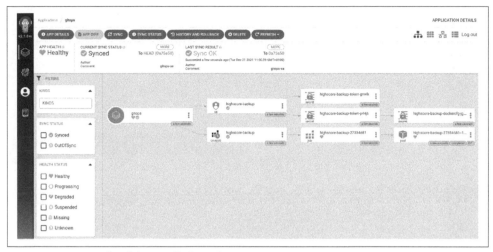

Figure 8-11. Details of the applied configuration

As you can see, Argo CD is aware of the CronJob and the jobs and pods it created. You can see when the last run was and that it ran successfully. If you select one of the pods, you can even inspect the job logs from inside the Argo CD UI.

Once set up, OpenShift GitOps allows you to easily manage cluster configuration in a Git repository and use your existing reviewing best practices to make sure everything deployed to the cluster is tracked. Undoing a change is as simple as reverting a commit in Git and is tracked the same way.

Managing Configuration of Multiple Clusters with OpenShift GitOps

You have seen how to easily apply a configuration from a Git repository to a cluster by deploying and configuring Argo CD using OpenShift GitOps. But how would you manage to configure more than a single cluster? Most likely you wouldn't want to install an operator to every single cluster manually to be able to manage its configuration.

Luckily, Argo CD supports this pattern out of the box. You can use one cluster to manage the configuration of all the clusters you want to maintain. Argo CD can manage the configuration of remote clusters the same as it manages the configuration of the cluster it's deployed to. All you need to make this work is a kubeconfig file that allows Argo CD the access it needs to deploy the necessary resources.

The easiest way to add a cluster to Argo CD is using the `argocd` CLI.

To download the CLI that fits the version of your Argo CD deployment, navigate to the documentation section, the bottommost icon on the left pane, in the Argo CD UI. On the page shown in Figure 8-12, select the build for your operating system.

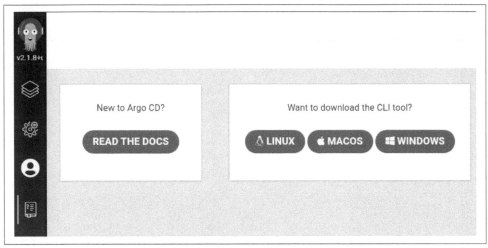

Figure 8-12. Download the Argo CD CLI from the Argo CD documentation UI

When the download is finished, be sure to make the binary executable and move it to somewhere inside your PATH:

```
$ mv ~/Downloads/argocd-linux-amd64 /usr/local/bin/argocd
```

```
$ chmod +x /usr/local/bin/argocd
```

Now you can log in to Argo CD using the OpenShift login as you did in the UI. Log in to the same hostname that you used to access Argo CD in the web browser:

```
$ ./argocd-linux-amd64 login --insecure\ ❶
  --sso\ ❷
  argocd-server-gitops.apps.mycluster.com:443
Opening browser for authentication
Performing authorization_code flow login:
https://argocd-server-gitops.apps.mycluster.com/api/dex/auth?[...]
Authentication successful
'admin' logged in successfully
Context 'argocd-server-gitops.apps.mycluster.com:443' updated
```

❶ The `--insecure` flag is necessary only when you don't have a trusted certificate on the Argo CD route.

❷ The `--sso` flag tells the CLI to initiate the login flow in a web browser.

This command should fire up a login page in your web browser. If it doesn't, click the provided link to log in. Afterward, you can use the `argocd` CLI to communicate with the Argo CD deployment.

To add a new cluster to Argo CD, use the `argocd cluster add` command. If you're logged in to the cluster in your current session, you can add it by specifying its context name. Optionally, you can specify a separate kubeconfig file:

```
$ ./argocd-linux-amd64 cluster add --kubeconfig kubeconfig.yaml othercluster ❶
WARNING: This will create a service account `argocd-manager` on the cluster
referenced by context `othercluster` with full cluster level admin privileges
Do you want to continue [y/N]? y
INFO[0001] ClusterRole "argocd-manager-role" created
INFO[0002] ClusterRoleBinding "argocd-manager-role-binding" created
Cluster 'https://api.othercluster.com:6443' added
```

❶ The kubeconfig file *kubeconfig.yaml* contains the configuration to access the cluster. The context name of the cluster inside the kubeconfig file is `othercluster`.

You can see the cluster has been added successfully by running the following command:

```
$ ./argocd-linux-amd64 cluster list
SERVER                                          NAME          STATUS
https://api.othercluster.com:6443               othercluster  Successful ❶
https://kubernetes.default.svc (1 namespaces)   in-cluster    Successful ❷
```

❶ The cluster you just added.

❷ The in-cluster configuration, which is used to manage configuration of the cluster that Argo CD is deployed to.

You can also see the new cluster in the Argo CD UI in the web browser, as shown in Figure 8-13.

Figure 8-13. A second cluster is added to the cluster list in Argo CD

You can now create a new application as you did before, this time referencing the cluster you just added. After the resources are synchronized, you will be able to see the resources created by Argo CD.

Log in to the cluster you just added and run the following commands if you deployed the example resources from above:

```
$ oc get cronjob -n gitops
NAME               SCHEDULE     SUSPEND   ACTIVE   LAST SCHEDULE   AGE
highscore-backup   * * * * *    False     0        <none>          16s

$ oc get sa -n gitops
NAME               SECRETS   AGE
builder            2         6s
default            2         6s
deployer           2         6s
highscore-backup   2         4s
pipeline           2         6s
```

The application configurations are stored in resources in the namespace that Argo CD is deployed to. The configuration to access othercluster also will be stored inside the cluster with the Argo CD deployment as a secret:

```
$ oc get secret -n gitops othercluster -o yaml
apiVersion: v1
data:
  config: <kubeconfig file content>
  name: othercluster
  server: api.othercluster.com:6443
kind: Secret
metadata:
  annotations:
    managed-by: argocd.argoproj.io
  creationTimestamp: "2021-12-23T15:08:03Z"
  labels:
    argocd.argoproj.io/secret-type: cluster ❶
  name: othercluster
  namespace: gitops
type: Opaque
```

❶ Argo CD uses the argocd.argoproj.io/secret-type: cluster label to detect new secrets that reference a cluster it's supposed to manage.

This provides you with another way of adding clusters and configuring the synchronization: Instead of using the CLI and UI, you can also create application resources and secrets using the oc CLI, or manage them using Argo CD.

Summary

Site Reliability Engineers have an inner fear of manual work, including managing the configuration of the software they are operating. If the software an SRE team operates is OpenShift, most of the configuration can be represented in text files, so they can be versioned in the same way that source code is versioned.

In this chapter, you learned how to turn the traditionally manual effort of configuring software into an automated workflow similar to managing source code.

Everything the SRE team deploys to a cluster they manage will be versioned, reviewed, and can be undone using a well-known reviewing process, for example, the pull-request workflow used by GitHub. Even a continuous integration process can be put in place on the configuration to automatically validate changes before merging them to the cluster configuration repository and deploying them to clusters.

Similar to software deployment, practices like canary testing or A/B deployments are possible. Test automation may be a bigger effort and associated with higher costs for OpenShift configuration than for smaller software deployments, as the test probably requires the deployment of a new cluster each time a change triggers an integration test run.

With OpenShift GitOps, OpenShift includes all the tools you need to manage the configuration of one, or dozens, of OpenShift clusters.

OpenShift GitOps can be installed from OperatorHub, just like OpenShift pipelines. Operators are a way to interact with resources deployed to OpenShift, often custom resources that come with the operator, like Argo CD deployment resources. While you installed operators and used them to install software to your OpenShift cluster so far, you can also develop custom operators and deploy them to your cluster. Operators can also help to automate a certain part of the cluster operations.

Developing custom operators will be covered in the next chapter.

## CHAPTER 9

Developing Custom Operators to Automate Cluster Operations

Manuel Dewald

At the heart of every OpenShift cluster runs a set of controllers, working relentlessly to turn the desired state of resources the cluster manages into an actual state.

Each run of a control loop aims to bring the actual state closer to the desired state. The desired state is defined declaratively in OpenShift resources. A control loop can check the actual state and figure out which actions are necessary to get one step closer to the desired state.

The actual state can be read from various sources, and in many cases the API Server can be queried to get it, depending on the goal of a resource.

A good example is the relation between ReplicaSets and pods. A ReplicaSet defines how many pods of a given specification should run. All pods managed by the ReplicaSet can be identified by a common label. The control loop can query the API Server for the number of actual pods with this label. If the number is lower than the desired number as defined by the ReplicaSet resource, it can start more pods until the number matches.

When the ReplicaSet is scaled down, the control loop figures out there are suddenly more pods than desired by the ReplicaSet and delete some of them with a DELETE call to the API Server.

The control loops run endlessly and compare the desired with the actual state, so even when a pod is manually deleted, the control loop creates a new one so the desired state of the ReplicaSet matches the actual state.

Not only can a control loop communicate with cluster-internal components to query and manipulate the actual state, but it can also communicate to external components, like the cloud provider. For example, when a service like LoadBalancer is created on a cluster that's deployed to a cloud provider, the controller typically communicates with the cloud provider to create a LoadBalancer resource. When done, the status of the service resource is updated so other components can query the details of the LoadBalancer, such as an external IP address, without querying the cloud provider themselves.

This mechanism is a powerful aspect of OpenShift and Kubernetes that helps automate the tasks an operator would otherwise need to do manually: decide how many instances are needed, roll out new versions of a container image, and so forth.

In homage to the operator whose job is made easier by these inexhaustible controllers, this paradigm is also called the Operator pattern.

As a human operator of OpenShift clusters, you can also leverage the mechanism of the Operator pattern to automate tasks that are not already automated by the OpenShift control plane. To do so, you can build your own custom operator and deploy it to your OpenShift cluster.

Throughout this book you have already met different operators:

- OpenShift Pipelines is an operator used to manage Tekton deployments.
- OpenShift GitOps is an operator used to manage Argo CD deployments.
- cert-manager Operator is an operator deployed to automate certificate renewal using Let's Encrypt for your web services.

Operators can include a custom resource type, with which you can extend the OpenShift API itself. These resource types are called Custom Resource Definitions (CRD).

OpenShift itself already contains some CRDs that extend the Kubernetes API. You can query them by running `oc get crds` on your OpenShift cluster. You probably remember some of the CRDs in the list from earlier in this book, like `ingresses.config.openshift.io`, which is a core resource of OpenShift but an extension to the Kubernetes control plane:

```
$ oc get crds

[...]
ingresscontrollers.operator.openshift.io
ingresses.config.openshift.io
installplans.operators.coreos.com
[...]
```

Instances of a CRD are called Custom Resources (CR). They are objects that you can interact with just as you can interact with the core resources of Kubernetes, like pods, services, or deployments. You can create them with `oc apply -f my-resource.yaml` and edit them once created with `oc edit resourcetype my-resource`.

Chapter 3 identified a problem with the cert-manager Operator: It doesn't support routes out of the box, so we need to work around it by using an ingress resource. This chapter guides you through bootstrapping your own operator that closes this gap.

 The operator built in this chapter is not meant to replace cert-manager Operator, but showcase the development of a new operator from scratch using a scenario that traditionally causes toil for IT operations. If you want to automatically issue TLS certificates for your services running on OpenShift, use cert-manager Operator with an ingress as a workaround as described in Chapter 3.

The full source code of the resulting operator can be found on GitHub (*https://oreil.ly/osknR*). This book explains only the most interesting aspects of building the operator.

Operator SDK

You can build an operator with every programming language that you can run inside a container; it could even be a bash script using the oc command to query the API server.

However, many good frameworks are available that can make your life significantly easier when it comes to operator development. When you start automating operations tasks using operators on OpenShift, it's likely that you won't stop after implementing the first operator. It's better to split out the different tasks than overstuff a single operator with all the different kinds of automation you need to implement.

With that in mind, it's also advisable to stick with similar patterns across the different operators you build and maintain to make switching between feature development in each of them as easy as possible. This becomes even more important when multiple teams maintain a set of operators. Contributing to an operator that another team built should be made as easy as possible if you consider sharing the maintenance responsibilities.

Whichever framework you decide to use, it's probably best to use it across all the operators you build. This chapter uses Operator SDK to bootstrap an operator.

Operator SDK offers three different options for implementing your own operator: Ansible, Helm, and Go. Which one you use depends on your requirements and personal preference. This chapter shows you how to get started and build a new operator using the Go programming language.

When it comes to Go, Operator SDK uses Kubebuilder (*https://kubebuilder.io*), so the project layout is similar and should even be compatible, allowing you to switch back and forth between the two. This has been introduced between the versions 0.x and

1.x of Operator SDK. Thus, when you inspect older operators built with Operator SDK, they may look very different than 1.x operators, and you need older versions of Operator SDK to interact with the operator repositories.

Operator SDK is a toolset that helps with many typical tasks you need to fulfill when building an operator, including:

- Creating and initializing a new operator repository from scratch
- Building and running it on your local computer
- Wrapping the operator code into a container image
- Pushing the container image to a container registry
- Deploy it to an OpenShift cluster

If you plan to publish your operator on OperatorHub, Operator SDK also helps you create the necessary artifacts used by the Operator Lifecycle Manager (OLM). Publishing an operator on OperatorHub allows others to easily install and use it, similar to how Chapter 5 does with the OpenShift Pipelines operator.

Operator Design

Before you start implementing the operator, it's probably a good idea to think of what the design of the operator should look like. Figure 9-1 gives an overview of the involved components and resources.

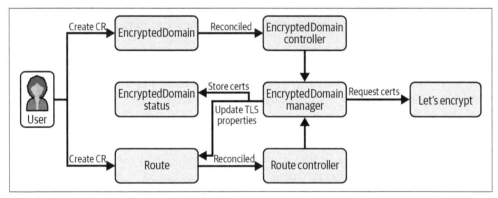

Figure 9-1. Let's Encrypt Operator design overview

The primary resource the operator acts on is the EncryptedDomain, in which a user can specify for which hostnames the operator should renew certificates. This resource type is installed using a CRD when the operator itself is installed. To configure the hostnames to be managed by the operator, the user can specify a regular expression per EncryptedDomain resource. The operator matches the regular expression against hostnames of routes on the OpenShift cluster.

Each time a new route is created or changed, the operator also needs to check whether an existing EncryptedDomain object matches the hostname specified. If so, the operator knows that it has to manage the TLS certificates of this route.

That means the operator needs two controllers: one that observes and reconciles EncryptedDomains, and one that observes and reconciles routes.

To ensure that for each hostname there is only one certificate, the TLS certificates are stored in the status of the EncryptedDomain resources. The operator can look them up when a new route is created for an existing hostname—for example, specifying a different path. Whenever an existing certificate is found, the operator also needs to check its expiry time and renew it before it expires.

To request or renew certificates, the operator talks to an Automatic Certificate Management Environment (ACME), for example, Let's Encrypt. The endpoint the operator uses to request certificates is called the CA directory. It can be configured by the user in the EncryptedDomain resources.

Requesting new certificates is done using the HTTP-01 (*https://letsencrypt.org/docs/ challenge-types*) challenge. The challenge itself is implemented in the lego (*https:// go-acme.github.io/lego*) Go library, but the operator needs to make sure that HTTP traffic reaches the operator during the challenge execution. The operator needs to create a temporary route for the challenge, along with a service and deployment to forward traffic back to the operator pod to complete the challenge.

When a new certificate is requested or found in an existing EncryptedDomain resource, the operator updates the TLS properties of the matching route. This enables TLS communication for the matched route, using a valid certificate that is renewed automatically before it expires. TLS is terminated at the edge.

A future improvement, which is outside the scope of this simple example implementation, could be to make the TLS termination configurable and expose the certificates as secret for use by other services, as the OpenShift ACME Operator does.

Bootstrapping the Operator

To bootstrap a new Go operator, the first step is installing Operator SDK itself. Download and install the latest version as described in the Operator SDK documentation (*https://sdk.operatorframework.io/docs/installation*). The commands and output may slightly change depending on which version you install. The example operator and this chapter are based on Operator SDK version 1.17.

Operator SDK comes as a CLI tool: After installing, this chapter assumes it's available as the command `operator-sdk`.

When initiating a new Go-based operator, Operator SDK generates a *go.mod* file in the folder where you run it. The module is named according to the repository name you pass to Operator SDK. Replace the repository name `github.com/OperatingOpen shift/le-operator` in the following commands with the destination you're planning to push the operator to. You can also just pretend you would publish it to some repository but not do it; all commands work just the same. If you don't specify a repository name, Operator SDK sets a default module name in *go.mod*.

Run the following commands to create a new folder and initialize a Go operator in it:

```
$ mkdir le-operator

$ cd le-operator

$ operator-sdk init --plugins go/v3 --domain \
  operatingopenshift.com --repo github.com/OperatingOpenshift/le-operator

Writing kustomize manifests for you to edit...
Writing scaffold for you to edit...
Get controller runtime:

$ go get sigs.k8s.io/controller-runtime@v0.11.0
Update dependencies:

$ go mod tidy
Next: define a resource with:

$ operator-sdk create api
```

The Operator SDK guides you through the process of initializing your new operator by even giving you a hint of what you are probably looking to do next.

Indeed, the next thing you should do is think about the API to interact with your operator. The API of an operator is always an OpenShift resource. Either your operator works on existing resources, or it comes with its own CRD. The API allows users to create resources that are managed by the operator and influence its behavior.

Initialize a CRD that allows users of the operator to specify for which routes on the cluster it should manage SSL certificates:

```
$ operator-sdk create api \
  --group letsencrypt --version v1beta1 --kind EncryptedDomain

Create Resource [y/n]
y
Create Controller [y/n]
y
Writing kustomize manifests for you to edit...
```

```
Writing scaffold for you to edit...
api/v1beta1/encrypteddomain_types.go
controllers/encrypteddomain_controller.go
Update dependencies:
$ go mod tidy
Running make:
$ make generate
go: creating new go.mod: module tmp
Downloading sigs.k8s.io/controller-tools/cmd/controller-gen@v0.8.0
[...]
Next: implement your new API and generate the manifests (e.g. CRDs,CRs) with:
$ make manifests
```

Operator SDK asks if you want to create the resource (the API) and the controller scaffolding. Answer both questions with y to get everything you need to implement a controller that operates on EncryptedDomain objects. As suggested by the last line of the output, run the make command to build the CRD YAML that you can apply to install the new custom resource type:

```
$ make manifests

controller-gen rbac:roleName=manager-role crd webhook paths="./..."
output:crd:artifacts:config=config/crd/bases
```

The command runs controller-gen to generate YAML templates in the *config/crd/ bases* folder of your repository. The output YAML is based on the type you can implement in the Go files. Right after initiating the new API, there are only the default fields and one single example property in the spec of the resource:

```
---
apiVersion: apiextensions.k8s.io/v1
kind: CustomResourceDefinition
metadata: [...]
spec:
  group: letsencrypt.operatingopenshift.com
  names:
    kind: EncryptedDomain ❶
    listKind: EncryptedDomainList
    plural: encrypteddomains
    singular: encrypteddomain
  scope: Namespaced
  versions:
  - name: v1beta1
    schema:
      openAPIV3Schema:
        description: EncryptedDomain is the Schema for the encrypteddomains API
        properties:
          apiVersion: [...]
          kind: [...]
          spec:
            description: EncryptedDomainSpec defines the desired state
              of EncryptedDomain
```

```
            properties:
              foo: ❷
                description: Foo is an example field of EncryptedDomain.
                  Edit encrypteddomain_types.go to remove/update
                type: string
            type: object
          status: ❸
            description: EncryptedDomainStatus defines the observed
              state of EncryptedDomain
            type: object
        type: object
    served: true
    storage: true
    subresources: ❹
      status: {}
[...]
```

❶ These properties define how instances of your new resource type are identified in YAML files and the CLI (singular and plural) on an OpenShift cluster. For example, users can list all resources in a namespace with `oc list encrypteddomains`. This is similar to how they interact with other resources, like pods with `oc list pods`.

❷ The example attribute added to the API by Operator SDK. All attributes come with a description that helps users understand objects using `oc explain`.

❸ This part can be used to store the status of a resource. The status should be primarily used to communicate the status to the outside world, not to influence how the operator handles a resource.

❹ The status is a subresource of the EncryptedDomain CRD. This means updates to the status are requests to a separate API endpoint of the OpenShift API server. Requests to the status endpoint ignore changes to the spec and vice versa.

Compare the CRD YAML to the corresponding Go type that has been generated in *api/v1beta1/encrypteddomain_types.go*:

```go
// EncryptedDomainSpec defines the desired state of EncryptedDomain ❶
type EncryptedDomainSpec struct { ❷
        // INSERT ADDITIONAL SPEC FIELDS - desired state of cluster
        // Important: Run "make" to regenerate code after modifying this file

        // Foo is an example field of EncryptedDomain.
        // Edit encrypteddomain_types.go to remove/update ❸
        Foo string `json:"foo,omitempty"`❹
}
```

❶ This comment is used to generate the description in the CRD.

❷ The type generated for our new API. Using the Kubernetes client in Go to query the OpenShift cluster you can get objects of this type to interact with.

❸ Comments for properties of a type are used to generate descriptions for fields in the CRD.

❹ The example property generated by Operator SDK. The json tag defines the property name in JSON and YAML representations of resources.

Update the API spec in the Go file and regenerate the CRD by running make mani fests to see how the CRD gets updated. For our operator you can add a first field that you can use later to identify for which hostnames the operator should request certificates:

```
// EncryptedDomainSpec defines the desired state of EncryptedDomain
type EncryptedDomainSpec struct {
  // MatchingHostnames is a regex describing which
  // hostnames to generate certificates for.
  MatchingHostnames string `json:"matchingHostnames,omitempty"`
}
```

The spec in the CRD reflects the changes:

```
spec:
description: EncryptedDomainSpec defines the desired state of EncryptedDomain
properties:
    matchingHostnames:
    description: MatchingHostnames is a regex describing which hostnames
        to generate certificates for.
    type: string
```

Using this mechanism, you don't have to bother with keeping YAML and Go code in sync but can focus on writing your code and defining the necessary types in Go. Operator SDK will handle creating the necessary resources for you.

Setting Up a CA Directory for Development

Developing an OpenShift operator is, in many cases, like any software engineering project. Setting up a development environment is one of the parts that needs to be done for every project and is often a hurdle for new developers to get started with a project.

Operator SDK helps to onboard new colleagues if they are familiar with developing operators, as it makes operator repositories all look similar. However, the business logic of an operator may still require a special setup, as the business logic is what makes the operator unique and ultimately justifies its existence.

The business logic of the example Let's Encrypt operator requires an external ACME endpoint to work with. For development, you don't want to require every developer to have a public accessible cluster, which they need to request certificates from an ACME provider like Let's Encrypt.

With OpenShift Local, developers get a functional OpenShift cluster that is accessible only on their local machines, which saves development costs and gives developers more control over the cluster itself. To solve the problem of public access to the cluster, you can deploy your own CA directory for development purposes to the OpenShift Local cluster. The operator and the CA directory can access each other from within the cluster, without the cluster being exposed to the internet.

Luckily, with Pebble (*https://github.com/letsencrypt/pebble*) Let's Encrypt provides a solution for exactly this problem. The purpose of Pebble is to stand up a CA directory that you can run yourself. It's not meant as a production deployment for internal TLS certificates but a CA directory for developers implementing clients, like the Let's Encrypt operator.

To deploy Pebble to the `le-operator-system` namespace on your cluster, run the following commands:

```
$ oc new-project le-operator-system

Now using project "le-operator-system" on server "https://api.crc.testing:6443".

$ oc apply -f https://raw.githubusercontent.com/OperatingOpenShift/\
le-operator/main/hack/pebble.yaml

configmap/pebble-config created
deployment.apps/pebble created
service/pebble created
```

This YAML file contains three resources:

- *ConfigMap pebble-config* configures Pebble to use the ports 443 and 80 for the certificate request challenges. They are used to verify a domain is owned by whoever wants to request a certificate for it. Since the OpenShift router listens on these ports even in OpenShift Local, and the challenge requests access the domains through the router, Pebble needs to use the ports 443 and 80. By default, Pebble uses ports 5002 and 5001.

- *Deployment pebble* deploys Pebble and mounts the ConfigMap `pebble-config` so Pebble can use it.

- *Service pebble* creates a service that exposes the CA directory so it can be accessed from inside the cluster. This chapter deploys the operator to the same namespace as Pebble, so it can request certificates at *https://pebble:14000/dir*.

Now you're all set to develop an operator that talks to your local CA directory.

Designing the Custom Resource Definition

The CRD your operator delivers is the API that users or depending software use to interact with it. That means you need to think about what input and output you want to provide to users of the operator and make that available in the CRD.

The input of the operator consists of:

- The hostnames to request and renew certificates for. The operator allows specifying a regular expression to match hostnames.
- The email address to use for the registration with the CA directory.
- The URL of the CA directory.
- (For development) A flag that allows disabling the TLS validation of the CA directory. This is needed to use an internal CA directory that itself doesn't have a valid TLS certificate.

Add these fields to the EncryptedDomainSpec struct in *api/v1beta1/encrypteddomain_types*:

```
// EncryptedDomainSpec defines the desired state of EncryptedDomain
type EncryptedDomainSpec struct {
  // MatchingHostnames is a regex describing which
  // hostnames to generate certificates for.
  MatchingHostnames string `json:"matchingHostnames,omitempty"`

  // CA directory Endpoint to use for certificate requests
  CADir string `json:"caDir,omitempty"`

  // Ignore invalid certificate on CADir
  CADirInsecureSSL bool `json:"caDirInsecureSSL,omitempty"`

  // Mail address to use for registration with CA directory
  RegistrationMail string `json:"registrationMail,omitempty"`
}
```

The spec part of the CRD defines the input API of the operator. Communication of the current observed state to the outside of the current reconciliation should happen via the status subresource. Keep in mind that when applying resources with oc apply, the status is ignored by the API server. This means you should make sure that the status only contains items the operator can reproduce when a CR gets recreated and design your operator and CRDs accordingly. Sometimes, the operator needs to put output data into the spec, as well: if the data is important for the processing or the user and cannot be reproduced.

A simple thought experiment to verify if a given piece of information should go to the spec or status is to imagine transferring a CR from one namespace to another by deleting and reapplying it. Would the operator be able to reproduce the information without leaking any resources? Then it should go to the status. Would the user lose important information or would the operator leak external resources? Then it should probably be part of the spec or some persistent storage like a database.

The status of the EncryptedDomain CRD is defined by the `EncryptedDomainStatus` struct in *api/v1beta1/encrypteddomain_types*:

```
// EncrypteddomainStatus defines the observed state of Encrypteddomain
type EncryptedDomainStatus struct {
  // INSERT ADDITIONAL STATUS FIELD - define observed state of cluster
  // Important: Run "make" to regenerate code after modifying this file
}
```

After initial generation with Operator SDK the `EncryptedDomainStatus` struct is still empty. A common pattern is to add a `status` property that communicates if the CR is currently being processed, if the observed state matches the desired state, or if an error occurred while reconciling the resource.

The EncryptedDomain CRD also needs a way to store the certificates that have been generated so they can be reused across routes. In addition, it needs to generate and store a private key used for the registration. Both could also be stored in a secret, but for the simplicity of this example, they are stored in the status subresource.

By conducting this experiment you can verify the status is a good place: when the user deletes and recreates a CR in a different namespace, the operator would go and renew certificates for all the managed routes. No important data would be lost as the TLS certificates and keys can be reproduced easily.

Each EncryptedDomain can match multiple routes with different hostnames, so the certificates should be stored in a list. A separate struct `GeneratedCertificate` allows you to store the hostname and certificate data. Add the following two properties to the `EncryptedDomainStatus` struct and create the `GeneratedCertificate` struct to allow the operator to store a private key and a list of certificates in each EncryptedDomain.

```
// EncryptedDomainStatus defines the observed state of EncryptedDomain
type EncryptedDomainStatus struct {
  // GeneratedCertificates holds all certificates the operator has generated
  // for a given CR
  GeneratedCertificates map[string]GeneratedCertificate
                                    `json:"generatedCertificate,omitempty"`

  // PrivateKey is the private key used for certificate requests
  PrivateKey string `json:"privateKey,omitempty"`
}
```

```
// GeneratedCertificate holds the key and certificate generated for a
// given hostname
type GeneratedCertificate struct {
  // Hostname is the hostname for which this certificate is valid
  Hostname string `json:"hostname,omitempty"`

  // Certificate is the TLS certificate
  Certificate string `json:"certificate,omitempty"`

  // Key is the certificate private key
  Key string `json:"key,omitempty"`
}
```

The attributes of the `GeneratedCertificate` struct can be used by the operator to update routes that have the exact same hostname with valid TLS certificates, similar to what you did manually in "Redirecting Traffic to TLS Route" on page 42 to transfer certificates between different routes.

Regenerate the CRD YAML by running `make manifests`. The CRD status in *config/crd/bases/letsencrypt.operatingopenshift.com_encrypteddomains.yaml* now contains the updated status definition. The GeneratedCertificate struct is represented as a list of objects in the CRD:

```
status:
  description: EncryptedDomainStatus defines the observed state
    of EncryptedDomain
  properties:
    generatedCertificates:
      additionalProperties:
        description: GeneratedCertificate holds the key and certificate
          generated for a given hostname
        properties:
          certificate:
            description: Certificate is the TLS certificate
            type: string
          hostname:
            description: Hostname is the hostname for which this certificate
              is valid
            type: string
          key:
            description: Key is the certificate private key
            type: string
        type: object
      description: GeneratedCertificates holds all certificates the operator
        has generated for a given CR
      type: object
    privateKey:
      description: PrivateKey is the private key used for certificate requests
      type: string
  type: object
```

The updated CRD allows users to specify EncryptedDomains as shown in Example 9-1.

Example 9-1. Example EncryptedDomain resource

```
apiVersion: letsencrypt.operatingopenshift.com/v1beta1
kind: EncryptedDomain
metadata:
  name: encrypteddomain-sample
  namespace: default
spec:
  matchingHostnames: ".*-arcade.apps-crc.testing$"
  caDir: "https://pebble:14000/dir"
  registrationMail: "le-operator@operatingopenshift.com"
```

This example EncryptedDomain matches all routes with generated hostnames created in the arcade namespace, as they match the hostname pattern. The operator uses the pebble deployment generated in the same namespace as the operator to register domains for this EncryptedDomain.

Installing the CustomResourceDefinition

Now that the API of the operator is defined and generated into the CRD YAML in the file *config/crd/bases/letsencrypt.operatingopenshift.com_encrypteddomains.yaml*, you need to install the CRD to your OpenShift cluster. For this purpose, Operator SDK prepared a specific target in the *Makefile*.

Run the following command to install the CRD you created in the previous section:

```
$ make install
[...]
kustomize build config/crd | kubectl apply -f -
customresourcedefinition.apiextensions.k8s.io/
  encrypteddomains.letsencrypt.operatingopenshift.com created
```

The `install` target runs `kustomize` to generate all manifests in the *config* folder. Kustomize (*https://kustomize.io*) is a tool to make YAML files configurable so they can be created once and easily customized to match different use cases. When you inspect the files in the *config* folder you can find many different templates that are used for installing and running the operator. Right now, you only need the CRD, which is applied to the cluster as any other Kubernetes resource by the `make` target: With `kubectl apply -f`.

Operator SDK can be used to build operators for vanilla Kubernetes, not only OpenShift. Hence, it uses Kubernetes libraries and commands, rather than the specific OpenShift toolchain. For this reason, the *Makefile* uses the kubectl CLI instead of oc. The usage of both CLI tools is very similar. However, the operator built in this chapter cannot be used on vanilla Kubernetes, as it assumes applications are exposed using routes, which are available only on OpenShift.

After installing the CRD, you can already create the example CR Example 9-1, although nothing generates certificates for it, as the operator is not yet running, nor does it contain any logic:

```
$ oc apply -f sample-encrypteddomain.yaml
encrypteddomain.letsencrypt.operatingopenshift.com/encrypteddomain-sample
    created
```

The next step is to build some logic into the EncryptedDomain controller and run it to reconcile the example resource you just created.

Local Operator Development

Deploying and running the operator on an OpenShift cluster can be done by building a container, pushing that container to a container registry, and then deploying the operator as any other application running on OpenShift.

However, for the development environment of the operator, building a container, pushing and pulling it, even from the OpenShift internal registry, is too much effort. When developing code, it's important to be able to iterate quickly, do small changes, and run the code as if it all was running on the local device.

For operator development, you often need to interact with a real cluster, but you can still run the code on your local machine and connect it to an OpenShift cluster, for example, your local OpenShift Local environment. Operator SDK provides a make target that you can use for exactly this purpose. Make sure you're logged in to the OpenShift cluster that you want to run the operator against before starting the operator on your local machine. Then start the operator with the following command:

```
$ make run
controller-gen [...]
controller-gen [...]
go fmt ./...
go vet ./...
go run ./main.go
[...] controller-runtime.metrics  metrics server is starting to listen
                              {"addr": ":8080"}
[...] setup  starting manager
[...] starting metrics server  {"path": "/metrics"}
```

```
[...] controller.encrypteddomain  Starting EventSource
    {"reconciler group": "letsencrypt.operatingopenshift.com", [...]
[...] controller.encrypteddomain  Starting Controller
    {"reconciler group": "letsencrypt.operatingopenshift.com", [...]
[...] controller.encrypteddomain  Starting workers
    {"reconciler group": "letsencrypt.operatingopenshift.com", [...]
```

The run make target builds and starts the operator. You can see the output of the
operator as it runs indefinitely, waiting for EncryptedDomains to reconcile. Press
Ctrl-C to stop the operator again and build some logic into the controller for EncryptedDomains.

Operator SDK generated a boilerplate controller with a `Reconcile` function in
controllers/encrypteddomain_controller.go. It looks similar to the following, marking
where you should put the logic of your controller with a comment:

```
func (r *EncryptedDomainReconciler) Reconcile(ctx context.Context,
  req ctrl.Request) (ctrl.Result, error) {

  _ = log.FromContext(ctx)

  // TODO(user): your logic here

  return ctrl.Result{}, nil
}
```

The `Reconcile` function is the entry point to your own code. It is called each time an
observed resource is created, updated, or removed. First, create some code that parses
the request to reconcile a resource and get the resource in the form of an object of the
type you defined earlier:

```
import (
  letsencryptv1beta1 "github.com/OperatingOpenshift/le-operator/api/v1beta1"  ❶
  "k8s.io/apimachinery/pkg/api/errors"  ❷
  [...]
)

[...]

func (r *EncryptedDomainReconciler) Reconcile(ctx context.Context,
  req ctrl.Request) (ctrl.Result, error) {

  log := ctrl.Log.WithName("controller").WithName("encrypteddomain")

  domain := letsencryptv1beta1.EncryptedDomain{}  ❸
  err := r.Get(ctx, req.NamespacedName, &domain)  ❹
  if errors.IsNotFound(err) {
    return ctrl.Result{}, nil  ❺
  }
  if err != nil {
    return ctrl.Result{}, err
  }
```

```
log.Info("reconciling EncryptedDomain " +
    domain.Name + " in namespace " + domain.Namespace) ❻

    return ctrl.Result{}, nil
}
```

❶ Import the types you defined earlier in the api package.

❷ Import the errors package used for checking common error types.

❸ Create an empty EncryptedDomain object to fill it with the data from the current request.

❹ Read the reconciled resource from the API Server and store it in the object domain.

❺ In case the resource can't be found anymore, ignore the request. If another error occurs while reading the resource, stop reconciling. See "The Reconcile Function" on page 216 for a detailed explanation of the return codes.

❻ Log the name and namespace of the resource that's currently being reconciled.

Run the code again using make run, and you should see the log output for the resource you created by applying Example 9-1:

```
$ make run
go fmt ./...
go vet ./...
go run ./main.go
[...] controller-runtime.metrics  metrics server is starting to listen
                                   {"addr": ":8080"}
[...] setup  starting manager
[...] starting metrics server  {"path": "/metrics"}
[...] controller.encrypteddomain  Starting EventSource
[...] controller.encrypteddomain  Starting Controller
[...] controller.encrypteddomain  Starting workers
[...] controller.encrypteddomain  reconciling EncryptedDomain
                                   encrypteddomain-sample in namespace default
```

As you can see, the operator read the resource from the cluster and printed its name and namespace. While the operator is running, you can also delete and recreate the resource or create it in a different namespace, using a separate terminal to watch the operator picking it up again.

The Reconcile Function

Each time you see the newly created log output, the `Reconcile` function of the EncryptedDomain controller has been called for a request that includes information about the resource being reconciled. Using the name and namespace included in this request object, the operator queries the API server for the full object to reconcile.

That means, each time a new resource is created or an existing resource changes, the `Reconcile` function is called. Even when you update the resource using the client you used to query it, a new request is put into the reconcile queue and reconciled by the controller again to ensure each change went through the reconcile loop. Therefore, it's a good practice to return from the `Reconcile` function whenever you applied a change to the resource being watched by the controller.

The return value of the `Reconcile` function consists of two values, a `Result` struct, and an error. Whenever your `Reconcile` function returns an error, a new request to reconcile the same resource is put into the reconcile queue to try to resolve the error on the next run. There is an exponential back-off built into the operator, so it won't run in an endless loop without a wait between the runs when an error was returned.

Using the `Result` struct, you can also influence how the operator treats your return code. You can force a requeue of the current request by returning an object like the following:

```
result := ctrl.Result{
    Requeue:      true,
    RequeueAfter: 5 * time.Second,
}
return result, nil
```

This `result` object causes the operator to requeue the request after five seconds. This can be useful when the operator needs to wait for an external dependency, for example, a pod coming up, without blocking the reconcile loop.

You always need to be aware that the `Reconcile` function can be called multiple times for a single resource, caused by external changes to it but also changes by the operator itself. You need to make sure that when a resource reaches the desired state and gets reconciled again, the controller doesn't change anything. When a reconciliation is stopped at any point in time because an error occurred or because you applied a change, always make sure the operator is able to pick up the resource again, understand the actual state, and continue working to reach the desired state.

In other words, your `Reconcile` function should be idempotent. No matter how often it's called, the output should be the same if the actual and desired state have both not changed. Reaching this goal can best be achieved by splitting it up into idempotent subroutines, each checking their portion of the desired state, applying changes if necessary, and deciding if they should stop the current request.

Deploying the Operator

After baking the first logic into your operator, you may want to know if it's able to run inside your OpenShift cluster. To deploy it, as with any other application deployed to OpenShift clusters, it needs to become a container image.

Operator SDK generates make targets for everything around building, pushing container images, and deploying the operator to a cluster.

The first step is building the container image. The *Makefile* in your operator folder has a target docker-build. If you want to use a different container engine than Docker for building and pushing the image, you need to update these targets and replace the docker command with something else.

A useful pattern if you want to support both podman, an alternative to the Docker command, and Docker itself is to figure out if the podman command is available and use the docker command as a fallback. The syntax in the commands used in the make targets is compatible between Docker and Podman. This behavior can be achieved by updating the docker-build and docker-push targets in the *Makefile*:

```
CONTAINER_CMD ?= podman ❶
ifeq ($(shell command -v ${CONTAINER_CMD} 2> /dev/null),) ❷
  CONTAINER_CMD = docker
endif

.PHONY: docker-build
docker-build: test ## Build docker image with the manager.
  ${CONTAINER_CMD} build -t ${IMG} . ❸

.PHONY: docker-push
docker-push: ## Push docker image with the manager.
  ${CONTAINER_CMD} push ${IMG} ❹
```

❶ Allow overriding the CONTAINER_CMD variable when calling make, defaulting to podman if none is provided.

❷ Figure out if the provided command stored in CONTAINER_CMD is available. If not overwritten, it will check for the podman command. If it is not available, change the CONTAINER_CMD variable to docker as fallback.

❸ Instead of docker, use the command stored in the CONTAINER_CMD variable to run the build command.

❹ Instead of docker, use the command stored in the CONTAINER_CMD variable to run the push command.

With these changes, a user can decide which container engine to use or let the Makefile use whichever is available, prioritizing Podman over Docker.

Run the following command to build the container image of your operator. Make sure you set the IMG variable to a value that allows you to push the image to a container registry accessible by your cluster, for example, Quay (*https://quay.io*):

```
$ make docker-build IMG=quay.io/operatingopenshift/le-operator
[...]
STEP 1: FROM golang:1.16 AS builder
STEP 2: WORKDIR /workspace
--> Using cache 1997d380ff5106968bc77f561b9385d8bed5b115f7cd26fe99bf85ca0849931d
--> 1997d380ff5
STEP 3: COPY go.mod go.mod
--> d420fb9fb04
STEP 4: COPY go.sum go.sum
--> 3e5b2725674
STEP 5: RUN go mod download
--> ea860cedda9
STEP 6: COPY main.go main.go
--> 6e85bb3bf7e
STEP 7: COPY api/ api/
--> 71984243c3e
STEP 8: COPY controllers/ controllers/
--> 1925076019b
STEP 9: RUN CGO_ENABLED=0 GOOS=linux GOARCH=amd64 go build -a -o manager main.go
--> 89e5dc4f4a0
STEP 10: FROM gcr.io/distroless/static:nonroot
STEP 11: WORKDIR /
--> Using cache b072cf0fe482146400c096280961a63a02e7a7a22787472db774d9c0e6803558
--> b072cf0fe48
STEP 12: COPY --from=builder /workspace/manager .
--> 1fc4c2f0347
STEP 13: USER 65532:65532
--> 0cbe848aefe
STEP 14: ENTRYPOINT ["/manager"]
STEP 15: COMMIT quay.io/operatingopenshift/le-operator
--> 28b98a8ed51
Successfully tagged quay.io/operatingopenshift/le-operator:latest
28b98a8ed51a4e24bd8d25ef515d9187d480fa76718099ca3c920d12751ce83b
```

While the operator image is being built, you can follow the steps provided by the Dockerfile. As you can see, it uses the golang base image to build the operator and in a second stage the distroless/static image, which results in a minimal image for running the operator. The resulting image for this operator, which currently contains mostly boilerplate and dependencies, is around 50 MiB in size.

The next step is to push the image to the container registry:

```
$ make docker-push IMG=quay.io/operatingopenshift/le-operator
podman push quay.io/operatingopenshift/le-operator
Getting image source signatures
Copying blob 0cbbaac2769c done
Copying blob fd6fa224ea91 skipped: already exists
Copying config 28b98a8ed5 done
Writing manifest to image destination
Storing signatures
```

Make sure you are logged in to the corresponding container registry, so the push command can store the image in the container registry.

Before deploying the image to the cluster, make sure the image can be accessed from the OpenShift cluster. If you're using Quay, the easiest way is to make the image public in the Repository Settings on the Quay website (*https://quay.io*), as shown in Figure 9-2.

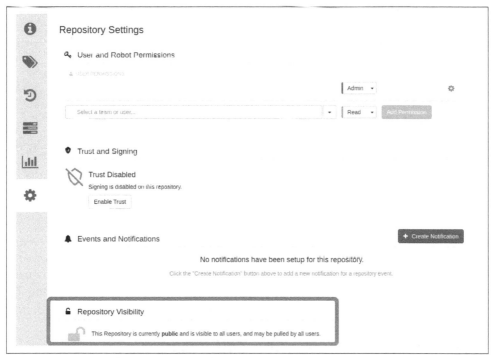

Figure 9-2. Setting the repository visibility in Quay

The final step is deploying the operator to the OpenShift cluster. Unsurprisingly, there is a make target for the operator deployment, available for you to use:

```
$ make deploy IMG=quay.io/operatingopenshift/le-operator
controller-gen rbac:roleName=manager-role crd webhook paths="./..."
   output:crd:artifacts:config=config/crd/bases
cd config/manager && kustomize edit set image controller=controller:latest
```

```
kustomize build config/default | kubectl apply -f -
namespace/le-operator-system created
customresourcedefinition/encrypteddomains.letsencrypt.operatingopenshift.com
  configured
serviceaccount/le-operator-controller-manager created
role.rbac.authorization.k8s.io/le-operator-leader-election-role created
clusterrole/le-operator-manager-role created
clusterrole/le-operator-metrics-reader created
clusterrole/le-operator-proxy-role created
rolebinding/le-operator-leader-election-rolebinding created
clusterrolebinding/le-operator-manager-rolebinding created
clusterrolebinding/le-operator-proxy-rolebinding created
configmap/le-operator-manager-config created
service/le-operator-controller-manager-metrics-service created
deployment.apps/le-operator-controller-manager created
```

The `deploy` target updates the artifacts in the *config* folder, rebuilds all artifacts from the templates using kustomize, and applies them to your OpenShift cluster. You should now find a pod in the namespace `le-operator-system`, running the operator and producing output similar to when you ran it locally:

```
$ oc get po -n le-operator-system
NAME                                                  READY   STATUS    AGE
le-operator-controller-manager-6bd648bbbd-8khb5       2/2     Running   4m8s

$ oc logs le-operator-controller-manager-6bd648bbbd-8khb5 manager \
  -n le-operator-system
controller-runtime.metrics   metrics server is starting to listen
setup   starting manager
starting metrics server   {"path": "/metrics"}
[...]
controller.encrypteddomain   reconciling EncryptedDomain encrypteddomain-sample
                             in namespace default
```

Deploying the operator to the cluster includes creating the CRD, the operator name-space, a service account with all the necessary permissions to run the operator, and the deployment that manages the operator pod. Whenever any of these changes, either because you updated the template or a new RBAC rule is generated by `controller-gen`, run `make deploy` to update the resources in the OpenShift cluster.

Creating and Updating OpenShift Resources

Fast-forward the implementation effort of the Let's Encrypt operator a little bit and say you figured out all the necessary steps to renew a certificate. You created a separate package `encdomain` with a struct `EncryptedDomainManager` that manages the certificate renewal and is able to create a new certificate for a hostname that belongs to a route on your OpenShift cluster. To do so, the `EncryptedDomainManager` needs to create OpenShift resources itself, namely ConfigMaps, deployments, services, and routes.

The struct itself is quite simple:

```
type EncryptedDomainManager struct {
  client client.Client
}
```

The Kubernetes client provided by the boilerplate code is capable of reading and manipulating OpenShift resources. The EncryptedDomainManager can be initialized with a client from within the Reconcile function:

```
func (r *EncryptedDomainReconciler) Reconcile(ctx context.Context,
req ctrl.Request) (ctrl.Result, error) {
  m := encdomain.New(r.Client)
  [...]
}
```

Take a look at the following method of the EncryptedDomainManager, which creates the route to handle the HTTP-01 challenge:

```
import (


  ctrl "sigs.k8s.io/controller-runtime"
  routev1 "github.com/openshift/api/route/v1"

  "k8s.io/apimachinery/pkg/api/errors"
  "k8s.io/apimachinery/pkg/types"
  [...]
)

[...]
func (r *EncryptedDomainManager) ensureAcmeRoute(ctx context.Context,
  route routev1.Route) (err error) {

  log := ctrl.Log.WithName("controller").WithName("EncryptedDomain/ensureRoute")

  // Create route for hostname:5002/.well-known/acme-challenge
  desiredChallengeRoute := routev1.Route{
    ObjectMeta: metav1.ObjectMeta{
      Name:      route.Name + "-acme-challenge",
      Namespace: route.Namespace,
      Labels: map[string]string{
        UsageLabel: "acme-challenge",
      },
    },
    Spec: routev1.RouteSpec{
      Host: route.Spec.Host, ❶
      Path: "/.well-known/acme-challenge", ❷
      To: routev1.RouteTargetReference{
        Kind: "Service", ❸
        Name: route.Name + "-acme-challenge",
      },
      Port: &routev1.RoutePort{
```

```
      TargetPort: intstr.FromInt(5002),
    },
  },
}

challengeRoute := routev1.Route{}
err = r.client.Get(ctx, types.NamespacedName{
  Name: desiredChallengeRoute.Name,
  Namespace: desiredChallengeRoute.Namespace
}, &challengeRoute) ❹
if err != nil {
  if !errors.IsNotFound(err) {
    return
  }
  // Challenge route doesn't exist
  log.Info("Creating challenge route " + desiredChallengeRoute.Spec.Host +
    " in namespace " + desiredChallengeRoute.Namespace)
  err = r.client.Create(ctx, &desiredChallengeRoute) ❺
  return
}
log.Info("Updating challenge route " + desiredChallengeRoute.Spec.Host +
  " in namespace " + desiredChallengeRoute.Namespace)
challengeRoute.Spec = desiredChallengeRoute.Spec
err = r.client.Update(ctx, &challengeRoute) ❻
return
}
```

❶ The route that is created for the HTTP-01 challenge uses the same hostname as the original route for which the operator is about to request a certificate.

❷ The path of the new route is different, configuring the OpenShift router to forward requests to *route-hostname/.well-known/acme-challenge* to the service specified for this route.

❸ The service behind the challenge route. It is created with a function ensureAcmeSvc, which is very similar to ensureAcmeRoute.

❹ Get a route resource in the desired namespace with the name of the desired route to figure out if it already exists. It may have been created in a previous run of the Reconcile function for the same resource. If it doesn't exist, an HTTP return code 404 is returned by the API Server, reflected by an error in Go.

❺ If the API server returns 404, it means the operator should create the route.

❻ If the route already exists, update it so it fits your needs. The function could potentially additionally check if an update is even needed, but the update call won't change anything if the route already matches the expectations.

It's a common pattern to first try to get the resource you want to create, and then check if it matches the one you're about to create. If it doesn't exist, it's created according to your needs. Update the resource only if the route already exists but doesn't match your needs.

This behavior makes for a good idempotent subroutine of the `Reconcile` function because if the desired state, in our case, the matching route for the challenge, is already there, it doesn't do anything. If for some reason the route doesn't match, the operator creates or updates it to match the expectations.

Specifying RBAC Permissions

The methods you've seen previously use a Go client to interact with the OpenShift API Server. This is comparable to commands you run from the command line with the `oc` CLI. To create resources, such as routes, your user needs to have the necessary permissions, as described in Chapter 4.

The operator is running with the permissions of a service account that you created with the `make deploy` command. This means you must ensure everything you do in the operator code is included in the RBAC rules for the operator service account. This is a point where you often see different behavior when running the operator locally then deployed to the cluster. When you run the operator locally, it connects to the cluster using your configuration as your user, which usually has more privileges than the operator service account.

For this reason, you always need to verify that the operator still works as expected from inside a cluster before deploying your code, in the best case using a CI that verifies the behavior.

Luckily, you won't have to write all the RBAC YAML manually but can use Kubebuilder directives directly within your source code. Some of these permissions are already in the boilerplate code generated by Operator SDK. You can add similar comments to your code to give the service account more permissions.

The following comment grants the necessary permissions to create the route necessary for the HTTP-01 challenge:

```
//+kubebuilder:rbac:groups=route.openshift.io,
    resources=routes,verbs=get;list;watch;create;delete;update;patch
//+kubebuilder:rbac:groups=route.openshift.io,
    resources=routes/custom-host,verbs=get;list;watch;create;delete;update;patch
```

The kubebuilder directives usually get very long, especially as they contain fully qualified resource groups and potentially long lists of verbs. Please note that Kubebuilder doesn't support new lines in these directives. However, splitting the lines is necessary to fit the lines within the margins in this book.

When `controller-gen` regenerates the kustomize template, the new permissions are added, for example when you run `make deploy` or `make manifests` again:

```
$ make manifests
controller-gen rbac:roleName=manager-role crd webhook paths="./..."
  output:crd:artifacts:config=config/crd/bases

$ cat config/rbac/role.yaml
---
apiVersion: rbac.authorization.k8s.io/v1
kind: ClusterRole
metadata:
  creationTimestamp: null
  name: manager-role
rules:
[...]
- apiGroups:
  - route.openshift.io
  resources:
  - routes
  verbs:
  - create
  - delete
  - get
  - list
  - patch
  - update
  - watch
- apiGroups:
  - route.openshift.io
  resources:
  - routes/custom-host
  verbs:
  - create
  - delete
  - get
  - list
  - patch
  - update
  - watch
```

As you can see, `controller-gen` is invoked by the `make manifests` command, which regenerates CRDs and other templates based on the source code. The comments you added to the operator are appended to the ClusterRole that is generated for the operator. The ClusterRole is bound to the operator service account using a ClusterRoleBinding.

Routing Traffic to the Operator

To run the HTTP-01 challenge the operator uses the lego library, which opens a port to verify the domain name you want to get a certificate for. To forward the traffic of the ACME challenge to the operator, the controller creates a route in OpenShift with the corresponding path; see "Creating and Updating OpenShift Resources" on page 220.

However, the route needs to be created in the same namespace as the input route for which the operator requests a certificate since OpenShift doesn't allow you to create a route with a custom hostname that already exists in a different namespace.

Additionally, routes can forward traffic only to services in the same namespace. Hence, to allow forwarding traffic, we need to create a deployment, service, and route to forward the traffic to the operator in a different namespace. Figure 9-3 visualizes the flow of the request from the CA directory to the operator.

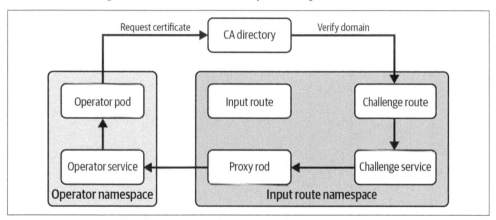

Figure 9-3. Request flow from the CA directory to the operator

The service in the operator namespace needs to be created only once and can be added statically to the *config* directory. The deployment, service, and route need to be created per input route, or at least once per hostname. This means the operator should also clean up those resources when it's finished with the certificate renewal.

The cleanup can be done similarly to creating and updating requests, using the Delete function of the Kubernetes client:

```
func (r *EncryptedDomainManager) CleanupAcmeChallenge(ctx context.Context,
  route routev1.Route) error {

  deployment := appsv1.Deployment{ ❶
    ObjectMeta: metav1.ObjectMeta{
      Name:      route.Name + "-acme-challenge",
      Namespace: route.Namespace,
    },
  }
  err := r.client.Delete(ctx, &deployment) ❷
  if err != nil && !errors.IsNotFound(err) { ❸
    return err
  }

  svc := corev1.Service{
    ObjectMeta: metav1.ObjectMeta{
      Name:      route.Name + "-acme-challenge",
      Namespace: route.Namespace,
    },
  }
  err = r.client.Delete(ctx, &svc)
  if err != nil && !errors.IsNotFound(err) {
    return err
  }

  challengeRoute := routev1.Route{
    ObjectMeta: metav1.ObjectMeta{
      Name:      route.Name + "-acme-challenge",
      Namespace: route.Namespace,
    },
  }
  err = r.client.Delete(ctx, &challengeRoute)
  if err != nil && !errors.IsNotFound(err) {
    return err
  }
  return nil
}
```

❶ Create a minimal Deployment object for deletion: only namespace and name are required.

❷ Delete the deployment.

❸ To ensure idempotency of this function, it needs to ignore the case where the deployment doesn't exist, so subsequent cleanup will be done if the previous Delete calls fail for some reason.

This design allows renewing certificates for routes in different namespaces than the operator namespace. An alternative design would be to have the operator manage certificates only in the namespace it is deployed to. This would make for a simpler implementation, but it would also require the user to deploy it to every namespace they want to manage certificates in.

Adding Additional Controllers

So far the operator is able to manage TLS certificates of routes when reconciling EncryptedDomains. However, a user of the operator would most probably expect it to immediately detect new route resources and generate certificates for them, rather than wait for the next reconciliation of the matching EncryptedDomain.

To allow the operator to reconcile additional resources, you need to add and implement an additional controller. This additional controller will not need its own custom resource definition, but instead, it will reconcile route resources. The route API is already installed on every OpenShift cluster, so we can write a controller for it and use it without installing an additional CRD.

To generate the boilerplate code for an additional controller, run the following command, which tells Operator SDK to generate code for the controller but skip the CRD generation:

```
$ operator-sdk create api --controller --resource=false \
  --kind Route --group routes.openshift.io --version v1
Writing kustomize manifests for you to edit...
Writing scaffold for you to edit...
controllers/route_controller.go
Update dependencies:
$ go mod tidy
```

This command generates a new controller in *controllers/route_controller.go* where you can add code to generate certificates when a new route resource is created.

Since the code that handles the certificate generation is split out into its own package, the code of this controller is fairly simple.

The controller first will need to figure out if there is an EncryptedDomain resource matching the route hostname. If there is more than one, the operator needs to decide which one should manage the certificates of the route to avoid competition between EncryptedDomains. Then it needs to check if there is already an existing certificate in the corresponding EncryptedDomain and if so add it to the route. If no certificate is found, the request process needs to be initiated.

To get started, you first need to tell the controller which resource kind it should reconcile. This step was not necessary for the EncryptedDomain controller, as the CRD and types have been generated by Operator SDK. Compare the function Setup

WithManager of the EncryptedDomain controller shown in Example 9-2 with the function of the route controller in Example 9-3.

Example 9-2. controller/encrypteddomain_controller.go

```
// SetupWithManager sets up the controller with the Manager.
func (r *EncryptedDomainReconciler) SetupWithManager(mgr ctrl.Manager) error {
  return ctrl.NewControllerManagedBy(mgr).
    For(&letsencryptv1beta1.EncryptedDomain{}).
    Complete(r)
}
```

Example 9-3. controller/route_controller.go

```
// SetupWithManager sets up the controller with the Manager.
func (r *RouteReconciler) SetupWithManager(mgr ctrl.Manager) error {
  return ctrl.NewControllerManagedBy(mgr).
    // Uncomment the following line adding a pointer to an instance of the
    // controlled resource as an argument
    // For().
    Complete(r)
}
```

As you can see, Operator SDK already provided a comment with a hint about what to do. Since it doesn't know where to find the type that you want to watch using this new controller, it can't generate that code for you. In case of the route controller, we can import the type from the module github.com/openshift/api/route/v1:

```
import (
  routeapi "github.com/openshift/api/route/v1"
  [...]
)

// SetupWithManager sets up the controller with the Manager.
func (r *RouteReconciler) SetupWithManager(mgr ctrl.Manager) error {
  return ctrl.NewControllerManagedBy(mgr).
    For(&routeapi.Route{}).
    Complete(r)
}
```

As with the EncryptedDomain controller, you can now go ahead and implement the Reconcile function, starting with reading the resource the request is about:

```
func (r *RouteReconciler) Reconcile(ctx context.Context,
  req ctrl.Request) (ctrl.Result, error) {

  log := ctrl.Log.WithName("controllers").WithName("Route")

  m := encdomain.New(r.Client) ❶
```

```
    route := routev1.Route{}
    err := r.Get(ctx, req.NamespacedName, &route)  ❷
    if errors.IsNotFound(err) {
      return ctrl.Result{}, nil
    }
    if err != nil {
      return ctrl.Result{}, err
    }

    log.Info("Reconciling route: " + route.Name)

    label, ok := route.Labels[encdomain.UsageLabel]
    if ok && label == "acme-challenge" {  ❸
      log.Info("Ignoring acme-challenge route")
      return ctrl.Result{}, nil
    }
    [...]
}
```

❶ To renew certificates, the same logic is reused that the operator uses in the EncryptedDomain controller.

❷ Read the resource that the operator is about to reconcile. If the resource is not found, return from Reconcile but don't requeue the request.

❸ Skip routes that are generated by the operator.

One thing to keep in mind while implementing this controller is that to renew certificates, the operator creates route resources in the cluster. These resources should be ignored by the route controller, as they do not require new certificates. For this purpose, a label is added to these routes by the operator so they can be identified easily.

When implementing an operator, be aware that any change that you make to a resource is recognized by the cluster and likely will initialize further processing of the resource. This processing can happen within the same operator by enqueuing another request or in a different control loop in another API server or operator.

Updating Resource Status

As discussed in "Operator Design" on page 202, the operator stores the certificates it generates for routes inside the EncryptedDomain status. The status is a subresource of the EncryptedDomain resource that requires sending requests to a separate endpoint.

This is mostly hidden within the client library the operator uses. The only difference is that instead of calling functions like client.Update(), you need to call their status counterparts like `client.Status().Update()`. The parameters passed to the status functions are the same.

The following code shows an example status update, which adds a requested certificate to an EncryptedDomain resource:

```
domain.Status.GeneratedCertificates[route.Spec.Host] =
  letsencryptv1beta1.GeneratedCertificate{
    Hostname:    route.Spec.Host,
    Certificate: route.Spec.TLS.Certificate,
    Key:         route.Spec.TLS.Key,
  }

log.Info("Updating encrypteddomain status " + domain.Name)
err = r.client.Status().Update(ctx, &domain)
if err != nil {
  return err
}
```

As you can see, the `Status().Update()` function takes the full EncryptedDomain object, although it will update only the status. Likewise, the `Update()` function gets an object that can contain a status, but it will update only the spec of the resource.

In contrast to updating, reading the status doesn't require a separate request. The status subresource is included in the response to a `GET` call and populated by the client in the object read, as in the following code, which takes a certificate that already exists in an EncryptedDomain and writes it to a route.

```
domains := letsencryptv1beta1.EncryptedDomainList{}
r.client.List(ctx, &domains, &options) ❶

[...]

route.Spec.TLS = &routev1.TLSConfig{ ❷
  Certificate: domain.Status.GeneratedCertificates[route.Spec.Host].Certificate,
  Key:         domain.Status.GeneratedCertificates[route.Spec.Host].Key,
}

log.Info("Certificate already exists. Updating route " + route.Name)
err = r.client.Update(ctx, &route)
```

❶ By calling the `List()` function, the client will query and return all EncryptedDomains.

❷ After identifying the right EncryptedDomain to use, the certificate can be read from the EncryptedDomain status.

In this code, no additional function call is necessary to read the status of the EncryptedDomain. The status is populated after reading the EncryptedDomain resource with the `List()` function. The same applies to getting an object with `Get()`.

Summary

Developing custom operators allows you to extend OpenShift by adding new resources to the API and adding processing logic on API resources. This allows you to leverage the OpenShift API to automate operations tasks. Operators allow users to interact with your software using the tools they already know and use to interact with OpenShift itself or other operators. This interaction can be humans creating custom resources that your operator is managing using the oc CLI or a GitOps workflow. Other software, for example, other operators, also may need to collaborate with your operator using a client library. This allows standardizing how users or services communicate with other services in your environment.

Developing an operator is not how every service running on an OpenShift cluster should be implemented. Everything above the platform level will most likely use a different kind of API that fits the need of users of the service, outside of the OpenShift cluster itself.

However, for software that mainly interacts with the OpenShift cluster itself and is used by the same people or services that interact with the OpenShift API, it provides an easy-to-use way and makes for a uniform interface across services.

Using frameworks like Operator SDK allows you to easily get started with your new operator and to create operators that look familiar to your developers if they are all based on the same framework. This allows new developers to start contributing quickly if they are already familiar with other operators that utilize the same toolkit.

## CHAPTER 10

Practical Patterns for Operating OpenShift Clusters at Scale

Manuel Dewald

Throughout this book, you've learned a lot of practical tips when it comes to operating OpenShift clusters: how to get a cluster installed, installing a specific software application, be it business software or software to help you operate the cluster, and knowing the security implications of running software on OpenShift.

You also learned about OpenShift operators that help you to automate several aspects of cluster operations, such as running a CI/CD system or configuring a cluster using the GitOps methodology. Chapter 9 showed how to implement your own operator to automate an operations piece that's specific to your situation.

All this information aims to help you build and operate single or multiple OpenShift clusters in your specific environment. OpenShift adds lots of functionality to Kubernetes to make working with Kubernetes easy for you. That being said, OpenShift cannot answer every organizational consideration. That's where your job, as an operator of OpenShift clusters, starts.

This last chapter will give you a few indications to help you build or steer an organization that operates OpenShift clusters toward using the SRE approach. The focus of this chapter is on operating multiple clusters: a fleet of OpenShift clusters.

Cluster Lifecycle

Operating OpenShift clusters starts with installing a new cluster for the user who needs it, for example, an internal development organization. Sure, you can install a cluster manually, but soon there will be another organization that wants a cluster, and a third, and a couple months later you have a zoo of clusters, each of which is slightly different from the others.

That's not where you want to be. Installing updates in this diverse environment will be painful, applying configuration changes will break single clusters while others will survive, and there is little chance someone knows how all the clusters are configured or how.

Instead, you want your clusters to be as similar as possible, and the best way to achieve this is by automating the whole cluster lifecycle from installation until deprovisioning. In the best case, you need to only kick off the automation to get a cluster ready to hand over to your user, or even make the provisioning and deprovisioning a self-service.

Of course, that means you need to build some kind of software to do the automation. This software needs to run somewhere, and for that, you need infrastructure available for your team. OpenShift itself can be a good choice for running your automation. Using it yourself will help you understand OpenShift and get an idea of what it means to use your service and run software on your platform.

The OpenShift installer has a lot of different configuration options to allow OpenShift to run in as many different environments as possible. You should answer as many of those configuration options as possible for your user. Does your service really need to run on all cloud providers, or is deciding on one good enough for your company? This decision may even be required by the business already. How will users log in to the cluster? You probably can automatically integrate clusters with your company Identity Provider (IDP) and just delegate the permissions to the right part of the organization. That way, your users don't need to bother with setting up an IDP.

Uniform OpenShift Clusters

The more decisions you can make for your users, the more your clusters will look the same, and the easier it will be to operate them. Also, the better you automate the lifecycle and the better the user's experience of your tooling, the easier it will be to rebuild a cluster instead of trying to fix it after some manual action broke it.

There is also an open source project built to automate the OpenShift cluster lifecycle: Hive (*https://github.com/openshift/hive*) is a cluster management software built as an operator. You can deploy it to an OpenShift cluster, and creating new clusters is initiated by applying resources to this cluster. It also allows managing CRs that are applied to all or a selection of your clusters with custom resource definitions called SyncSets and SelectorSyncSets.

Cluster Configuration

Managing multiple clusters means managing the configuration of multiple clusters. The previous section stressed keeping all clusters as similar as possible to each other when installing them, so working with them later is the same, no matter which cluster you're looking at. However, the configuration will change after installing the clusters. Rebuilding the cluster with every change you want to apply may seem ideal from a consistency standpoint, as it would allow making the cluster configuration immutable, but it's not a practical strategy in many cases.

That means you need to build a system that manages the configuration of your OpenShift clusters. The goal should be the same as for the lifecycle management: the cluster configuration should be as similar as possible for all clusters. In some cases, you may need to handle a set of clusters differently than others, but the vast majority should be the same. This will make operating the clusters much easier than having to inspect the configuration of every single cluster when investigating a problem.

A good idea is to use a GitOps approach to manage your configuration. The easiest way is to have a cluster that holds all software to manage all your clusters, deploy Argo CD to it, and have it synchronize a Git repository with all configuration objects to all your clusters. Chapter 8 explains how to install and use Argo CD to manage configuration for OpenShift clusters using the GitOps approach. As Argo CD is working with OpenShift resources, adding credentials for accessing a new cluster can be automated as well.

As mentioned, Hive has custom resource definitions that allow you to synchronize the configuration to managed clusters as well, so if you decide to use it for lifecycle management, it can also help you with configuring clusters. However, the hurdle to getting started with Hive is slightly higher than setting up Argo CD on your cluster, and it doesn't come with a nice UI to explore the functionality. Once you're used to it, however, it's a powerful tool to help you manage your OpenShift clusters.

Logging

Accessing and searching logs on a single cluster can be done in many different ways. Although deploying a log aggregator to the cluster can make searching your application logs easier and can be done in OpenShift using the approach described in Chapter 7, some still prefer to access logs using `oc logs -n my-namespace my-pod`.

However, when managing multiple clusters, logging in to a single cluster in case of a problem, searching for the right pod to look at, and searching through these logs have a couple of disadvantages:

Logs may be gone

If the problem you're investigating results in a crashing container, you may not be able to find the right logs. You can view logs of previous containers using `oc logs -p`, but the previous container may have exited for a different reason.

Logging in takes time

When you need to log in to a cluster to investigate the logs of a given application, you are already spending a good amount of investigation time. In the best case, you should only log in to the cluster to apply some manual mitigation, which should be a rare case.

Investigating problems across clusters is hard

If you have a problem and wonder if that's happening on other clusters as well, you will have a hard time figuring it out depending on the logs of a specific pod if you have no option for searching logs across clusters. Logging in to many clusters in parallel is possible and there is tooling to support you, but still, it's a time-consuming effort.

Luckily, OpenShift supports forwarding the logs of your clusters to a central location using the log forwarding feature of the Cluster Logging Operator (*https://oreil.ly/ WKePR*). With log forwarding, you can configure all your clusters to forward logs to an external system, which can be a log aggregator you deploy and manage, like the ELK stack (*https://oreil.ly/pbxXJ*), or one managed by a third-party service.

Now all you need to do is give your SREs access to the log aggregation service to allow them to search logs across clusters.

Monitoring

Similar to storing logs in a central location, it is possible to forward metrics from the on-cluster monitoring stack to an external aggregation like Thanos (*https://thanos.io*) using a remote write (*https://oreil.ly/sBJ3h*) configuration.

This practice allows you to store metrics for a longer period without attaching large and expensive storage to every cluster. You can keep the retention period short within the cluster and still keep historic metrics in the central long-term storage.

While it is advisable to keep your alerting rules in the single cluster configuration, it's often helpful to start an investigation by looking at the historic behavior of the related metrics and whether the behavior of an alerting cluster is similar to what you see on others.

In addition, if you want to build dashboards across your managed clusters to visualize how you're performing against your defined SLOs, a central aggregation that has all the metrics available for at least the window of the SLOs is indispensable.

Alerting

All the self-healing capabilities of OpenShift, all the automation you build to remediate common problems, and all the care you take while crafting RBAC rules to prevent issues with permissions will not prevent all incidents. It's part of the SRE life to be on call for problems that could not be foreseen or are not (yet) automated. In a distributed system like OpenShift, things can, and will, go wrong. That's why you have a built-in monitoring and alerting stack that you can plug into your favorite alerting infrastructure using the configuration for Alertmanager.

Alerts in OpenShift come in different severities. The meanings for those alert levels as defined in the kubernetes-mixin project (*https://oreil.ly/WA7fo*) are as follows:

- Critical: An issue that needs to page a person to take instant action
- Warning: An issue that needs to be worked on but in the regular work queue or during office hours rather than paging the on-call person
- Info: Supports troubleshooting process by informing about a nonnormal situation for one or more systems but is not worth a page or ticket on its own

—Kubernetes Mixin

Alert Levels for Custom Alerts

When defining new alerts, stick with this definition to avoid alerting on problems that are good to know but don't need to page on-call staff. Also, while writing new alerts, you should always favor building symptom-based alerts over cause-based alerts. See Chapter 7 for a detailed explanation of building alerts based on symptoms and Chapter 5 in the SRE Workbook (*https://sre.goo gle/workbook/alerting-on-slos*).

Being on call for a system that is paging purely on cause-based alerts will quickly lead to a situation where the on-call staff needs to prioritize on their own which alerts should be worked on, as the queue will fill up as service adoption increases. Alerting on symptoms means alerting on issues that your customers care about. That doesn't mean a cause you can detect is irrelevant. When troubleshooting a symptom-based alert, like an increased error rate, it's incredibly helpful to look at lower-level cause-based alerts to get all the context and figure out the reason for the error rate increase.

Our advice is to page on-call staff on critical alerts, but keep warning and info alerts visible as context. Additionally, warning alerts should make up a proactive queue in a different place than your primary alerting system. In some cases, you may find it useful to change the severity of critical alerts built into OpenShift as they may be purely cause based. Build your symptom-based alerts on your SLOs, as no one can answer the question of what those SLOs are in your specific context.

It's also important to know what you are on call for. Is it only for the cluster health and the applications you're managing to support the cluster? Or are you on call for applications that your users deploy to the cluster?

If you're not responsible for the applications deployed by your users, make sure you don't get alerted for them and offer user-workload management for them to run their monitoring and alerting stack as described in "User Workload Monitoring" on page 130.

Automation

Hiring SREs means hiring software engineers to solve operations problems. It's easy to let yourself drift into writing a small bash script to solve a particular problem. It doesn't seem important to have a test for this little piece of automation. You may not even know how long it'll be required to stay.

Sometimes it's necessary to provide a quick solution for a specific problem, and that may be fine. But you should treat all automation you build as software.

Even if it is only that small bash script, make sure it is reviewed and managed centrally. Whenever possible, your automation should run from a central place, like a Tekton Pipeline, not on a developer machine. This ensures that the environment is configured as expected and nothing on the developer machine interferes with the automation.

And, wherever possible, the automation should not be a script. It should be a tested piece of software, with a release and testing strategy, and a CI/CD pipeline to verify and deploy each release. Your confidence in software that is tested and deployed in the same way many times a day will be much higher than confidence in a bash script that's lingering around in a Git repository and no one knows when it worked the last time.

Also for changing your automation software, the confidence will be much higher than the confidence in changing a bash script where you barely understand what all those `sed`, `grep`, and `awk` commands, chained together with | characters do.

On Call

How you organize the shift work for your SRE team depends heavily on your organizational structure and the scale of your service. This section is meant to be a blueprint for when you're getting started with a relatively small number of clusters, like 10–20. Iterate your processes as you grow.

Primary On Call

Primary on call is the person holding the pager. If nothing is done, primary on call will watch the queue of lower-level alerts to figure out if there is a pattern in those or work on a ticket queue. Primary is freed up from project work for the time being on shift.

Backup On Call

Backup on call is available to hop on calls to pair up with primary on call whenever necessary. On call should be encouraged to pair-operate as often as possible for improved knowledge sharing and a lower possibility of breaking things while remediating an issue. When the primary is overwhelmed with alerts or the ticket queue is growing, backup will jump in to share the burden. Backup is expected to leave project work any time during the shift. If calling the backup doesn't help clear the queue or handle the load, all project work should be paused until the operational load is under control again. Focus on improving the shift before releasing new features.

Shift Rotation

The shift rotation should be automated. People should be able to trade shifts on their own as necessary. Every engineer in the SRE organization should be on shift every couple of weeks, independent of their level. It's easier to effectively prioritize SRE work across the organization if you experience the shift work yourself.

If possible, leverage time zones to distribute engineers across the globe.

If you need engineers to be on call at night, make sure the number of pages is manageable. An engineer shouldn't need to get up every night to fix an alert that doesn't impact any users.

After the shift, engineers should take time to reflect on how it went and where they see room for improvement. The outcome of a busy shift should be treated as a high-priority work item and worked on as soon as possible. The highest priority of every SRE team should be to improve the time on shift and reduce the number of alerts to a minimum.

Ticket Queue

Use a ticketing system to track issues your users face. Even if they usually first reach out via email or in chat, get into the habit of asking them to open a ticket for you and convince them it'll be resolved. This helps to prevent a culture where the one being the loudest gets help first, which is a stressful situation for on-call staff.

Incident Management

Incidents happen. They shouldn't happen daily but, from time to time, a situation requires SREs to team up and resolve it as soon as possible. If such a situation occurs, everyone should know exactly what to do. In other words, you should have an incident management process that everybody understands and follows.

Figure 10-1 gives an overview of what a simple incident management process could look like. It's divided into the following stages:

Report
> The incident needs to be declared using defined communication channels. The incident process is initiated.

Resolve
> The incident is investigated and the problem mitigated until the problem is resolved.

Review
> After the incident is closed, everyone involved adds the details necessary for a root cause analysis (RCA). A postmortem meeting is conducted to review what happened, if it can be prevented in the future, and how well the incident management process worked.

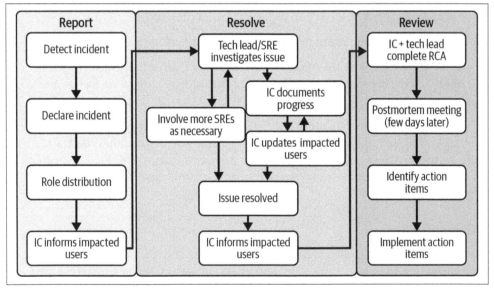

Figure 10-1. Example incident management process

As with shift scheduling, it depends on your organization and its scale how this process will look. The following factors should be considered when designing an incident management process.

When to Declare an Incident

Your incident management process should make it clear to everyone when to declare an incident. Is a single master node being unresponsive a reason to declare an incident? Probably not, but when the whole OpenShift control plane is unreachable, you may want to declare an incident. There are situations in between, and it's hard to define how to decide if an issue is an incident, but a team of sensible SREs will be able to come up with a good explanation. A good start is defining a time frame for how long an SRE should debug on their own before calling for help.

If the decision is made to declare an incident, it's important to document how to declare it. Note concrete communication channels, like mailing lists, chat channels, status pages, and so on.

Inform the Customer

It's also important to notify the customer, the user of your cluster, about the outage. Make sure it's obvious to SREs how to reach out to users in a written form, for example, via email. In addition to the first notification, customers should be kept up to date as the incident continues and is investigated. Typically, customers want to hear that you're working on the problem and about progress you have made.

When the incident is over, your customers will be happy to hear you accomplished the mission and everything is back to normal again.

Define Roles

The first step after declaring an incident should be to decide who takes which role in an incident. Define the different personas in your incident-management process. The following two roles should be the minimum, so at least two people are investigating an incident and not a single SRE left on their own:

- Tech lead
- Incident commander (IC)

The tech lead is the engineer who detected the issue, started the investigation, and declared the incident. In the on-call structure shown in "On Call" on page 238, this will be the primary on call in most cases. Until the incident is resolved, the tech lead will continue the investigation and reach out for helping hands if necessary, for example, to follow different paths in the investigation at the same time.

The tech lead and whoever is available when the incident is declared make a quick decision on who going to act as incident commander going forward, and the incident commander takes over the organizational tasks momentarily.

The incident commander is one of the engineers who reacted to the declared incident to help out. The incident commander takes care of all organizational tasks around an incident, including the following:

- Updating the customer
- Documenting the timeline of the incident for a later retrospective
- Facilitating retrospective meetings
- Finding additional engineers when necessary

Incident Timeline

The incident commander should document the beginning and end of an incident, as well as all the ad-hoc changes made during the investigation or problem remediation, along with the time they are made. This is necessary for a postmortem meeting to recap what happened and determine any action needed to prevent such incidents from happening.

If a decision is made to alter a cluster that will need to be undone later, this kind of change must be recorded so the information doesn't get lost as the incident continues.

Document the Process

The incident management process should be documented in a place where everyone on the team can find it easily. Make sure you have a clear outline of the process so even in face of an incident the steps can be quickly revised and followed.

Train Incident Management

Train the process with the team to make sure everyone understands it. Facilitate small, fake incidents just to practice the process. They don't need to involve creative problem solving but should allow participants to execute all the steps in the process, including incident declaration, role distribution, timeline keeping, and customer notification.

Postmortem

The postmortem meeting should happen, at the latest, a few days after the incident occurred. Everyone involved should participate, and the whole team should be invited to join if interested. Review the timeline, write down action items to prevent incidents, and discuss how investigation and remediation could be improved.

Sometimes things break because of an introduced bug or a bad decision. While investigating the incident, the tech lead may even make a mistake and worsen the situation. Effective postmortem meetings need to stay away from blaming anybody for what happened. Mistakes happen, and they provide opportunities to learn from them. If necessary, remind yourself and the team how important it is to create a blameless culture for the team.

Accessing OpenShift Clusters

It should be a rare occasion that the SREs need to access single clusters. However, in the face of an incident, it's not atypical that certain information needs to be gathered from the cluster or manual actions need to be done, for example, rescheduling a pod to a different node, or replacing a malfunctioning node.

You need to make sure accessing the clusters is as easy as possible for your SREs, so they can log in to clusters and make the necessary changes. It's helpful to audit which actions an SRE does in case it's necessary to review what happened, for example for a root cause analysis. However, make sure your processes don't prevent SREs from doing what's necessary because of the hurdle of accessing a cluster or the paper trail that an on-cluster investigation creates for them.

A simple way to make clusters accessible is adding the same IDP to all clusters that all SREs have access to. For example, using a GitHub team that includes all team members.

The Stage Is Yours

Starting with installing a new cluster, deploying and securing applications, automating builds and operations, and holding the pager for production clusters, you now have a good starting point to operate OpenShift clusters using an SRE approach.

Thank you for sticking with us all the way to the end of the book. We hope you're taking some practical advice with you that helps you with your own journey.

All the resources used in this book can be found at GitHub (*https://github.com/Opera tingOpenShift*). If you have any questions, feel free to reach out to us. You can find us on social media using our handles @manueldewald and @RiRa12621.

Index

A

A/B deployments, 197
access control, 68 (see also Role-Based Access
    Control (RBAC))
ACME (Automatic Certificate Management
    Environment), 203
add mappingMethod, 61
Alerting Rules, 119
Alertmanager
    AlertmanagerConfig custom resource, 123
    Cluster Monitoring Operator and, 122
    configuring from console UI, 127
    configuring via secrets, 123
    practicing alert routing, 124
    purpose of, 122
    silencing alerts, 129
    User Workload Monitoring, 130
alerts (see also monitoring and observability)
    accumulating toil through, 2
    mitigating problems, 167
    patterns for, 237
    symptom-based alerts, 1
Ansible, 201
application code changes, 77
application updates, 169
applications
    deploying from Git repositories, 29-31
    uninstalling, 31
Argo CD
    installing, 185-188
    managing cluster configuration with,
        189-193
    managing configuration of multiple clusters,
        193-196

B

backup on call, 239
backups, 170
base image changes, 77
BlackBox exporter, 150
build artifacts, cleaning up, 82
build automation
    OpenShift image builds, 73-87
    overview of, 110
    Red Hat OpenShift Pipelines, 87-110
build process, inspecting, 83
burn rate, 148

ARO (Azure Red Hat OpenShift), 8
auto-generated DNS names, 34
automated deployment, 185
automated testing, 185, 197
Automatic Certificate Management Environ-
    ment (ACME), 203
automation (see also custom operators)
    automating persistence, 170-173
    cluster configuration, 182-183
    creating snapshots, 173-176
    patterns for, 238
    types of tasks prime for, 168-170
    types of work in OpenShift, 167
    using CronJobs for, 176-182
    using OpenShift GitOps, 184-196
Azure Red Hat OpenShift (ARO), 8

C

CA directories, 207
canary testing, 197
cert-manager, 45

cert-manager Operator, 201
Certificate Authority (CA), 60, 207
certificate renewals, 169
CI/CD (continuous integration/continuous
    delivery), 1
claim mappingMethod, 61
CLI (command line interface), 65
Client ID, 60
Client Secret, 60
closed-box monitoring, 150
Cluster Monitoring Operator
    benefits and drawbacks of, 112
    jsonnet imports and, 112
    Prometheus Operator, 114-129
    purpose of, 111
    upstream dependencies and, 114
cluster operators, 111
Cluster Version Operator, 111
cluster-monitoring-config configmap, 123
ClusterLogForwarder resource, 158
ClusterLogging
    background on, 154
    benefits of, 154
    configuration, 157
    installation, 154-156
ClusterRoleBindings, 63
ClusterRoles, 62
clusters
    automating operation of, 199-201 (see also
        automation)
    configuring, 182-183
    managing configuration with OpenShift
        GitOps, 184-196
    patterns for operating, 233-243
    planning size of, 12-16
    security issues in accessing, 59-61
    visual impressions of, 136-140
code examples, obtaining and using, x, 243
code, deploying on OpenShift (see also build
    automation)
    automating, 185
    cleaning up applications, 31
    deploying applications from Git reposito-
        ries, 29-31
    deploying custom operators, 217-220
    deploying existing container images, 27-29
    project creation, 26
    switching between projects, 26
    version control systems, 184

command line interface (CLI), 65
comments and questions, xi
console dashboards, 136
Container Storage Interface (CSI), 171
continuous integration/continuous delivery
    (CI/CD), 1, 197
control plane nodes, sizing recommendations,
    14
core vitals, 144
CR (Custom Resources), 115, 200
crc binary, 10
CRD (Custom Resource Definitions), 62, 115,
    200, 209-212
CronJobs
    automated VolumeSnapshots, 176-180
    task automation with, 176
CSI (Container Storage Interface), 171
custom alerts, 237
custom operators
    adding additional controllers, 227-229
    automating cluster operations with, 199-201
    benefits of, 231
    bootstrapping operators, 203-207
    creating and updating resources, 220-223
    defining Custom Resource Definitions
        (CRD), 209-212
    deploying, 217-220
    installing CustomResourceDefinition, 212
    local operator development, 213-215
    operator design, 202
    Operator SDK, 201
    Reconcile function, 216
    routing traffic to operators, 225
    setting up CA directories, 207
    specifying RBAC permissions, 223-225
    updating resource status, 229
Custom Resource Definitions (CRD), 62, 115,
    200, 209-212
Custom Resources (CR), 115, 200
custom S2I images, 84-87

D

dashboards, 136
database backups, 170
deployed services, accessing, 31-33
deployment (see build automation; code,
    deploying on OpenShift)
deployment resources, 27
docker build strategy, 74-81

domain name system (DNS)
    auto-generated DNS names, 34
    creating public DNS name as subdomain, 33
    creating unique subdomains, 35
    querying services in different namespaces,
      32
    reusing domain names, 35
    routing based on DNS names, 54

E

EncryptedDomain, 202, 210
EventListeners, 89
external load balancers, 37 40

F

firefighting work, 167

G

generate mappingMethod, 61
GET verb, 63
Git repositories, deploying applications from,
    29-31
GitHub, 184
GitLab, 184
GitOps
    benefits of, 184
    installing, 185-188
    managing cluster configuration with,
      189-193
    managing configuration of multiple clusters,
      193-196
    version control using, 184
Go programming language, 201
Godot engine, 84
Grafana, 137-140, 158
Grafana Operator
    creating instances, 161
    dashboards, 164-166
    data sources, 161-163
    installation, 159-160

H

Helm, 201

I

IaC (Infrastructure as Code), 184
idempotency, 94
identity providers (IdP), 59

image builds (see OpenShift image builds)
incident management
    declaring incidents, 241
    defining roles, 241
    documentation, 242
    informing customers, 241
    postmortems, 243
    process for, 240
    timeline, 242
    training and practice, 242
infra nodes, 15
Infrastructure as Code (IaC), 184
installation
    basic, 17-24
    local clusters with OpenShift Local, 8-11
    OCP (OpenShift Container Platform), 8
    OKD, 7
    OpenShift-as-a-Service, 8
    planning cluster size, 12-16
installer-provisioned infrastructure, 17-24
instance-ip header, 33
instances, sizing recommendations, 12
Internet Security Research Group (ISRG), 40

J

jsonnet templating language, 112

K

kube-prometheus, 112, 114
kubeadmin, removing, 67
Kubebuilder, 201, 224
kubectl, 10
Kubernetes, 5, 7, 112, 213
kubernetes-mixin, 114, 237
Kustomize, 212

L

language detection, 81-83
least privilege principle, 62
Let's Encrypt service, 40, 44-50, 202, 208
load balancers, 37-40, 144
logging
    ClusterLogging, 154-158
    log forwarding, 158
    Loki, 158
    patterns for, 235
LogQL, 158
Loki, 158

lookup mappingMethod, 61

M

maintenance tasks, 167
mappingMethod, 61
masters, sizing recommendations, 13
metrics
    persisting, 115
    visualizing, 136-140
mixins, 114, 237
monitoring and observability
    Cluster Monitoring Operator, 111-136
    in-cluster stack, 111
    logging, 154-158
    patterns for, 236
    service oriented monitoring, 143-154
    visualizing metrics, 136-140, 159-166

N

namespaces, versus projects, 26
NodePort, 37
nodes
    infra nodes, 15
    sizing recommendations, 12

O

Oauth configuration, 61
observability (see monitoring and observability)
oc command line utility, 10
OCM (OpenShift Cluster Manager), 9
OCP (OpenShift Container Platform), 8
OKD, 7
OLM (Operator Lifecycle Manager), 202
on call structure, 238-239
OpenShift
    as a tool for SRE, 4
    automating updates, 180-182
    benefits and challenges of, 1, 5
    discovering dashboards shipped with, 136
    installing, 7-24
    installing updates, 169
    purpose of, 1
    role of Kubernetes in, 112
OpenShift Cluster Manager (OCM), 9
OpenShift Container Platform (OCP), 8
OpenShift Dedicated (OSD), 8
OpenShift image builds

custom S2I images, 84-87
docker build strategy, 74-81
Source-to-Image (S2I) builds, 81-83
supported build strategies, 74
OpenShift Local, 8-11
OpenShift-as-a-Service, 8
openshift-monitoring namespace, 122
Operator Lifecycle Manager (OLM), 202
Operator SDK, 201
operators (see custom operators; individual operator names)
OSD (OpenShift Dedicated), 8

P

passthrough TLS termination mode, 51
patterns
    accessing clusters, 243
    alerting, 237
    automation, 238
    cluster configuration, 235
    cluster lifecycles, 233
    incident management, 240-243
    logging, 235
    monitoring, 236
    on call structure, 238-239
Pebble, 208
persistence, automating, 170-173
Pingdom, 150
pipelines (see Red Hat OpenShift pipelines)
pods, accessing services from, 31, 199
port-forwarding, 29, 33
postmortems, 243
primary on call, 239
principle of the least privilege, 62
projects, versus namespaces, 26
Prometheus Operator
    alert routing, 124
    Alertmanager custom resource, 122-136
    AlertmanagerConfig custom resource, 123
    creation of, 114
    custom resources, 115
    persisting metrics, 115
    Prometheus custom resource, 115
    PrometheusRules custom resources, 118
    purpose of, 115
    querying using PromQL, 117
    Service Monitor custom resource, 131
Prometheus Query Language (PromQL), 117, 158

PrometheusRules custom resource, 118
Pyrra, 151-154

Q

questions and comments, xi

R

RBAC (see Role-Based Access Control (RBAC))
Reconcile function, 216
Recording Rules, 118
Red Hat OpenShift Pipelines
    composing pipelines, 99-104
    continuous integration pipelines, 104-110
    example deployment pipeline, 87
    implementing tasks, 92-98
    installing, 90-92
    overview of, 88-90
Red Hat OpenShift Service on AWS (ROSA), 8
repetitive maintenance tasks, 167
ReplicaSets, 199
requests, distribution of, 32
resources
    creating and updating, 220-223
    deployment resources, 27
    in OpenSource, 62
    route resources, 33-36
    service resources, 28
review process, 185, 197
Role-Based Access Control (RBAC)
    command line interface, 65
    RoleBindings and ClusterRoleBindings, 63
    roles and ClusterRoles, 62
    specifying permissions in custom operators,
        223-225
RoleBindings, 63
ROSA (Red Hat OpenShift Service on AWS), 8
Route Monitor Operator, 150
route resources, 33-36
    routing by auto-generated DNS names, 34
    routing by path, 35
running workloads (see workloads)

S

S2I builds (see Source-to-Image (S2I) builds)
SCC (security context constraint), 28
secrets, configuring Alertmanager via, 123
security
    cluster access, 59-61

restricted security context constraints, 28
Role-Based Access Control (RBAC), 61-66
ServiceAccounts, 66
threat modeling, 67
workloads, 68-72
security context constraint (SCC), 28
self-provisioned infrastructure, 24
Service Level Indicators (SLI), 144
Service Level Objectives (SLO), 1, 145-150
service oriented monitoring
    challenges of, 143
    Service Level Indicators (SLI), 144
    Service Level Objectives (SLO), 145-150
    tools, 150-154
service resources, 28
ServiceAccounts, 66
services
    accessing deployed services, 31-33
    exposing services, 33-40
    querying services in different namespaces,
        32
    securing with TLS, 40-57
shift left, 166
shift rotation, 239
Site Reliability Engineering (SRE)
    automating software operations, 168
    benefits of, 3
    challenges of, 5
    definition of term, 1
    goal of, 3
    on call structure, 238-239
    OpenShift as a tool for, 4
    versus traditional operations teams, 2
SLI (Service Level Indicators), 144
SLO (Service Level Objectives), 1
snapshots
    automating, 176-180
    creating, 173-176
software development, 184
Source-to-Image (S2I) builds
    automatic language detection, 81-83
    custom images, 84-87
    goals of, 81
SRE (see Site Reliability Engineering (SRE))
SSL certificates, 169
Statuscake, 150
steps, 89
structured logging, 154
supplemental material, obtaining, x, 243

symptom-based alerts, 1

T
tail pod logs, 154
tasks, 89
Tekton
    downloading, 91
    pipelines in, 92
    resources involved in pipelines, 89
    steps in, 89
    viewing, creating, and deleting objects, 91
testing, automated, 185, 197
threat modeling, 67
ticket queues, 239
Time Series Database (TSDB), 115
TLS (transport layer security)
    encrypted communication to the service,
        51-57
    Let's Encrypt service, 44
    redirecting traffic to TLS route, 42
    securing services with, 40
    specifying TLS certificates, 40
toil
    definition of term, 2
    goal of upper limit for, 2
    in traditional operations teams, 2
traceability, 184
transport layer security (see TLS (transport
    layer security))
TriggerBinding resource, 90

TSDB (Time Series Database), 115

U
unique identifier (UID), 28
updates
    application, 169
    automating, 180-182
    installing, 167, 169
User Workload Monitoring, 130
users, provisioning automatically, 59

V
version control, 184, 197
visualization (see Grafana Operator)
VolumeSnapshots, 176-180

W
webhooks
    generic, 78
    GitHub, 79
    more build triggers, 80
    triggering builds with, 77
workloads
    accessing deployed services, 31-33
    arcade platform example application, 25
    deploying code, 26-31
    exposing services, 33-40
    securing services with TLS, 40-57
    security issues, 68-72

About the Authors

Rick Rackow is a seasoned professional who has worked on cloud and container adoption throughout his career. As Site Reliability Engineer on Red Hat's OpenShift Dedicated team, Rick manages and maintains countless OpenShift clusters at scale and ensures their reliability every day by developing and following the best practices the reader will learn in this book.

Manuel Dewald has worked as a site reliability engineer at Red Hat since 2019. In his role, he's keeping the lights on for OpenShift clusters atop of the major public clouds.

Previously, he worked as a software engineer, participating in DevOps practices in different development teams. With all the challenges of this setup, he decided to change to a role focused on operating software, while keeping the focus on software engineering to solve operations challenges.

He's passionate about open source software and good software engineering practices. From time to time, you can find him complaining about missing tests even on the smallest projects, which are solving only a little pain of the operations team.

Manuel speaks at conferences and meetups about utilizing the OpenShift build infrastructure, best practices for implementing Kubernetes operators, and agile practices in SRE teams. He writes blog posts about Kubernetes operators, agile practices, and Raspberry Pi projects on *https://blog.redhat.com* and *https://opensource.com*.

Colophon

The animal on the cover of *Operating OpenShift* is an oval butterflyfish (*Chaetodon lunulatus*).

Oval butterflyfish get their name from the disk-like shape of their small, thin bodies. The color of their body is a pinkish-yellow that transitions to a pure yellow on the head and lower body. A vertical black band runs across their face and through their eyes. Purplish stripes run horizontally across their body. Their tails are also striped in black and white.

Oval butterflyfish are reef dwellers that can be found in the Pacific Ocean around Australia, Japan, Indonesia, and Hawaii. They live in coastal, coral-rich habitats that are anywhere from three to thirty meters deep. They utilize their pointed snouts to feed off of live coral polyps along the reef.

Because their sole food source is live coral and they require ample swimming space, they are not recommended for household aquariums. However, these fish are capable of being bred in captivity if their environmental needs are met. The abundance of oval butterflyfish found in their natural habitat results in a conservation status of least concern.

Many of the animals on O'Reilly covers are endangered; all of them are important to the world.

The cover illustration is by Karen Montgomery, based on an antique line engraving from Lydekker's *Royal Natural History*. The cover fonts are Gilroy Semibold and Guardian Sans. The text font is Adobe Minion Pro; the heading font is Adobe Myriad Condensed; and the code font is Dalton Maag's Ubuntu Mono.

Lightning Source UK Ltd.
Milton Keynes UK
UKHW050905080123
414917UK00005B/4